The Observer Years
ORWELL

GEORGE ORWELL, the pen name of Eric Blair, was born in Motihari in India on 25 June 1903, where his parents were both members of the Indian Civil Service. He was educated at Eton, after which he joined the Indian Imperial Police Force in Burma in 1922. He wrote both novels and non-fiction during the 1930s, including his first book, *Down and Out in Paris and London* (1933) and *The Road to Wigan Pier* (1937). *Homage to Catalonia* (1938) documents his experiences in the Spanish Civil War when he fought for the Loyalist forces. It was not until the publication of *Animal Farm* in 1945 and *Nineteen Eighty-Four* in 1949, however, that he found fame as a novelist. Essentially a political writer, throughout his career Orwell contributed to many newspapers and periodicals, most famously *Tribune*, the *Observer*, and the *Manchester Evening News*. His 'As I Please' column was produced for the left-wing magazine *Tribune*, where he was appointed Literary Editor in November 1943. He continued to write articles and book reviews until shortly before his death on 21 January 1950.

'This is a splendid assemblage, to whose compilers I doff my hat.'
D. J. Taylor, *The Spectator*

'Fifty years on, these ephemeral pieces still display a marvellous acuity and freshness and go some way to explaining why Orwell is such an influential English writer for the generations that followed.'
Robert McCrum, *Observer*

'An absorbing haul that reflects a fascinating period... Orwell's pieces, which flowed effortlessly from his typewriter after he first tried them out on colleagues in the form of monologues fuelled by "strong tea and hand-rolled cigarettes of strong shag", are remarkable for both perceptiveness and prescience... And 70 book reviews, on topics from poetry to potholing, indicate Orwell's range.' Christopher Hirst, *Independent*

'My bedside reading includes yet another Orwell collection, but this time of his writings for the *Observer* from 1942 onwards; this includes his news reporting, which is excellent, if confidently opinionated, and his book reviews... I've been enjoying these in particular. Orwell's brusque certainty can bring you up short – Dostoevsky's *The Brothers' Karamazov*, for instance, is "heavy going"... It is full of strange sideways glints, too. Orwell reviewed a biography of Atlee by the young Roy Jenkins and, after studying the photographs, he decided that he agreed with the *Daily Mail*: the Labour leader's head "is the same shape as Lenin's". But the main thing is that, in the case of every book, Orwell tells you roughly what it's about and roughly what it says. This quaint old habit could be revived today.' Andrew Marr, *Daily Telegraph*

'The book stayed beside my bed to be dipped into from time to time: but the dips became more frequent and longer and pretty soon I was re-reading pieces... Nothing he writes is without interest... A handy, one volume selection of Orwell's journalism... Get this as a tribute to Orwell's clarity, good sense and good faith.' Nicholas Lezard, *Guardian*

'No one on the left in Britain seems to be able to discuss anything for very long without saying, "What would George have thought?" This collection of writings includes stories, profiles, articles and book reviews, and covers the period between 1942 and 1948... A very welcome addition to the growing tide of Orwelliana.' David Lea, *Bookseller*

'This collection of George Orwell's journalism is a glory. In all his newspaper articles, Orwell upheld the virtue of good writing combined with intellectual and emotional engagement. His work endures remarkably well... Amongst his peers, only Orwell wrote such trenchant and enduring newspaper copy.' *Scotland on Sunday*

'Orwell's rigorous prose and clarity of thought can be enjoyed by anyone, be it in the context of a piece on the question of India or a review of a biography of Charles Dickens.' *Metro*

'A captivating, educating read.' *Good Book Guide*

The Observer Years

ORWELL

The Observer

Atlantic Books
London

First published in 2003 by Atlantic Books,
on behalf of Guardian Newspapers Ltd.
Atlantic Books is an imprint of Grove Atlantic Ltd.

This paperback edition published by Atlantic Books in 2004.

10 9 8 7 6 5 4 3 2 1

A CIP catalogue record for this book is available
from the British Library

ISBN 1 84354 326 5

Research by Gavin McGuffie, Siân Wynn-Jones, Allan Price,
Dominique Smith, Ellie Geraghty, Mary Kouba, Alison Wills,
Newsroom, Guardian and Observer Archive and Visitor Centre,
Gill Furlong, Head of Special Collections, UCL Library

Designed by Richard Carr
Typeset by FiSH Books, London
Printed in Great Britain by Mackays of Chatham Ltd

Grove Atlantic Ltd
Ormond House
26–27 Boswell Street
London WC1N 3JZ

CONTENTS

The Reviews

INTRODUCTION

INTRODUCTION

GEORGE ORWELL wrote his first piece for the *Observer* in February 1942. His relationship with the paper had begun almost a year earlier, however, when he met David Astor, its proprietor and later its editor. Astor instinctively took to Orwell; his 'absolute straightforwardness, his honesty and his decency', and their close friendship underpins these pieces which Orwell wrote for the *Observer* throughout the 1940s.

Astor wanted to update the paper, which he felt had been politically and editorially stifled by its outgoing editor, J. L. Garvin. He introduced a column intended to stimulate debate, called 'Forum', and commissioned Orwell to write the first. In this pioneering piece, 'India Next' (p. 2), Orwell made the radical case for Indian independence, signalling the *Observer*'s longstanding opposition to British colonialism, which would cost Astor thousands of readers when he led the paper out against the Suez campaign in 1956. Ironically, Orwell's first contribution to the *Observer* appeared directly beneath Garvin's last, on 22 February 1942.

Cyril Connolly, an old friend of Orwell's, was editing the books pages, and he commissioned Orwell to write a series of reviews on subjects close to his heart – Dickens (p. 82), Burma (p. 86), de Gaulle (p. 84). Things went well until the cautious editor, Ivor Brown, spiked one of Orwell's more radical pieces. Orwell wrote furiously to Connolly, refusing to write for 'papers which do not allow... at least a minimum of honesty.' Astor must have worked hard to keep Orwell on his fledgling team, for although he continued to contribute political pieces, it was a year before he wrote for the books pages again.

Orwell wrote on a wide range of topics for the *Observer*, from the Spanish Civil War (pp. 22, 95, 153, 213) to the history of Eton (p. 225); from the evacuation of problem children (p. 24) to Oscar Wilde's socialism (p. 74); and from anti-semitism (p. 104) to the Home Guard (of which he was a dutiful member) (pp. 10 and 26). His articles were rattled off, like most of his journalism, at top speed. His friend George Woodcock was amazed to see him composing directly on the typewriter, neither amending nor revising. He thought Orwell's fluency was explained by 'the extent to which his writing was tied into his existence'. Orwell 'liked to talk out his ideas in long monologues over cups of strong tea and hand-rolled cigarettes of black shag and not long afterward one would see the evening's talk appearing as an article'.

In November 1943, Orwell began contributing a book review every fortnight to the *Observer*, a pattern which would continue until May 1946. At the same time, he started work on *Animal Farm*, which was finished by the end of February 1944. The reviews he wrote during this period provide a fascinating companion to the making of a masterpiece. In both the novel and his literary journalism, he grappled with the contradictions within socialism, coming to difficult conclusions which isolated him from those on both the left and the right.

It took Orwell most of 1944 to find a publisher as courageous as he was. Victor Gollancz rejected *Animal Farm* because it was too hostile to communism; T. S. Eliot rejected it on behalf of Faber because it was too sympathetic; and Jonathan Cape rejected it on the advice of a friend at the Ministry of Information who felt that the fable mirrored too neatly the development of the Soviet Union, at that time a crucial ally. Cape wrote to Orwell, saying: 'the choice of pigs as the ruling caste will no doubt give offence to many people, and particularly to anyone who is a bit touchy, as undoubtedly the Russians are'. In the margin of this letter, Orwell simply wrote 'balls'.

The following Sunday, he replied to Cape in the form of a book review – of *The Sociology of Literary Taste*, by L. L. Schucking (p. 125) – in which he complains that writers are beholden to 'the arbitrary decision of publishers'. 'In effect' says Orwell, 'the "patron" has come back again, but he is a patron enormously less civilised, less tolerant, less individual and more powerful than in the past.' The feudal patron 'was probably not a harder master than Dr Goebbels, or even the M.O.I., and his literary taste was probably better.' Ironically, Cape's contact at the Ministry of Information, Peter Smollett, was later unmasked as a Soviet spy. For a time, he had been Astor's favoured candidate to edit the *Observer*.

In March 1945, Astor sent Orwell to cover the Allied advance into Germany. He was delighted to find Hemingway's name on the guest list at his Paris hotel, and rushed up to his room to introduce himself – as Eric Blair. Hemingway had never heard of him. 'Well what the hell do you want?' he demanded, thinking that Orwell was just another British correspondent. Orwell tried again: 'I'm George Orwell'; at which Hemingway produced a bottle of Scotch from under the bed, exclaiming: 'Why the hell didn't you say so? Have a drink. Have a double.' This was Orwell's account. According to Hemingway, Orwell came to find him looking 'fairly nervous and worried' and asked to borrow a gun, as he was afraid that Stalinist agents were out to get him amid the mayhem of liberated Paris. Hemingway lent him a .32 calibre Colt.

Orwell followed the Allies to Cologne and found it devastated. 'After years of war it is an intensely strange feeling to be at last standing on German soil', he wrote on 24 March (p. 37). 'The Herrenvolk [master race] are all round you, threading their way on their bicycles between the piles of rubble or rushing off with jugs and buckets to meet the water cart.' Orwell's reports from this period (pp. 28–63) are filled with a sense of wonder that, only a few miles from London, this other world, no less real, has been shielded from view for six years by hatred and propaganda.

On 29 March, Orwell's wife Eileen died. He barely interrupted his work to return home for her funeral. Once back in England he threw himself into his work. In the April 1946 issue of *Horizon*, he published the essay 'Politics and the English Language', in which he bemoaned the state of contemporary journalism and gave some strongly worded advice for would-be writers: 'A man may take to drink because he feels himself to be a failure, and then fail all the more completely because he drinks. It is rather the same thing that is happening to the English language. It becomes ugly and inaccurate because our thoughts are foolish, but the slovenliness of our language makes it easier for us to have foolish thoughts.' Astor had a copy of this essay distributed to every new *Observer* writer. Even now, it is quoted in the house style guide. The bit about drinking has never had much impact, but Orwell's criticism of slovenly language is still taken very seriously.

Astor continued to lean on Orwell for advice and companionship, and to offer personal and professional assistance. When Orwell's health declined, he retired to the Hebridean island of Jura, where Astor owned property. When Orwell decided to marry from his sick bed in University College Hospital, it was Astor who procured the necessary licence from

Lambeth Palace. And when he died a few months later, Astor found him a grave at Sutton Courtenay in Oxfordshire.

Everything Orwell wrote for the *Observer* was written for Astor, steering a course for him through the horrific muddle of the 1940s, and helping to establish the paper's anti-colonialist, socially aware voice. He wrote exactly a hundred articles for the *Observer*, all published here. Sad, angry, sometimes severe and often witty, they all display Orwell's combination of lofty ideals and painful self-awareness. 'If you look into your own mind, which are you, Don Quixote or Sancho Panza?', he once asked. 'Almost certainly you are both.' It was the tension between these two sides, the reaction between idealism and cynicism, which gave Orwell his peculiar energy, and which did so much to determine the feel of Astor's *Observer*.

JONATHAN HEAWOOD, *Observer*

THE ARTICLES

1942–48

INDIA NEXT

I N ten of the blackest weeks in our national and imperial history one piece of really good news has passed almost unnoticed by the British public. This is the treaty recently signed between Britain and Abyssinia.* Though there are several criticisms that could be levelled against it, the treaty does demonstrate that Britain's claim to be fighting for international decency is justified. The Italians annexed Abyssinia after a cowardly war of aggression, and the British fought to set it free: the inference ought to be obvious enough.

And yet in Asia, given our present policy, the propaganda value of the Abyssinian treaty is doubtful, or worse than doubtful. And meanwhile the Japanese pan-Asiatic propaganda, a thin disguise for an obviously predatory purpose, makes headway all over Asia, even among people who are hardly if at all deceived by it.

So far as southern Asia is concerned, there is probably no real answer to Japanese propaganda except military victories. India, however, is a different matter and in India it is precisely those forces that have been most hostile to us in our imperial capacity which are our potential allies against Japan and against Fascist aggression generally.

It is easy for even the most ignorant person to grasp that Indian aspirations towards independence are menaced by the Japanese advance, and in addition, nearly all of the most gifted and active among Indian intellectuals are sympathetic towards China and Soviet Russia. Yet it remains true that Japanese propaganda makes headway. What answer can we make to the Japanese cry of 'Asia for the Asiatics'? Only that the Japanese claims are lies and that Japanese rule would be worse than our own. It is true, but it is not inspiring. In a positive sense, we promise nothing, we hold out no picture of the future. It is hardly to be wondered at if the poorer classes argue that they could not be worse off under the Japanese than they are at present, and sections of the intelligentsia are so blinded by hatred of Britain that they are half ready to betray Russia and China.

Meanwhile India, the second greatest population centre in the world, is not effectively in the war. The number of troops raised hitherto is relatively tiny, and war production is pitiful. This would be a serious matter even if the situation can be stabilised in Asia, but with the Japanese navy in the Indian Ocean and the German armies threatening the Middle East, India becomes the centre of the war – it is hardly an exaggeration to say, the centre of the world. For a long time to come, possibly for years, it may have to act as a supply base from which men and munitions of war can be poured out in two directions, east and west.

How is that huge effort to be made possible? Clearly we have got to win the enthusiasm of the peoples of India; their passive obedience is not enough. And the one sure way of arousing their enthusiasm is to convince them that Indian independence is possible if Britain wins the war and impossible if Japan wins. We cannot do that by promises nor by resounding phrases about liberty and democracy; we can only do it by some concrete unmistakable act of generosity, by giving something away that cannot afterwards be taken back. The Abyssinian treaty was a pointer in the right direction. It was a gesture of a kind that our enemies cannot emulate, and it can be repeated on a vaster scale in India.

The general lines of the settlement we should make in India are now clear enough. First, let India be given immediate Dominion status, with the right to secede after the war, if she so desires. Secondly, let the leaders of the principal political parties be invited at once to form a National Government, to remain in office for the duration of the war. Thirdly, let India enter into formal military alliance with Britain and the countries allied to Britain. Fourthly, let a trade agreement be drawn up for the exchange of necessary commodities and the reasonable protection of British interests, terminable some stated number of years after the end of the war.

This plan seems less Utopian now than it would have seemed a year or two ago. There are obvious difficulties in its execution – the Hindu– Moslem rivalry is the most obvious – but the menace of outside attack makes this a propitious moment for getting over them. Both China and USSR would welcome a settlement along some such lines as these, and so would at any rate the bulk of American opinion. Our record in India is one of the easiest targets of the Isolationists. Above all, by such a settlement, we should take the wind out of the sails of Axis propaganda once and for all. By helping China and freeing India we should have appropriated 'Asia for the Asiatics' to our own use and turned it from a lie into something at least approaching a reality.

We have learned from the events in Malaya – or at least that is the lesson we ought to have learned – that to concede nothing is to lose everything. The implication of the treaties with Abyssinia and Iran is that a generous act performed at the right moment can substitute genuine partnership for the inherently unsatisfactory relationship of master and servant.

* The 1942 Anglo-Ethiopian agreement confirmed Ethiopia's status as a sovereign state, Britain assisting the build-up of state apparatus whilst retaining some administrative control.

8 March 1942

MOOD OF THE MOMENT

THE British people are in a more thoughtful mood than at any time since 1940, and this time there is no bombing and – seemingly – no imminent invasion to turn their discontent outwards.

They have a feeling of frustration because of continued military defeats, they are angry about the Black Market and the muddle over production, and they are interested, for almost the first time within living memory, in the problem of India. They are anxious for Army reform and for a clearer definition of war aims – above all, anxious for the new Government to demonstrate speedily that it represents a change of policy and not merely a change of personnel.

If one had to sum up the prevailing mood in a phrase, the best would probably be 'Make Democracy Real'. The concrete demands which are put forward on every side are only the symptoms of an underlying malaise. The general public are not competent to decide on details of policy, and probably they realise that they are not competent. But what they do know, or what they deeply feel, is that Britain is too much tied to the past and to an outworn social system. They feel that there is more waste, more inequality of wealth, more thwarting of intelligence, more nepotism, more privilege, than a nation which has been two years at war can afford.

The changes in the Government and, above all, the inclusion of Sir Stafford Cripps [a prominent Marxist socialist, pacifist, and critic of Churchill], have raised hopes which may turn out to be extravagant. Even people normally uninterested in politics feel this to be a turning-point. They are ready for the most sweeping changes and the most cruel sacrifices, if need be. Let the Government's next move be visibly in the direction of making democracy more real, and the mass of the people will follow without bothering too much about the hardships that lie by the way.

---

19 April 1942

MOOD OF THE MOMENT

THERE is not much grumbling about the Budget. Common ale at tenpence a pint and cigarettes at ten for a shilling, unimaginable a few years ago, now seem hardly worth bothering about. In so far as Sir Kingsley Wood [Chancellor of the Exchequer, 1940–43] is criticised, it is less for what he has done than for what he has not done. The fact is that this is not a Budget which 'soaks the rich'. In the matter of direct taxation it benefits the lowest income groups, but it imposes no fresh burdens on the higher groups. It is not much use demonstrating to the common man that, on paper, large incomes don't exist nowadays: they exist, in fact, as he knows by the evidence of his eyes.

It is still not true – and everyone below £500 a year knows it – that we are 'all in it together', as we felt ourselves to be for a little while during the big air-raids. That is why discussions of the Budget lead on irrelevantly to remarks about the basic petrol ration or speculations about the price limit in the forthcoming ban on luxury meals. The British people are not envious as peoples go, but they would like to feel, now, with the enemy at several of the gates, that we ARE all in it together, sharing the petty hardships as well as the great ones.

Since 1940 public opinion in this country has generally been a little ahead of the Government. It has demanded – sometimes within the limits of the possible and sometimes not – an invasion of Europe, more aid to Russia, and a tougher attitude towards hostile neutrals. This week the announcement of the Budget swings attention back to home affairs. 'Cut us to the bone – but cut us ALL to the bone' would probably express what people are thinking. They want equality of sacrifice at home just as they want effective action abroad, and it is probably a sound instinct which tells them that the two things are interconnected.

---

29 November 1942

IN THE DARLAN COUNTRY

B EFORE the war French Morocco, like much of North Africa, lived partly on its picturesqueness, ultimately traceable to poverty. Except for the climate, every feature that attracted the tourist really depended on the fact that the average human being's earnings were round about a penny an hour.

The most striking thing in Morocco is its barrenness. Of its seven million inhabitants the great majority are small peasants, cultivating a soil which is little better than desert. Down the Atlantic coast there is a strip of fertile land where a million tons of wheat are grown annually, but this is owned by a French syndicate which works it with gang labour. The Arab peasant stirs his dried-up soil with a primitive plough drawn by a cow and an ass yoked together, and grows crops of weed-infested barley and lucerne. For a few months there are fitful storms of rain, and then the streams swell, the grass springs up and the miserable domestic animals put on a little flesh, but for the rest of the year water is precious enough to be a cause of feuds and murders. Just as in Biblical times, landmarks are moved and streams suddenly diverted in the middle of the night. Part of the trouble is the lack of trees.

There are date palms, pomegranates and, where the French have settled, groves of oranges and olives, but except in the Atlas Mountains there are no wild trees at all. This is the result of hundreds of years of goat-grazing. Even in the thinly populated Atlas, where there are forests of oak and fir, the mountain-side round each village is bare as a slag-heap, thanks to the goats.

Arabs and French

Morocco differs from the majority of French colonies in that it has only recently been conquered (the fighting did not really end till 1934), and French cultural influences have barely touched it. Very few Moroccan Arabs speak French otherwise than in a sort of barbarous pidgin. In the way of education the French have done very little, and there are no universities and no class corresponding to the English-speaking intelligentsia of Egypt or India. In 1939, at any rate, there was no vernacular Press or Arab-owned French Press, nor any nationalist movement worth bothering about. The social relationship between French and Arabs is complicated by the fact of Morocco being so near Europe. Excellent motor roads run all the way from the Mediterranean shore to the desert beyond the Atlas, and the French lorry-driver, carrying with him the atmosphere of Marseilles, is as ready to sit down in the wayside bistro with an Arab as with a European.

In Casablanca there is a large French proletariat, drawing low wages, and everywhere there are small traders and shopkeepers living among the Arabs, but re-producing as well as they can the life of provincial France. On the other hand, the business community, the bureaucracy, and the army officers live in a more lordly, Anglo-Indian style, and there is a general tendency to treat the Arabs as charming but rather naughty children. Everyone tu-toies them, and the newspapers refer to them patronisingly as 'les indigènes' ('natives'). But the fact that the French working class have little colour prejudice – so that, for instance, French conscripts do not mind being put in the same barracks as African troops – makes for a friendly atmosphere, and has no doubt played its part in damping down nationalist feeling.

Political faiths

There are some 200,000 Europeans in Morocco, all French-speaking, though some of them are of Spanish origin. Since 1940 few Englishmen can have seen the interior of Morocco, and one can only guess at subsequent political developments, but in 1939, at any rate, the prevailing outlook among Europeans was semi-Fascist. The loyalties of the local Press ranged from Daladier to Doriot,* and the Fascist weeklies *Gringoire, Candide, Je Suis Partout,* and the rest of them, were on sale everywhere. The Left-wing parties had no foothold, even in Casablanca. During the Munich crisis the general apathy and cynicism, even among army officers, were very striking. Anti-Semitism was common, although the Moroccan Jews, who live in self-contained communities and are mostly petty craftsmen, present no real problem. Some nationalist feeling may also have increased among the Arabs as a result of the French defeat and the consequent slump in French prestige.

Morocco is now under the control of the United Nations, and merely to govern it, in the sense of preventing rebellion, is not likely to be difficult. The French have successfully ruled it through the phantom Sultan, who has already transferred his allegiance to ourselves. But whether Morocco can be brought actively into the war is another question, not answerable during the political interregnum. At present we appear to have guaranteed Admiral Darlan,† and if that means that we have guaranteed the existing regime, then Morocco will remain what it has always been – stagnant, feudal, and desperately poor. The long-term needs of the country are obvious enough. It needs more trees, more irrigation, better agricultural methods, better breeds of animals, more schools, more hospitals. All this means foreign capital and, inevitably, foreign protection, for a weak and backward country like Morocco cannot be genuinely independent.

But it would be a great pity if a positive short-term policy, capable of enlisting the Arabs on our side, cannot be evolved. Morocco is obviously important in the strategy of the war. The road and rail communication running from Casablanca to Tunis gives us a supply route far safer than we have had hitherto, and at the worst the possession of Casablanca would partly offset the loss of Gibraltar. In spite of its poverty, Morocco can export several valuable foodstuffs, and at need it could also produce at least 100,000 soldiers of the highest quality. The peace-time strength of the colonial army in Morocco was 50,000, of whom perhaps half would be Arabs. They were long-term volunteers, the Moroccan Arabs, unlike the Algerians or the Senegalese, not being French citizens and therefore not liable to conscription. The equipment of these troops was and probably still is old-fashioned, but as human material they would be hard to beat.

It seems unlikely, however, that Morocco will enter fully into the war effort unless the war can somehow be given a meaning from the Arab point of view. Basically it is a matter of economic restitution. The French exploitation of Morocco has not been particularly gross, but still it is exploitation, and any thinking Arab must be aware of this. Nearly all of the most fertile soil of the country, and all the modern industries, are in foreign hands.

'Deep changes'

Moreover, if Italian Libya is conquered and some fairly generous settlement arrived at there, it must have repercussions among the Western Arabs. The grosser injustices could be wiped out without interfering with the small French settler, though not, indeed, without bumping up against the big capitalist interests. If we want the Arabs on our side, we have got to promise them either autonomy or a higher standard of living, or both. And there is also the local French working class, whose interests are approximately the same as those of the Arabs. Whether the existing French authorities, whom we have so hastily guaranteed, will lend themselves to any genuine programme of reform seems very doubtful. But it is certain that in Morocco, as in so many other places, the mass of the people will not and cannot be actively with us unless we are ready to make deep changes in the status quo.

* Edouard Daladier was a Radical socialist and French premier from 1938 to 1940; Jacques Doriot was a French Communist who later fought with Germany during WWII.

† Admiral Jean Francois Darlan was High Commander in French north Africa during WWII.

THREE YEARS OF HOME GUARD

IT is close on three years since the eager amateurs of the LDV [Local Defence Volunteers] doctored shot-gun cartridges with candle-grease and practised grenade-throwing with lumps of concrete, and the value of the Home Guard [as the LDV was later renamed] as a fighting force can now be fairly accurately estimated.

Although it has never fought, its achievement has not been negligible. In the early days, the Germans, to judge by their broadcasts, took the Home Guard more seriously than it took itself, and it must at all times have been part of the reason for their failure to invade Britain. If it were even 5 per cent of the reason it would not have done so badly for a part-time and unpaid army.

The Home Guard has passed through three fairly well-defined phases. The first was frankly chaotic, not only because in the summer of 1940 the Home Guard had few weapons and no uniforms, but because it was enormously larger than anyone had expected.

An appeal over the radio, probably intended to produce 50,000 volunteers, produced a million within a few weeks, and the new force had to organise itself almost unhelped. Since opinions differed about the probable form of a German invasion, it organised itself in innumerable different ways.

Modern problems

By the middle of 1941 the Home Guard was a coherent and standardised force, seriously interested in street-fighting and camouflage, and reasonably well armed with rifles and machine-guns. By 1942 it had Sten guns and sub-artillery as well, and was beginning to take over some of the anti-aircraft defences. This third phase, in which the Home Guard is definitely integrated with both the Regular Army and Civil Defence, has its own problems, some not easily soluble.

During the past year it has been assumed that if the Continent is invaded the Home Guard will partly replace the Regular Forces in these islands, and the result has been the tendency to train it for mobile warfare. This has been made easier by the fall in the average age of the Home Guard. But in some ways the results have not been happy. With a part-time and frequently changing personnel, it is doubtful wisdom to imitate the training of Regular soldiers and, in any case, the Home Guard could not be made fully mobile even if transport existed for it.

Most of its members are also workers and, even in the case of invasion, the economic life would have to be carried on in any area where fighting was not actually happening.

Home ground

If Britain is ever invaded, the Home Guard will in practice fight only in its own areas and in smallish units. The steady tightening of discipline and the increasing contact with the Regular Army have been enormous advantages, but as a strategic plan it would probably have been better to stick to the original idea of purely local defence, and thus make use of the only advantage the amateur soldier has over the professional – that is, intimate knowledge of the ground he is fighting on.

But though the Home Guard has come to look and to be much more like an army than it was, its early days have left their mark on it. The training schools started by Tom Wintringham and others in the summer of 1940 did invaluable work in spreading an understanding of the nature of total war and an imaginative attitude towards military problems.

Even the then lack of weapons had its advantages, for it led to much experimenting in garages and machine shops, and several of the anti-tank weapons now in use are partly the result of Home Guard researches.

Non-political

Socially the Home Guard is not quite what it was at the beginning. Membership has changed rapidly with the call-up, and its tendency has been to settle into the accepted English class pattern. This was perhaps inevitable in an unpaid army in which it is difficult to do the work of an officer without having a car and a telephone.

But if its internal atmosphere is not truly democratic, at least it is friendly. And it is very typical of Britain that this vast organisation, now three years old, has had no conscious political development whatever. It has neither developed into a People's Army like the Spanish Government militias, as some hoped at the beginning, nor into an SA [*Sturm Abteilung*, the Nazi terrorist militia], as others feared or professed to fear. It has been held together, not by any political creed, but simply by inarticulate patriotism.

Its mere existence – the fact that in the moment of crisis it could be called into being by a few words over the air, the fact that somewhere near two million men have rifles in their bedrooms and the authorities contemplate this without dismay – is the sign of a stability unequalled in any other country of the world.

---

23 May 1943

PROFILE: SIR RICHARD ACLAND

LEAN, spectacled and young-looking for his thirty-six years, with an irresistible suggestion of a sixth-form boy – the kind of prefect who is not very good at games but makes up for it by force of character – Sir Richard Acland gives above all else an impression of earnestness. Even his enemies do not accuse him of insincerity. But it is not a solemn kind of earnestness either, merely the eager, buttonholing enthusiasm of a man who not only knows that he possesses the truth, but, what is more, knows that the truth is very simple and can be printed on a four-page leaflet.

If you ask Sir Richard Acland what is the central doctrine of Common Wealth, his small but growing political party, he will answer you more or less like this: Capitalism must be scrapped forthwith but Britain must 'go Socialist' under her own steam and in the way that accords with her past traditions. Nationalisation of industry – yes; class warfare – no; imperialism – no; patriotism – yes; collaboration with Russia – yes; imitation of Russian methods – no.

Simple, and even obvious, as such a programme may sound, it is original enough to have earned the hostility of the older Left-wing parties. And the by-election figures suggest that they have good reason to fear this youthful rival.

Much depends on phraseology, as Acland is well aware. Common Wealth dislikes labelling itself as 'Socialist', avoids the Marxist jargon and tries, not altogether successfully, to speak the language of the people.

Acland is a landowner and fifteenth baronet, but this describes only a part of his background. He comes of notable West Country Radical stock. His father, Sir Francis Dyke Acland, after holding other Government posts, was Asquith's Secretary to the Board of Agriculture in the first Coalition, and resigned office with his leader in 1916.

Lady Acland, a woman of singular sensibility and graciousness, who died in 1933, was a former President of the Women's National Liberal Federation and an ardent worker for the emancipation of women. Thus Richard Acland's politics are deeply rooted.

Holder of a seat at Barnstaple, for which he was elected as a Liberal, Acland has never experienced the ordinary discipline of a Left-wing party.

He likes to explain – eagerly, and even with a tendency to bang on the table – that the existing Left-wing parties have ruined themselves by ignoring three obvious facts. The first is that the 'dictatorship of the proletariat' is out of date. The proletariat by itself is no longer strong enough to dominate society and can only win with the help of the middle classes. Secondly, any political party which insults patriotism is doomed, at any rate in England. Thirdly, and above all, the real driving force behind the Socialist movement is and must be ethical and not economic. Hence the Common Wealth slogan, 'What is morally wrong cannot be politically right' – a clumsy slogan, but one with some appeal.

Grafted on to this is a rather indeterminate immediate policy which at times seems to promise everything to everybody. Common Wealth proposes to nationalise all the means of production, but it is also ready to pay compensation – full compensation to small property-owners, fractional compensation to big ones. It will stop exploiting the Empire, but will preserve the English standard of living. It will deal firmly with its opponents, but will permit freedom of speech. It will be anti-military, but will encourage patriotism. It will co-operate with anyone whose aims are reasonably similar.

In all this, no doubt, there is an element of Utopianism. But this much can be said: if common ownership is ever established in Britain, it will be by a party of approximately the kind that Acland is striving for, and not of the continental Marxist type.

Whether Sir Richard Acland will be the ultimate leader of that party is a different question. He himself says that he does not want to; he merely wants to bring a larger movement into being. His opponents, on the other hand, accuse him of a 'Führer complex' and declare that, if Common Wealth seemed likely to be swamped by a really nation-wide movement, Acland would walk out of it sooner than play second fiddle.

This judgement is probably coloured by jealousy. It is, in fact, not easy to imagine Acland as a political figure of the very first rank, either for good or evil. He has the single-mindedness of a dictator, but not the vulgarity, perhaps not even the toughness. More plausibly, his opponents say that Common Wealth is merely a product of the electoral truce and will wither away as soon as the Labour Party is free to campaign again.

Meanwhile, Common Wealth fights by-elections all over the country and wins a surprising number of votes. It may finally break, as all radical movements hitherto have broken, on the rock of the trade unions. Acland claims, and can produce figures to support him, that he has a strong following in the armed forces and is gaining ground in the factories, in spite of Communist opposition. He has at least had the wisdom not to look at Britain through pink spectacles or think in terms of that mythical animal the 'economic man'.

15 August 1943

WHERE TO GO – BUT HOW?

To know where to go and to know how to get there are two different mental processes, all too seldom combined in any one person. Political thinkers, in general, can be divided into two classes: the Utopian with his head in the clouds and the realist with his feet in the mud. Mr Edward Hulton, in spite of the shrewdness that brought *Picture Post* into being at the exact moment when the potential demand for it had begun to exist,* is nearer to the first class and more successful at pointing out desirable objectives than at surveying the actual political scene.

The new world that Mr Hulton wants is, broadly speaking, the kind of world that every sensible man wants, but the comparative powerlessness of sensible men is something that he is inclined to ignore. Throughout his book called *The New Age* (George Allen and Unwin, 7s. 6d.), the phrases 'we must', 'we should', 'the Government must', 'the Government should' recur again and again, on every subject from foreign policy to town planning and from finance to educational reform, with the implied assumption that if 'we' know what we want 'we' shall get it. But there is also the working-class assumption that 'they' (the higher-ups) will invariably prevent you from getting what you want, and though this is often over-pessimistic, it contains much truth.

Mr Hulton has not much use for the orthodox Socialist, and particularly for the Marxist doctrinaire. Now it is true that Marxism in the form in which it is usually preached makes a false estimate of the balance of forces, but it does keep sight of the fundamental truth that 'where your treasure is, there will your heart be also'. The social changes that Mr Hulton desires would only entail a diminution of power and privilege for a few people, but those few people are not easily removable, and what is more are not teachable. For as Marx rightly pointed out, the rich man will not only cling to his riches, but will construct philosophies to justify him in doing so.

But if Mr Hulton has his blind spots, his boldness and generosity more than make up for them. For five years he has acted as a sort of catalyst on public opinion, and what he writes is nearly always stimulating, even when it is silly. He stands for a number of things which no society has yet succeeded in combining, but which the ordinary thinking man in our age instinctively feels to be compatible. He stands for a world of plenty and a simple way of living, for a planned economy and individual freedom, for a European Federation and local autonomy, for democracy without uniformity, and for religion without dogma.

Though he is definitely to be classified as 'Left', he is a disbeliever in the class war, does not believe nationalisation to be the cure for everything, thinks the British ruling classes have their points, and is not notably anti-imperialist. The dinginess and out-of-dateness of contemporary England, its unenterprising business methods, its worship of stupidity, its ravaged countryside, its joylessness (Mr Hulton is markedly anti-puritan) fill him with considerable fury, but he has a mystical belief in the destiny of his own country and is quite certain that Britain must be the paramount influence in Western Europe after the war. In a slightly guarded way, he is pro-Russian, and he is also – perhaps this is only a temporary phenomenon, arising out of recent events – anti-American.

Now this epitomises the outlook of some millions of youngish people who are well aware that the present evils of the world are largely unnecessary, and Mr Hulton has done a great service, both here and in *Picture Post*, by acting as a sort of one-man Brains Trust.[†] The best quality of his mind is that he is genuinely anti-totalitarian, and no respecter of orthodoxy of any kind. In his search for remedies he flits blithely to and fro between democracy, aristocracy, Socialism, currency reform, federalism, imperialism, consumers' co-operatives, compulsory labour service, Youth Movements, and even – tentatively – polygamy. And there is little doubt that with his eclectic approach he gets nearer to the truth than he could get by clinging to some obsolete 'ism'.

Against the Conservative he maintains that 'sound finance' is nonsense, class privilege indefensible, and national sovereignty an anachronism. Against the Socialist he maintains that the class war is out of date, hedonism a danger, and pacifism a delusion. Above all, he insists on the need for common decency and an abandonment of the Machiavellianism practised by politicians and defended by intellectuals. As a statement of what the ordinary decent person under fifty *wants*, his book is adequate and it is not even so shallow as its hurried slipshod writing makes it appear. It is merely that, like most Liberals, he under-estimates the gulf between 'what' and 'how'.

Perhaps, after all, Mr Hulton could learn something from the doctrinaires whom he too lightly dismisses. At present there is a gap in his intellectual ladder. Common sense and good will are not enough; there is also the problem of overcoming ill will and invincible ignorance. Mr Hulton might do us all a service if he would turn his optimistic and inquiring mind towards that problem.

* Edward Hulton was the publisher of *Picture Post*, a groundbreaking magazine of photojournalism, produced 1938–57.

† *The Brains Trust*, first broadcast in 1941, was the precurser of the BBC radio's *Any Questions*.

13 February 1944

A HUNDRED UP

IT is now a hundred years since the final numbers of *Martin Chuzzlewit* were published, and though it came thus early in Dickens's career (it was his fourth novel if one counts *Pickwick* as a novel), it has more the air of being a pot-boiler than any of his books, except the *Sketches*. There cannot be many people living who could outline its plot from memory. Whereas books like *Oliver Twist* or *Bleak House* or *Great Expectations* have a central theme, which can in some cases be reduced to a single word, the various parts of *Martin Chuzzlewit* have not much more relationship to one another than the sounds produced by a cat walking across the piano. The best characters are 'supers'.

What do people remember when they think of *Martin Chuzzlewit*? The American interlude, Mrs Gamp, and Todgers's (especially Bailey). Martin Chuzzlewit himself is a stick, Mark Tapley a tedious paradox on two legs, Pecksniff a partial failure. It is ironical that Dickens should have tried, more or less unsuccessfully, to make Pecksniff into a monumental figure of a hypocrite, and at the same time, almost incidentally, should have painted such a devastating picture of hypocrisy in the American chapters. Dickens's comic genius is dependent on his moral sense. He is funniest when he is discovering new sins. To denounce Pecksniff did not call into play his special powers, because, after all, no one supposes that hypocrisy is desirable. But to see through the pretensions of American democracy or even, at that date, to see that Mrs Gamp was a luxury that society might well do without, did need the eye of a Dickens. The book's lack of any real central theme can be seen in its fearful ending. It is as though Dickens were dissolving into lukewarm treacle, and – as so often when he says something that he does not really feel – whole paragraphs of the final chapter will go straight into blank verse:

Thy life is tranquil, calm, and happy, Tam.
In the soft strain which ever and again
Comes stealing back upon the ear, the memory
Of thine old love may find a voice perhaps.
But it is a pleasant, softened whispering memory,
Like that in which we sometimes hold the dead,
And does not pain or grieve thee,
God be thanked.

Yet the man who could write this stuff could also record the conversations of Bailey, and could not only create Mrs Gamp but could throw in, just for good measure, that metaphysical puzzle, Mrs Harris.

The American chapters are a good example of Dickens's habit of telling small lies in order to emphasise what he regards as a big truth. No doubt many of the things he reports actually happened (other travellers of the time confirm him on some details), but his picture of American society as a whole cannot possibly be true: not only because no community is wholly bad, but because the chaos of real life has been deliberately left out. Every incident, every character, is simply an illustration of Dickens's thesis. Moreover, the strongest charge that he makes against the Americans, that they boast of being democratic while actually living on slave labour, is obviously unfair. It implies that American opinion as a whole acquiesced in slavery, whereas a bloody civil war was to be fought mainly on this issue only twenty years later. But, Dickens says these things in order to hit at what he feels to be the real fault of the Americans: their ignorant contempt for Europe and unjustified belief in their own superiority. Perhaps there *were* a few Americans who did not edit libellous newspapers or emit sentences like 'the libation of freedom must sometimes be quaffed in blood', but to lay too much stress upon them would have been to spoil the picture. After all, the business of a caricaturist is to make his point, and these chapters have worn very much better than *American Notes*.

The mental atmosphere of the American interlude is one that has since become familiar to us in the books written by British travellers to Soviet Russia. Some of these report that everything is good, others that everything is bad, but nearly all share the same propagandist outlook. A hundred years ago America, 'the land of the free', had rather the same place in the European imagination that Soviet Russia has now, and *Martin Chuzzlewit* is the 1844 equivalent of André Gide's *Retour de l'URSS*. But it is a sign of the changing temper of the world that Dickens's attack, so much more violent and unfair than Gide's, could be so quickly forgiven.

Martin Chuzzlewit stands somewhere near the turning-point of Dickens's literary development, when he was becoming less of a picaresque writer and more of a novelist. The times were changing with the rise of the new cautious middle class, and Dickens was too much alive not to be affected by the atmosphere he lived in. *Martin Chuzzlewit* is his last completely disorderly book. In spite of its frequent flashes of genius, it is difficult to feel that by following up this vein in himself, Dickens could have given us anything to compensate for the loss of *Hard Times* and *Great Expectations*.

---

4 June 1944

SURVEY OF 'CIVVY STREET'

THE surveys undertaken by Mass Observation from the beginning of the war onwards have revealed many different moods, but nearly all have suggested that Britain suffers from too little government rather than too much. Cheque after cheque has been drawn on the accumulated good will of the British people, but very little positive guidance has been given. They know what they are fighting against, but they have not been clearly told what they are fighting *for* or what the post-war world will probably be like. The new survey,* like some previous ones, gives warning that their patience and hopefulness may not be inexhaustible.

Although specifically concerned with demobilisation, it also deals with re-employment and reconstruction. It reveals not only widespread cynicism about 'after the war', but also a surprising vagueness. Thus, when a cross-section of the public was asked in November 1943 'whether the Government had announced any policy of post-war reconstruction', only 16 per cent thought it had. The corresponding percentage had actually been higher two years earlier. Most disquieting is the return to the 1918 frame of mind. Great numbers are convinced that 'it will be just like last time' and, as their memories of last time are not happy ones, the effects on morale are potentially bad.

Disbelief in the future is especially strong in the armed forces and among the Civil Defence workers. The soldiers (this is somewhat less marked in the women's services) want above all things to get out of uniform as soon as the war is over, and a number of people even think that there will be great discontent if demobilisation is not achieved rapidly. They know that the process of demobilisation is complicated, but are not confident that it will be done fairly or intelligently (memories of 'last time' are a heavy liability here) and, even more serious, they have no clear idea as to how long it ought to take. Meanwhile, countless soldiers cherish a private dream that they, as individuals, will somehow be able to get out of it when the fighting stops. The possible effects of this kind of thing in the immediate post-war period are obvious. They can only be countered by a clear statement from the Government which will let people know just how long they will be expected to stay in uniform and why.

So also with post-war employment. According to the Mass Observers' findings, a majority still expect large-scale unemployment after the war – another legacy from 'last time'. At the same time there is a growing consciousness that unemployment is an unnecessary evil. It is probably significant that the number of people expecting unemployment to return has not markedly altered over several years: there is no strong belief that our economic system will be radically changed. In general the feeling seems to be that most of our problems are soluble, but that the mysterious and all-powerful 'They' will prevent anything from being done. The result is increasing apathy and a determination – of course accentuated by sheer fatigue as the war continues – to sit back and have a good rest as soon as the guns stop firing.

It is a sign of the general lack of confidence in the future that in 1943, out of a random sample of Londoners, 46 per cent thought that there would be another world war after this one, and 19 per cent thought there might be. The majority of these thought that this new war would happen within twenty-five years. Faith in all the main political parties has dwindled, and there is a confused desire for more vigorous leadership combined with more genuine democracy.

Yet how ready for effort and sacrifice most people are, when they are given a good reason, can be seen in their attitude towards war-time controls. Nearly all of these have been accepted readily: even the withdrawal of white bread was approved by a four to one majority. Other more drastic measures, not actually put into force, would be generally approved. For example, the Mass Observers found a ten to one majority in favour of Government ownership of essential industries, and seven to one in favour of nationalisation of the mines.

Controls are even welcomed for their own sake, as having an equalising effect. On the whole, whenever the Government acts positively and explains what it is doing, even if what it is doing is to take something away, the people seem to respond. Certain events, such as the delay about 'Beveridge', and even the release of Mosley, have deeply shaken public confidence, but it is the failure to explain, to give a picture of the future, that apparently does the most harm.

It is unfortunate that much of the work done by Mass Observation should have to be financed by a private body which naturally only wants reports on a rather limited range of subjects. The present survey has one very serious omission: this is that it makes no reference to the war against Japan. The subject of demobilisation is complicated by the fact that Japan will almost certainly go on fighting, perhaps for years, after Germany is defeated. But the main conclusions reached by the Mass Observers can hardly be questioned.

Political consciousness has expanded greatly during the war, while belief in the existing leadership has shrunk. The belief that planned reconstruction is possible has grown, while the belief that it is *likely* has made no headway. There is a gap between the leaders and the led, and the deadly word 'They' saps confidence and encourages anarchic individualism. It is important that that gap should be closed before the war ends. For, as the Mass Observers point out, it will need as great an effort to win the peace as to win the war, and the people may shrink from making it unless they have a better notion than at present of where they are going.

* The Journey Home by Mass Observation (published for the Advertising Service Guild by John Murray). [Original footnote.]

THE EIGHT YEARS OF WAR: SPANISH MEMORIES

THE Spanish Civil War, curtain-raiser of the present struggle and one of the most tragic as well as one of the most sordid events that modern Europe has seen, began eight years ago next Friday.

The issue of the Spanish war was decided outside Spain, and by the time that it was a year old realistic observers were able to see that the elected government could not win unless there were some radical change in the European situation. In the first period of the war, which lasted just under a year, the struggle was essentially between Franco's professional soldiers and Moors on the one side and the hurriedly raised militias of peasants and factory workers on the other.

In this period honours were about even, and no objective of first-rate importance changed hands.

Franco, however, was being reinforced on a massive scale by the Axis Powers, while the Spanish Government was receiving only sporadic doles of arms from Soviet Russia and the help of a few thousand foreign volunteers, mostly refugee Germans. In June 1937 the resistance of the Basques collapsed and the balance of forces tipped heavily against the Government.

Starvation comes

In the meantime, however, the Government had quelled the revolutionary disorder of early days, smoothed out the struggles between factions, and trained its raw forces. Early in 1938 it had a formidable army, able to fight on for the year or so that food supplies would last out.

Dr Negrin and the other rulers of Government Spain probably realised that they could not win by their own efforts, but they were justified in fighting on since the political outlook in Europe still might change. The obviously approaching world war might break out during 1938; the British Government might abandon its policy of non-intervention.

Neither event happened, and towards the end of 1938 the Russians withdrew their help. Government Spain had long been hungry and was now definitely starving.

As the Fascist forces drove across Catalonia, hordes of refugees streamed into France, machine-gunned by Italian aeroplanes and interned behind barbed-wire as soon as they arrived.

Early in 1939 Franco entered Madrid and used his victory with the utmost ruthlessness. All political parties of the Left were suppressed, and countless people executed or imprisoned. If recent reports are true, half a million people or 2 per cent of the population of Spain are still in concentration camps.

Axis intervention

The story is a disgusting one, because of the sordid behaviour of the Great Powers and the indifference of the world at large. The Germans and Italians intervened in order to crush Spanish democracy, to seize a strategic keypoint for the coming war and, incidentally, to try out their bombing planes on helpless populations.

The Russians doled out a small quantity of weapons and extorted the maximum of political control in return. The British and French simply looked the other way while their enemies triumphed and their friends were destroyed. The British attitude is the hardest to forgive, because it was foolish as well as dishonourable.

It had been obvious from the start that any foreign country which supplied arms to the Spanish Government could control or at least influence that Government's policy. Instead, the British preferred to make sure that Franco and Hitler should win, and at the same time that the affection and gratitude of the Spanish people should be earned by Russia and not by Britain.

Aid from Russia

For a year or more the Spanish Government was effectively under Russian control, mainly because Russia was the only country to come to the rescue. The growth of the Spanish Communist Party from a few thousands to a quarter of a million was directly the work of the British Tories.

There has been a strong tendency to push these facts out of sight and even to claim Franco's hostile 'non-belligerency' as a triumph for British diplomacy. Rather should the true history of the Spanish war be kept always in mind as an object lesson in the folly and meanness of Power Politics. Nothing, indeed, redeems its story except the courage of the fighting-men on both sides and the toughness of the civilian population of Loyalist Spain, who for years endured hunger and hardship unknown to us at the worst moments of war.

---

13 August 1944

THE CHILDREN WHO CANNOT BE BILLETED

A valuable piece of sociological work has been done by Mrs Marie Paneth, the Austrian authoress, whose book *Branch Street*, recently published by Allen and Unwin, brought to light some rather surprising facts about the slum conditions still existing here and there in the heart of London.

For nearly two years Mrs Paneth has been working at a children's play centre in a street which she chooses to conceal under the name of Branch Street. Though not far from the centre of London, it happens to be a 'bad' quarter, and it is quite clear from her descriptions that when she first went there the children were little better than savages. They did indeed have homes of sorts, but in behaviour they resembled the troops of 'wild children' who were a by-product of the Russian civil war. They were not only dirty, ragged, under-nourished and unbelievably obscene in language and corrupt in outlook, but they were all thieves, and as intractable as wild animals.

A few of the girls were comparatively approachable, but the boys simply smashed up the play centre over and over again, sometimes breaking in at night to do the job more thoroughly, and at times it was even dangerous for a grown-up to venture among them single-handed.

Won their confidence

It took a long time for this gentle, grey-haired lady, with her marked foreign accent, to win the children's confidence. The principle she went on was never to oppose them forcibly if it could possibly be avoided, and never to let them think that they could shock her. In the end this seems to have worked, though not without some very disagreeable experiences. Mrs Paneth believes that children of this kind, who have had no proper home life and regard grown-ups as enemies, are best treated on the 'libertarian' principles evolved by Homer Lane, Mr A. S. Neill and others.

Though not a professional psychologist, Mrs Paneth is the wife of a doctor, and has done work of this kind before. During the last war she worked in a children's hospital in Vienna and later in a children's play centre in Berlin. She describes the 'Branch Street' children as much the worst she has encountered in any country. But, speaking as a foreign observer, she finds that nearly all English children have certain redeeming traits: she instances the devotion which even the worst child will show in looking after a younger brother or sister.

It is also interesting to learn that these semi-savage children, who see nothing wrong in stealing and flee at the very sight of a policeman, are all deeply patriotic and keen admirers of Mr Churchill.

Forgotten corner

It is clear from Mrs Paneth's account that 'Branch Street' is simply a forgotten corner of the nineteenth century, existing in the middle of a comparatively prosperous area. She does not believe that the conditions in which the children live have been made much worse by the war. (Incidentally, various attempts to evacuate these children were a failure: they all came under the heading of 'unbilletable'.)

It is impossible to talk to her or read her book without wondering how many more of these pockets of corruption exist in London and other big towns. Mrs Paneth has managed to keep in touch with some of the children who were previously under her care and have now gone to work. With such a background they have neither the chance of a worthwhile job nor, as a rule, the capacity for steady work. At best they find their way into some blind-alley occupation, but are more likely to end up in crime or prostitution.

The surprise which this book caused in many quarters is an indication of how little is still known of the underside of London life. The huge slum areas that existed within living memory have been cleared up, but in a smaller way there is obviously still a great deal to do. Mrs Paneth was astonished and gratified that her book, which casts a very unfavourable light on this country, received no hostile criticism.

Probably that is a sign that public opinion is becoming more sensitive to the problem of the neglected child. In any case, it would be difficult to read the book without conceiving an admiration for its author, who has carried out a useful piece of civilising work with great courage and infinite good-temper.

But 'Branch Street' still exists, and it will go on creating wild and hopeless children until it has been abolished and rebuilt along with the other streets that have the same atmosphere.

15 October 1944

HOME GUARD LESSONS FOR THE FUTURE

Now that the danger of any serious attempt at German invasion has obviously passed, the Home Guard can be safely disbanded, and it becomes possible to see its activities in perspective and even to draw some general inferences about part-time irregular armies.

We do not know how the Home Guard would have fought if it had been called upon: almost certainly it would have given a good account of itself any time after 1941, and would have had a considerable nuisance value even in 1940. As things turned out its functions were purely preventive and, granted that its existence did help to make the Germans think twice about invasion, it gave extraordinarily good value at very low cost to the community as a whole. It is worth reflecting on the amount of extra work that can be safely demanded of the citizens of a democratic State without effective compulsion and almost without pay.

The ordinary Home Guard private who is now retiring after four years' service will certainly not have given up less than 1,200 hours of his spare time: more probably it would be about 4,000 hours, or many more in the case of an officer. During those four years he will have been paid in fees for guard duties (similar to those paid to fire-watchers) round about £85.

Pre-Army training

Otherwise he will have cost the community nothing except his uniform, a certain amount of ammunition, and wear and tear of weapons, the rent of a few premises, and the salaries of a very few Regular Army instructors. And, in addition, during the second two years of its existence, the Home Guard has given valuable preliminary training to tens of thousand of youths who would later enter the Regular Forces.

More important, symptomatically, than the cheapness of an army of this type is its voluntary character. Conscription was introduced after about two years, but it was probably aimed at getting younger recruits and was not strictly necessary for the purpose of keeping up numbers. Between a million and two million men had been raised by voluntary means. Moreover, at the beginning discipline rested entirely upon good will. Officers and NCOs had no power of coercion whatever. Later, legal penalties were introduced for absenteeism and indiscipline, but they were a very weak substitute for military punishments, and they were applied in only a few cases. There were many units where no prosecution was ever instituted, and some unit commanders announced from the start that they did not intend to make use of their legal powers.

If one asks 'What held the Home Guard together?' the answer can only be 'The Germans'. The idea behind it was simply the primitive instinct to defend one's native soil, and to an astonishing extent it failed throughout its four years to develop any political colour. Foreign-born recruits remarked with surprise that they listened to scores of lectures on military technique, but never to one on the origins of the war. The inherited or early acquired patriotism on which the Home Guard depended is not necessarily inexhaustible, even in Britain, and it is possible to point out ways in which a force of this kind could probably be made more effective should it be needed again.

Political symptom

Briefly, such a force should be, and probably could be, more democratic and more conscious of what the war is about. It should be more exactly aware of its own aims, military as well as political. The Home Guard suffered from the start from an uncertainty as to whether it was a guerrilla force or an adjunct to the Regular Army. And it would have been more democratic as well as more efficient if it had had a higher proportion of paid personnel. In the absence of paid instructors the commissioned ranks were frequently filled by people with fairly large incomes, so that the Home Guard mirrored the existing class-structure even more exactly than the Regular Army. In the circumstances of a foreign invasion these things could be serious weaknesses. But they are all remediable and meanwhile the Home Guard has played its part, both as a military force and as a political symptom. No authoritarian State would have dared to distribute weapons so freely.

---

4 March 1945

OCCUPATION'S EFFECT ON FRENCH OUTLOOK

Different political thinking

Paris, 3 March

The visit of M. Bloault, French Foreign Minister, to London continues to be keenly discussed, and beneath the warm expressions of Franco-British friendship one can discern in part of the Press a faint uneasiness about the probable British attitude on the subject of the Rhine frontier.

Nevertheless, so far as one can gather from random conversations, the French are still somewhat in the dark about certain aspects of public opinion in Britain. The two peoples have had a totally different political development over five years, and their future relationship will probably be happier if the points of disagreement are brought into the open as early as possible.

One of the first things that strikes a newcomer is that almost any Frenchman has a far tougher attitude towards Germany than almost any Englishman. I have been impressed by this in private conversations even more than in reading the newspapers and it applies not merely to Communists and 100 per cent Gaullists, but to Socialists and members of the Left-wing Resistance groups.

There are, of course, individual variations, but there seems hardly to be such a thing as a Frenchman who does not assume that dismemberment of Germany, the dismantling of German war industries, heavy reparations, forced labour and military occupation over a long period are the minimum needs for French security.

Pacifism disappears

The real situation in France would be hard to assess even if internal communications were better. Some of the main forces are not operating on the surface. Irreconcilable enemies are observing a temporary truce, the Press is timid, and great numbers of people are made apathetic by privation.

But so far as the articulate minorities go, the effect of the occupation seems to have been a harshening of political thought and the disappearance of various trends once looked upon as progressive. Pacifism, for instance, seems to have disappeared completely. Not only did some of the leading pacifists discredit themselves by collaborating, but the desire to see France reappear as soon as possible as a great military power, with a large mechanised army, seems universal.

The ultra Left sects, which were not absolutely negligible in pre-war France, seem also to have vanished. Some groups of Trotskyists do manage to exist and publish an illegal paper, but they evidently have little influence. The nexus of ideas, Army–Fatherland–Glory seems to have re-established itself to an extent that is surprising when one remembers that it is only a decade or so since French Left-wingers thought it proper to denounce the Versailles Treaty as an iniquity, and to cover such figures as Foch and Clemenceau with abuse.

Anti-imperialist propaganda has faded out of the picture. De Gaulle's statement that Indo-China, once liberated, would be integrated more closely into the French Empire, without interference from outside powers, was received without comment.

Birth-rate anxiety

Another phenomenon, not strictly political but symptomatic of the change in the mental climate, is the widespread anxiety about the state of the French birth-rate. Left-wing newspapers and reviews carry articles discussing the best way to encourage maternity and deploring the practice of deliberate limitation of families – an attitude which is well justified but which would have been considered reactionary only a few years ago.

Since, in the long run, the enforcement of policy depends on the common people, the present divergence of French and British political thought has its dangers. In a way, France is politically to the left of Britain. The ruling class is largely discredited, and, on the other hand, there is comparatively little overt opposition to such projects as the nationalisation of major industries.

But the internationalist and humanitarian ideas once thought inseparable from Socialism have receded, and respect for Democracy has probably been weakened. This has not happened to the same extent in England and the fact ought to be made clear to the French people. In particular, it ought to be made clear that the British public is very unlikely for any length of time to support a peace settlement that appears vindictive, and certainly will not support any policy that entails a permanent army of occupation.

On the other hand, we ourselves ought to make a better effort to understand the French point of view.

No matter to whom you talk in this country, you are soon brought up against the same fact – that Britain has not known what it is like to be occupied.

Agitation for 'purge'

It is impossible to discuss the 'purge' for instance, without being reminded of this. [See also p. 52, below.]

The people who would like to see the 'purge' in full swing – and some of them say freely that they believe several thousand executions to be necessary – are not reactionaries and not necessarily Communists, they may be thoughtful, sensitive people whose antecedents are Liberal, Socialist, or non-political.

Your objections always get much the same answer: 'It's different for you in England. You can do things peacefully because there is no real division within the nation. Here we have to deal with actual traitors. It's not safe to let them remain alive.' So also with the attitude towards Germany. A highly intelligent Frenchman, brushing aside my suggestion that a Democratic Germany might arise when Hitler is gone, said to me: 'It's not a question of wanting revenge. It's merely that, after having had them here for four years, I have great difficulty in believing that the Germans are the same kind of people as yourselves.'

Some observers think that the present rather chauvinist cast of French thought is a superficial symptom and that quite other tendencies will show themselves when the war is safely won.

Meanwhile, whatever divergencies there may be, either in high policy or in public opinion, there appears to be no anti-British feeling in France.

If one may judge by Paris, France has never been more Anglophile and one is paid quite embarrassing compliments on the subject of Britain's lonely struggle in 1940 and on the 'très correct' bearing of the comparatively few British soldiers who are to be seen in the streets.

---

11 March 1945

CLERICAL PARTY MAY RE-EMERGE IN FRANCE

Educational controversy

Paris, 10 March

During this week, Paris has been discussing a yellow poster which appeared all over the city last Tuesday and which bore a title roughly translatable as 'Secularism versus National Unity'.

It was unsigned but obviously emanated from the Catholic Press, and it called for a public demonstration against anti-clerical intolerance.

The reference was clearly to some remarks made by a Communist speaker in the Assembly on the question of State subsidies to Catholic schools. The amount of private comment, as well as some guarded but acrimonious remarks in the Press, shows how important the issue is felt to be.

So far as it refers to education, the controversy between Clericals and anti-Clericals is very similar to the one that recently occurred in Britain. Under the Third Republic, education was secularised. Religious instruction in the State schools was voluntary, and though 'private' schools (meaning, in the great majority of cases, Catholic schools) were allowed to exist, they received no aid from the State.

Schools subsidy

The Pétain Government introduced compulsory religious instruction and subsidised the private schools to the extent of 500 million francs a year. It now appears, or at least it is generally believed, that the Provisional Government intends to continue with this arrangement. There has been no official statement to this effect but, at any rate, the Communist speaker in the Assembly who referred to the continuance of the subsidy was not contradicted.

The Catholics put forward the same argument as their co-religionists in Britain, i.e. that they pay taxes which help to support the State schools, and consequently that State aid for Catholic schools is an elementary act of justice. However, the issue is not merely educational. The Catholics now have a large and fairly vigorous Press, both daily and weekly, and some observers expect the re-emergence in the near future of Clericalism as a political force.

The special importance of this at the present moment is that women have now been given the vote. The Church has far more women than men among its followers and the appearance of any party which could be identified as the Church Party would be a serious development from the Left-wing point of view.

The Church ignored

Sectarian intolerance has always been fiercer in France than in Britain, even when no obvious political issue was involved. One reason, clearly, is that in France the Reformation failed. Not only did Protestantism cease long ago to be a political force, but there never developed the innumerable gradations of belief which exist in Britain and which make for tolerance and allow the established Church to survive. In France one had to be Catholic or nothing, and though at this moment bishops, generals, Communists and Socialists are uneasily collaborating, no one imagines that there is real friendliness between them.

For long past, great numbers of people in France have been wholly outside the orbit of the Church – many people prefer to be buried without any religious rite. For instance, some of the legislation of the Third Republic was provocatively anti-clerical. In the Left-wing political parties religious disbelief was almost obligatory and such figures as, for instance, the late Archbishop of Canterbury or the late George Lansbury* would have been hard to fit into the French political scene.

The occupation temporarily blurred the picture, because the distinction between resisters and collaborators was partly a distinction of character and cut across political divisions. It was true that the Pétain regime drew much of its support from the Church, and some of the hierarchy made themselves apologists of the Germans, but it could not be said that a Catholic as such was a collaborator or a pro-Fascist.

Communist protest

Individual Catholics everywhere took part in the Resistance Movement, and de Gaulle, the living symbol of France's will to fight, was himself a Catholic. Nor did the Catholic Press, in the early days of the liberation, strike out any independent line of its own. Now, however, it begins to appear as though the old battle between Clericals and anti-Clericals may re-open.

It was possibly significant that the first protest against the continuation of the subsidy came from a Communist member of the Assembly.

Although it has never succeeded in overcoming the suspicions of the Church, the Communist Party has for the greater part of the last decade been the least anti-clerical of the Left-wing parties. When the danger presented by Nazi Germany became obvious, the Communists saw that they must come to terms with the Catholics if possible, and they tried hard to do so.

It was in 1936 that Maurice Thorez[†] coined the phrase 'We hold out our hand to our Catholic comrades' and the same phrase is repeated – this time with a slightly menacing air – in Communist newspapers of the current week. During much of the intervening time the hand has remained held out, but the expected handshake has never quite happened.

Other topics much discussed in recent weeks have been the attempt of the deputies who voted for Pétain to get themselves reinstated; the campaign of the Parti Social Français (La Rocque's semi-Fascist party) for recognition as a legal party; the appearance of several new newspapers of noticeably Conservative tendency; and various scandals, which do not always get into print, connected with the purge.

These usually tell of the appointment of some notorious collaborator to some important post. From such odds and ends one has to make up one's picture, but all seem to point in the same direction: that is, to the wearing off of the surreal unity of the liberation period and the re-emergence of several of the political forces which dominated France before the war.

* George Lansbury, leader of the Labour Party 1932–35, was a committed Christian.

† Maurice Thorez: French Communist politician from 1920 until 1964.

---

18 March 1945

DE GAULLE INTENDS TO KEEP INDO-CHINA

But French apathetic on Empire

Paris, 17 March

General de Gaulle's recent broadcast on the fighting in Indo-China aroused much discussion, and the newspapers printed it in full with big headlines, though in many cases without commenting on it.

His earlier statement on Indo-China a few weeks ago had passed almost unnoticed, but the present crisis has set many people talking anew about the half-forgotten problem of the French colonies.

The broadcast included a warm tribute to the courageous fight put up by the French and Indo-Chinese troops, and also included the usual implied criticism of Britain and America, but its main object was evidently to emphasise the importance of France's part in the Pacific end of the war. De Gaulle is too good a soldier not to realise better than the majority of his countrymen that the position of France's remoter colonies will be precarious even after Japan is defeated, and doubtless it seems to him good policy to stake out as large a claim as possible in the forthcoming Pacific victory.

Some of what he said was exaggerated and misleading and he has been able to make similar statements before, precisely because the average Frenchman is only intermittently interested in imperial policy.

Not Empire-minded

This has been especially true since the liberation. Except when something violent happens, the French overseas territories hardly find their way into the French Press. It is only by dipping into quite obscure periodicals that one can learn, for instance, that in Algeria and Morocco, the Vichy apparatus is still largely functioning and the local Socialist and Communist Press is fighting for its life against heavily subsidised newspapers of reactionary tendency.

But, even when home affairs were less pressing, the word 'empire' has never aroused the same powerful emotions, for or against, in France as it does in England.

In England the anti-imperialist tradition of the Labour Party, inherited from the old Liberal Party, is no doubt partly hypocritical, but it exists and to some extent it influences policy.

In France, even before the disaster of 1940, it was always noticeable that the Left-wing parties had much less to say on this subject. No doubt this was partly because Frenchmen, as well as foreigners, tended to generalise too freely from the admirable lack of colour prejudice in France itself.

But one has also got to consider the psychological effects of the defeat, which have left so deep a mark on French political thought, even in extreme-Left circles.

Desire to be strong

It is curious that there is very little awareness here of the strategic dependence of the French Empire on other Powers. Large portions of it would be quite indefensible without American or British help and Indo-China, in particular, is very unlikely to remain in French possession without the agreement of China as well.

Yet one does not see admissions of this kind made in print or in public speeches, though thoughtful Frenchmen may make them in private. It is apparently more painful to have to admit in France that Madagascar lies within the British orbit than to admit in England that Jamaica lies in the American orbit.

The shock of the defeat naturally induced in almost everyone a desire to feel strong, and one can see the result in the unrealistic way in which strategic questions are often discussed.

One can see it again in the general tendency to attribute the defeat of 1940 primarily, though not wholly, to deliberate treachery. It is significant that Pétain [president of France during the Vichy regime] is often referred to in the Press as Pétain-Bazaine, thus being linked with the other great scapegoat of French history.

It would probably have made no difference to the outcome of the war of 1870 if the wretched Bazaine had held out in Metz for six weeks longer, but an identifiable traitor on whom to put the blame was no doubt helpful in the recovery of national pride. The recrudescence of the nationalistic outlook, product of defeat, is very marked in France at present and the equivocal attitude even of Communists and Socialists towards imperialism is one symptom of it.

Economic development

De Gaulle has not yet made any very comprehensive statement on imperial policy. From what he has said hitherto, his ideas seem to lie toward vigorous economic development and the raising of the standard of living of the colonial populations, rather than towards an extension of self-government.

One newspaper, reporting Wednesday's broadcast, stated hopefully that de Gaulle had promised 'a new status' to Indo-China, but the text of the broadcast does not seem to bear this out. Indeed, if his various pronouncements on this subject mean anything, they mean that he intends to keep Indo-China inside the French Empire and on as nearly as possible the same footing as before.

His speech aroused great interest, but, as usual, received no genuine criticism in the Press. It is an index of the state of the French Press that not a single paper pointed out that this was a matter on which China might have something to say.

Indeed, when such topics do get any discussion, it is usually not in the daily Press but in little struggling weeklies, whose pages are all too often chequered by blank spaces bearing nothing but the dismal word 'Censure'.

Maquis in Indo-China

A French Maquis [Resistance Movement] has been organised behind the Japanese lines in Indo-China, says Reuter. Its resistance to the Japanese occupation is backed by the French Provisional Government. How much assistance the Allies can give from outside is uncertain, but a small French military mission, under General Blaisot, has been attached to Lord Mountbatten's SEAC [South East Asia Command] HQ for some time.

---

25 March 1945

CREATING ORDER OUT OF COLOGNE CHAOS

Water supplied from carts

Cologne, 24 March

There are still 100,000 Germans living among the ruins of Cologne. Most of them, however, are living in the suburbs, where habitable houses are comparatively common.

The whole central part of the city, once famous for its romanesque churches and its museums, is simply a chaos of jagged walls, overturned trams, shattered statues and enormous piles of rubble out of which iron girders thrust themselves like sticks of rhubarb.

When the Americans first entered, many of the streets were quite impassable until the bulldozers had swept them clear. The town has no piped water, no gas, no transport, and only enough electrical power for certain vital jobs such as keeping the electric ovens of a few bakeries working. However, the Germans appear still to have fairly good stocks of food, and the military government – in this area a purely American concern – is tackling the job of reorganisation with praiseworthy energy.

It has arranged a primitive water supply in horse-drawn carts, it has set up a health service, it is issuing a weekly paper in German, and it is about halfway through the considerable labour of re-registering and finger-printing the entire population. This is a necessary preliminary to the issue of new ration books, and it also helps a little in the important task of sifting Nazis from non-Nazis.

In the first day or two of the occupation there was civilian looting on a large scale, and it was obviously necessary to enrol some civil police. Under the control of an experienced American police officer, a scratch force of about 150 Germans, unarmed and not in uniform, is already in being. With these and all other employees of the Military Government, the principle followed is never to employ a known Nazi in any capacity whatever.

AMG's good start

The new chief of police, for instance, is a Jew, who held the same post until 1933, when the Nazis evicted him. Three separate courts have been set up to try offences, ranging from espionage to infringement of traffic regulations. I attended the first sitting of the intermediary court, which deals with comparatively serious offences and has powers of imprisonment up to ten years. A young Nazi of rather unappetising appearance, who had been the social secretary of the Hitler Jugend,* was on trial, not for having belonged to this organisation – the Military Government has declared that belonging to the Nazi organisation is not an offence in itself – but for concealing the fact and attempting to withhold the list of members from the American authorities. He was sentenced to seven years' imprisonment and a fine of 10,000 marks, with an extra day's imprisonment for every mark that remained unpaid.

This would have seemed tolerably severe if such sentences were ever served in full, but he was obviously guilty and the fairness of the whole procedure was so impressive that even the German lawyer who defended him remarked on it. All in all the American Military Government seems to have made a very good start, though one may guess that difficulties will arise later when people have got over the bombing and the food situation becomes more acute.

Well clothed and fed

After years of war it is an intensely strange feeling to be at last standing on German soil. The *Herrenvolk* [master race] are all round you, threading their way on their bicycles between the piles of rubble or rushing off with jugs and buckets to meet the water cart.

It is queer to think that these are the people who once ruled Europe from the Channel to the Caspian Sea and might have conquered our own island, if they had known how weak we were. Propaganda, and especially their own propaganda, has taught us to think of them as tall, blond and arrogant. What you actually see in Cologne is smallish, dark-haired people, obviously of the same racial stock as the Belgians across the border, and in no way extraordinary. They are better clothed and, by the look of them, better fed than the people in France and Belgium, and they have newer bicycles and more silk stockings than we have in England: really there is no more to remark.

Aloof and hostile

The servility on which several observers have already commented did not particularly strike me. It is true that some of the inhabitants try to curry favour, hang round the offices of the Military Government at all hours and, when spoken to, doff their hats with a rather horrifying readiness, but the majority seem aloof and perhaps slightly hostile.

In some of the eyes that met mine, I caught a sort of beaten defiance which, if it meant anything, seems to me to mean that these people are horribly ashamed of having lost the war.

It is not true that all of them deny having ever been Nazis. Some of them admit when making the registration that they have been Party members, though they always claim that they were forced to join the Party against their will.

* Also known as the Hitler Youth. Compulsory youth arm of the Nazi party, for boys aged 15–18.

FUTURE OF A RUINED GERMANY

Rural slum cannot help Europe

A s the advance into Germany continues and more and more of the devastation wrought by the Allied bombing planes is laid bare, there are three comments that almost every observer finds himself making.

The first is: 'The people at home have no conception of this.' The second is: 'It's a miracle that they've gone on fighting.' And the third is: 'Just think of the work of building this all up again!'

It is quite true that the scale of the Allied blitzing of Germany is even now not realised in this country, and its share in the breaking-down of German resistance is probably much underrated. It is difficult to give actuality to newspaper or radio reports of air warfare, and the man in the street can be forgiven if he imagines that what we have done to Germany over the past four years is merely the same kind of thing as they did to us in 1940.

But this error, which must be even commoner in the United States, has in it a potential danger, and the many protests against indiscriminate bombing which have been uttered by pacifists and humanitarians have merely confused the issue.

World impoverished

Bombing is not especially inhumane. War itself is inhumane, and the bombing plane, which is used to paralyse industry and transport rather than to kill human beings, is a relatively civilised weapon. 'Normal' or 'legitimate' warfare is just as destructive of inanimate objects, and enormously more so of human lives.

Moreover, a bomb kills a casual cross-section of the population, whereas the men killed in battle are exactly the ones that the community can least afford to lose. The people of Britain have never felt easy about the bombing of civilians and no doubt they will be ready enough to pity the Germans as soon as they have definitely defeated them, but what they have still not grasped – thanks to their own comparative immunity –

is the frightful destructiveness of modern war and the long period of impoverishment that now lies ahead of the world as a whole.

To walk through the ruined cities of Germany is to feel an actual doubt about the continuity of civilisation. For one has to remember that it is not only Germany that has been blitzed. The same desolation extends, at any rate in considerable patches, all the way from Brussels to Stalingrad. And where there has been ground fighting, the destruction is even more thorough than where there has merely been bombing. In the 300 miles or so between the Marne and the Rhine there is not, for instance, such a thing as a bridge or a viaduct that has not been blown up.

Homeless millions

Even in England we are aware that we need three million houses and that the chances of getting them within measurable time seem rather slender. But how many houses will Germany need or Poland or the USSR or Italy? When one thinks of the stupendous task of rebuilding Cologne, Essen, Hamburg, Warsaw, Budapest, Kharkov, Odessa, Leningrad, and scores or hundreds of other European cities great and small – and rebuilding them at the end of six years during which all available labour has been squandered on war production – one realises that a long period must elapse before even the standards of living of 1939 can be re-established.

We do not yet know the full extent of the damage that has been done to Germany, but judging from the areas that have been overrun hitherto it is difficult to believe in the power of the Germans to pay any kind of reparations, either in goods or in labour. Simply to re-house the German people, to set the shattered factories working, and to keep German agriculture from collapsing after the foreign workers have been liberated, will use up all the labour that the Germans are likely to dispose of.

If, as is planned at present, millions of them are to be deported to the victorious countries for reconstruction work, the recovery of Germany itself will be all the slower. After the last war the impossibility of obtaining substantial money reparations – in short, of making the enemy pay for the war – was finally grasped, but it was less generally realised that the impoverishment of any one country reacts unfavourably on the world as a whole. It would be no advantage to turn Germany into a kind of rural slum.

ALLIES FACING FOOD CRISIS IN GERMANY

Problem of freed workers

Paris, 14 April

There are more and more reports, official and unofficial, telling of the difficulties now being experienced in dealing with the Allied and neutral deportees in German territory, generally referred to in the British Press as slave labour, but known officially as Displaced Persons.

The Displaced Persons do not include released prisoners of war, who are a separate problem and a somewhat easier one to handle.

When, only a few weeks ago, I visited a camp of 14,000 Displaced Persons in the Rhineland, I was struck by the sensible manner in which the American officers in charge were handling the job, and the obvious delight of the Displaced Persons at getting out of German hands. But at that time the problem was still of manageable proportions.

The extent to which it has swollen since then can be illustrated by a few figures. In France the Allied armies liberated 100,000 Displaced Persons, and in Germany west of the Rhine another 100,000. By the first week in April the number had risen to about one million, and it is now thought to be round about two million, with the prospect of many more to come, for there are at least seven million of these people in Germany and German-held territory; possibly as many as ten or twelve million, exclusive of war prisoners.

Escape, walk home

Meanwhile, the number actually rounded up is fewer by several hundred thousand than the number estimated as being in the areas which the Allied armies have occupied. As the German administration collapses, more and more Displaced Persons simply escape and take to the roads, often with the idea of walking back to their own countries by the shortest route, and the Allied authorities have several difficult problems to solve.

Obviously, before these people can be repatriated, some kind of sorting-out process is needed, both to prevent epidemics and to eliminate the spies and saboteurs who exist among them. This means that even French and Belgian deportees, whose homes are near at hand, have to be detained for several days, while most of the Russians and Poles will probably have to wait for some months before it is practicable to repatriate them.

It is not easy to find accommodation for these vast numbers of people, who include many children born in captivity, and the food problem is likely to become acute within a few months. In principle the responsibility for feeding the Displaced Persons falls on Germany, but this is only a financial measure and does not necessarily mean that actual food will always be forthcoming. Evidently a great deal depends on finishing the war quickly enough to allow this year's German harvest to be gathered in.

Farms disorganised

The Germans, who have been plundering all Europe for several years, still have or had recently good stocks of food, but their agriculture is now disorganised by the defeat, all the more so because it depends for labour largely on the Displaced Persons, who are now escaping or being released. Unless it can be set on its feet again by the late summer, the result is likely to be a disastrous food shortage, which will react indirectly on the Allied countries.

The great majority of Displaced Persons remaining under Allied care are Russians, Ukrainians, Poles and Italians.

The Western European deportees can usually be repatriated after only a short delay. Liaison officers drawn from the various countries concerned are attached to the military government.

It does not yet seem to have been definitely decided whether the return of a Displaced Person to his country of origin is or is not compulsory, and on this subject there are serious possibilities of disagreement between the Allied Governments.

Apart from stateless persons, of whom there are thousands in the German concentration camps, there is the minority of collaborators whose transference to Germany was voluntary, and the probably larger number of people who cannot be classed as collaborators, but have their own reasons for not wanting to go home.

Deportees better treated

It seems to be admitted that the Germans did not in all cases treat their deportees badly. At any rate, since they needed them for manual labour, they had the wisdom to feed them adequately – much better, it is generally agreed, than they fed their prisoners of war – and they seem often to have deported whole families rather than individuals and to have allowed the deportees to get married while in captivity.

In the circumstances, it will not be surprising if some of the Poles, especially those from Eastern Poland, and perhaps some of the Ukrainians as well, make efforts to remain where they are. The Soviet authorities are unlikely to acquiesce, and this awkward point will have to be settled in the near future.

In France, this particular difficulty does not arise, but there has been much unfavourable comment on the failure of the Government to organise suitable ceremonies of welcome for returned prisoners and deportees.

---

22 April 1945

BAVARIAN PEASANTS IGNORE THE WAR

Germans know they are beaten

Nuremberg, 21 April

To judge by the demeanour of the civilian population in this part of Germany, it is an understatement to say that the Germans now know they are beaten.

Most of them seem to regard the war as something already in the past and its continuation as a lunacy in which they have no part, and for which they need feel no responsibility.

To a surprising extent village life continues as usual, even in the middle of the fighting. The oxen still trudge slowly in front of the harrow while the guns echo from all the surrounding hillsides, and most of the peasants seem more afraid of being attacked by wandering Displaced Persons –

freed foreign workers – than of being hit by a stray shell. A day or two ago I entered the little village of Wimmelbach, west of Nuremberg, just after the landing units of the American Twelfth Armoured Division had passed through.

Just outside the village a smashed road-block, a corpse or two, an abandoned tank, and an orchard cratered by mortar shells marked the spot where the Germans had tried to make a stand. The village itself had been shelled. Several houses were burning. Immediately over the next hillside the self-propelled guns and heavy machine-guns had already opened fire on the next village and batches of miserably dressed German prisoners, their hands locked behind their heads, were being brought in by bored soldiers with carbines.

Youthful snipers

Amid all this the villagers were almost completely unconcerned. A little knot of elderly people, two women and a man, seemed to be in a state of distress, but as for the others they watched the irruption of the American Army with probably less interest than they would have given to a passing circus. Someone was loading manure on to a cart. There was the usual queue at the pump, and two old men were steadily sawing up logs on a trestle. Even the wretched parties of prisoners got hardly a glance of curiosity.

In this area what little civilian resistance there is (usually in the form of sniping) is almost entirely the work of youths between twelve and twenty. The other age groups seem indifferent or even friendly and relieved to see secure government established again. In some places German civilians have applied to the Military Government, not merely to protect them against the Displaced Persons, but even to provide anti-aircraft guns to keep the German planes away. The young men, who will obviously be the first source of trouble, are not much in evidence, most of them being in the army.

Almost anyone who is questioned, including prisoners, admits that the war is lost, and adds that resistance only continues because of a handful of fanatical Nazis, which is no doubt true. The decision to defend Nuremberg, for instance, was a political decision taken by the local SS commander against the wishes of both the army and the civilians.

Responsibility

This part of Germany has not suffered very greatly from the war; the people, especially the children, have obviously been very well fed, and the blitzing of Bavaria and Württemberg has not been so comprehensive as in the Rhineland and the Ruhr. It is true that, with the solitary exception of Heidelberg, the big towns have been flattened. Even the ancient university city of Würzburg is now a mere mass of ruins, though, fortunately, its medieval castle was too solid to be completely destroyed. But the villages and the pleasant little country towns, with their massive gateways, their baroque churches and their cobbled squares, have mostly escaped damage, except when they stood in the direct path of the fighting and did not produce their white flag promptly enough.

Away from the main road one would hardly know there was a war on if it were not for the occasional group of Displaced Persons, who trudge past carrying bundles of rags on their backs and keeping one eye open for stray chickens.

As one drives through this peaceful countryside with its winding roads fringed by cherry trees, its terraced vineyards and its wayside shrines, there is one question that raises itself over and over again. It is to what extent can the so obviously simple and gentle peasants who troop to church on Sunday mornings in decent black be responsible for the horrors of the Nazis?

The Nazi movement actually started in this part of Germany, and there can be no question about the enormity of the crimes it has committed, if only because the mass of evidence came so long before the war started.

But if one wants evidence of German cruelty, there is plenty of it here and now in the tales told by escaped prisoners and deportees.

The reason

Their condition partly depended on how long they had been prisoners, but the main dividing line was between those who did and those who did not receive Red Cross parcels. This camp contained some thousands of Russians who were herded together in wretched tents without side flaps and with no covering on the ground, so that they had to make themselves burrows in the sandy soil. Universally they were ragged and filthy, their faces drawn with hunger and misery and fresh typhus cases were occurring among them every day.

Even the British prisoners had been treated badly enough, most of them having been put to work in the Siberian coal mines and then, when the Red Army approached, were forced to march on foot all the way to Bavaria.

But they all spoke with indignation of the treatment given to the Russians. Only a few days before, in this camp, the German guards had opened fire and killed several Russians for crowding up to the wire when British and American prisoners tried to throw food over to them.

A British prisoner described how, on his arrival, he and his companions had thrown some soup over the wire to the Russians, and the starving Russians had promptly eaten it. Another told me of a camp in Siberia where, when a Russian prisoner died, his comrades would cover his body with a blanket and pretend that he was merely ill so that they could go on drawing his soup ration for a few days longer.

An American prisoner – an officer – summed up the situation by pointing to the scarecrow figures in the Russian encampment and remarking: 'The sole thing that has saved us from being in the same condition as those people there is our parcels from home.'

---

29 April 1945

THE GERMANS STILL DOUBT OUR UNITY

The flags do not help

With the US Third Army, Stuttgart, 28 April

The morning after the French First Army entered Stuttgart this week, the General commanding the 100th American Division sent a small detachment of tanks and infantry to make contact with them in the eastern suburbs of the town.

On the east bank of the Neckar a column found the French and then turned back. It was impossible for vehicles to cross the river, every bridge in the sixty miles between Heilbronn and Toeningen having been blown up. There was, however, a small footbridge which the Germans had not thought worth a charge of explosive, and two other correspondents and myself who were accompanying the Americans decided to go on foot.

On the other bank of the river groups of Displaced Persons, still delirious after twenty-four hours of liberty, were careering to and fro in looted cars and trucks, while others who had got hold of rifles were letting fly at pieces of driftwood in the stream.

The central part of the town, or what was left of it, had been thoroughly pillaged. The worst looting generally happens in the first hour or two after resistance collapses and is the work of German civilians and suddenly released prisoners and deportees.

Looting can be prevented, if at all, only by having the apparatus of Military Government ready before a town is captured, and in this case, no doubt owing to the unexpected suddenness with which Stuttgart collapsed, there was long delay.

Large-scale looting

Seventy-two hours after the French entered no proclamations had been posted and the whereabouts of the Military Government was undiscoverable, though some harmless-looking elderly men with armbands marked 'Polizei' were occasionally to be seen on the streets.

The disorder after the fall of Stuttgart was probably worse than usual because of the large-scale looting of wine. Empty bottles, and even half-full bottles, were littered all over the place. I had entered the town to the sound of rifle shots, and stray shots were still reverberating when I left two days later, though all pockets of resistance had long since been cleared out. The shots were merely an unofficial *feu de joie*.

Meanwhile, the French, disregarding the deportees and concentrating on the Germans, were combing the town house by house and arresting not only everyone in uniform, but every male civilian suspected of having belonged either to the Wehrmacht [German Army] or the Volkssturm [German home guard]. The toll of prisoners was so large that it was difficult to find places to put them in, and numbers of them had to be temporarily housed in the subway under the main railway station.

It is, above all, when one watches German prisoners being rounded up that a gulf seems to open between almost any Anglo-Saxon and almost any Continental European. One may recognise fully the need to destroy the German Army and to use no matter what means to do it, but one has to have lived under German rule before one can get an actual pleasure out of these scenes of humiliation.

Grim satisfaction

As the endless lines of prisoners trailed by, the deportees, and even some of the French soldiers, watched them with grins of quite frank delight.

'Just like us in 1940!' was a comment I heard several times. Some of these people even seemed to get a grim satisfaction in contemplating the ruin wrought by the bombs. I could not feel anything of the kind myself. Stuttgart, it is true, is a big town, and parts of it are still intact, but as usual it is the ancient central part of the town that has been flattened and the uninteresting residential suburbs which have escaped.

I had been billeted on some middle-class Germans in the suburbs. These people, like most of the Germans I have been able to talk to, were not only eager for the war to end quickly, but even more eager to see as much as possible of Germany occupied by the Americans and British, and as little as possible by the Russians and French.

Evidently it is still necessary to make the Germans understand that the Governments of the United Nations are in substantial agreement. At present the idea seems widespread that Russia, France, and Anglo-America are more or less hostile to one another and stand for quite different policies.

It is obviously dangerous to let this idea take root, and the failure to define the zones of occupation in advance, and the practice followed by the various armies of hoisting only their own national flag in the areas they occupy, have done something to encourage it.

FRANCE'S INTEREST
IN THE WAR DWINDLES

Paris, 5 May

Looking at the surface aspect of Paris it is a little difficult to believe that only last weekend a third of its electorate voted Communist, while another quarter voted for other extremist parties of the Left.

Paris has brightened up in the spring sunshine. Solid food is no more plentiful than it was when I came here two months ago, but there are lettuces and spring onions, even strawberries if you can pay for them, and it is warm enough to sit at café tables out of doors.

Clothes are still shabby, but the women's hats are more flamboyant than ever. If it were not for the ever-present American soldiers one would hardly take this for the capital of a country at war. In a little while, no doubt, flags will be flying and bells ringing to celebrate the final victory, but no extra flags have appeared as yet and, though Hitler's death did cause a certain stir, I could not overhear many spontaneous comments on it. Life goes on pretty much as usual, and the quest for food, fuel and amusement looms larger for most people than any external event.

And yet one could not truthfully say that there is no political activity. The municipal elections not only showed a nation-wide swing to the Left, but – what was perhaps even more significant – produced a very large poll. And there were also the May Day celebrations, when an enormous crowd of people filed through the streets chanting in unison: 'Pétain au Poteau!'*

Want France to be strong

What is one to make of this seeming combination of apathy and revolutionary sentiment? First of all it is widely agreed that France is far more interested in internal affairs than in the war. France's principal act of war was the Resistance which involved only a minority, and even now the number of people directly engaged in the war effort is tiny compared with that in Britain. Everyone wants France to be strong, to have a big army and reappear as a great Power, but the day-to-day detail of the war is not interesting.

Even the repatriated prisoners evoke very little enthusiasm. Every day hundreds of these men, in ragged, discoloured uniforms, jolt through the streets in lorries. The authorities give them a warm meal and a ceremony of welcome, but the passing crowds hardly notice them.

International affairs do not arouse the passions that they do in Britain. San Francisco is not much discussed, and neither the Greek nor the Polish issue provoked any very violent controversy.[†] The average Frenchman is interested first of all in France, and though he wants certain political reforms, what he wants above all things is to get back to normal, with enough to eat and better facilities for recreation.

Long cinema queues

Among the noticeable things in Paris are the long cinema queues and the large proportion of the dwindled Press given over to sport. Not only hunger, but boredom and the longing for a bit of amusement make up the background of the political scene.

The municipal elections showed a general Leftward slide. Communists won votes from Socialists, Socialists won them from Radicals, and in many areas the parties of the Right were almost obliterated. But one certainly cannot infer from this that France is on the verge of revolution. One has only to glance down any street to see that the people are in no mood for violent effort of any kind. In some ways, in spite of all that has happened, pre-war habits of mind seem to have lingered more strongly than they have in England. Distinctions of wealth are greater, or at any rate they are more obtrusive, and a larger proportion of people are engaged in menial occupations. Fifty per cent of the electorate have just voted Socialist or Communist, but the haberdashers still display top hats in their depleted windows and sandwichmen still trudge to and fro bearing advertisements for manicurists. However it may be when France is less hungry and when political discussion is less hampered by censorship and paper shortage, the general desire at present is for security and normality and not for drastic changes.

Reading the posters before the elections I was struck by the fact that all parties now promise almost exactly the same things. People nevertheless turn their eyes towards the Left because the Left is felt to stand not for bloody revolution, but for security of employment, family allowances and protection of the rights of labour. The Popular Front Government of 1936, which gave France certain elementary reforms it had never before had, is still fairly vividly remembered.

Uneasiness over purge

On the other hand, the Right is associated with certain vague but menacing entities called 'the trusts', which are held to be responsible for everything from the defeat of 1940 to the shortage of cigarettes.

The French Communist Party has a big membership as well as a strong hold on the general public and it contains a nucleus of hardened long-term members who still probably look forward to violent revolution as their ultimate objective. But the mass of its followers do not appear to want any such thing and certain points even in its declared policy are only doubtfully popular.

To begin with, in spite of 'Pétain au Poteau', it is doubtful whether the French masses wish for such a wholesale and vindictive persecution of collaborationists as the Communists demand. Certainly they are anxious that the biggest culprits shall not escape, but there seems to be a certain uneasiness about the moral aspects of the purge which, if carried out in a thoroughgoing way, would be all too often the punishment of the guilty by the guilty.

The other feature of Communist policy, which probably does not reflect popular opinion, is its anti-British orientation. Apart from the Vichyites, who are now lying low, the Communists are the only French political faction who are anti-British (and to a less extent anti-American) and they show it as plainly as is possible in the general muffling of the Press.

This is probably a matter of high policy – Britain being the possible leader of the Western bloc whose formation the USSR opposes – rather than an expression of the sentiments of ordinary French people, working class or middle class.

* 'Pétain to the stake!'

† The 1945 San Francisco Conference on International Organisation, convened to draw up the charter of the United Nations. Greece and Poland were under discussion by the Western Allies and the USSR over who would have most influence on them.

FREED POLITICIANS RETURN TO PARIS

TU leader sees De Gaulle

Paris, 12 May

Paul Reynaud, Yvon Delbos and Léon Jouhaux arrived in Paris two days ago. Jouhaux, the former leader of the French Trade Union Movement, has already been called to confer with de Gaulle, but is somewhat cagey about his political future.

He will not say whether he is likely to be offered a post in the present Government. He says he supports the de Gaulle Government and intends to return to political life immediately. At the coming General Election he will stand as an independent candidate.

Reynaud, Premier up to June 1940 and handed over by Pétain to the Germans after the Allied landings in North Africa in November 1942, spent the first six months of his captivity in an isolation cell in Oranienburg, but was afterwards removed to a fortress in the Tyrol, where he was incarcerated with other French political leaders.

He was well treated and spent his time in captivity writing a book on events leading up to the defeat.

There is, of course, a new political factor in the liberation of Herriot, Daladier, Reynaud and Blum. Of these, only Blum has fully maintained his reputation and his commanding position within his own party. Even when he had vanished into some concentration camp of unknown whereabouts, his name was still displayed on the front page of *Le Populaire* as editor-in-chief. Daladier is perhaps discredited for good. The Radicals have tried hard to build him up in recent months, but his internment of the Communist deputies in 1939 is not likely to be forgotten.

The celebrations

Nevertheless, all of these politicians are much better known to the general public than any member of the present Government except de Gaulle himself, and Daladier and Reynaud share with Blum the prestige of the Riom trial [an abortive trial of French leaders by the Vichy government] at which they behaved with courage and dignity. By this half-hearted attempt at terrorism the Pétainists did much to rehabilitate the regime they had overthrown and it is thought that at the coming General Elections the reappearance of Herriot, Reynaud and Daladier may do something to revive the fallen fortunes of the Radical Socialist Party.

Those whose memories went back long enough declared that the victory celebrations in Paris 'didn't come up to 1918', but they were certainly impressive, the more so because the news of the German surrender did not come with dramatic suddenness, but leaked out owing to various indiscretions after having been impatiently expected for weeks.

At least twenty-four hours before the official announcement everyone in Paris appeared to know the exact hour at which the cease-fire would sound, and one evening paper was seized by the police for spilling the news prematurely. Apart from the much discussed misdemeanour of one of the news agencies, the German Radio at Flensburg had made an announcement which was repeated by the French Radio and then contradicted a little while later.

After all this it was hardly surprising that there was an unofficial celebration on Monday night, with songs and processions in the streets and aeroplanes dropping many coloured flares among the chimney-pots. But the real excitement began early on Tuesday morning. Bands of youths and girls marched to and fro in military formation chanting 'Avec Nous! Avec Nous!' and gradually swelling their numbers until by midday the crowds were so enormous that many of the main streets and squares were quite impassable. They remained so the whole of Tuesday and the whole of Wednesday. Some people did go home for part of Tuesday night, while others subsided on to benches or patches of grass and snatched a few hours' sleep.

At three o'clock on Tuesday afternoon I managed to force my way near enough to a loudspeaker in the Place de la Concorde to listen to the official announcement.

De Gaulle speaks

There had been rumours that the whole thing might have to be postponed. Then came de Gaulle's voice: 'The war is won. This is victory.' The people did not break into a cheer, but listened attentively to the rest of the speech, and then stood in reverent silence while the National Anthems of all the leading Allies were played over.

For several days the newspapers maintained a kind of self-censorship, keeping unpleasant topics in the background as much as possible, but there are certain questions both of home and foreign policy that it is impossible to ignore for any length of time. It cannot be said that present-day French newspapers ever discuss foreign politics with much freedom, but there are obvious signs of discord over the San Francisco Conference and Russian policy generally. The question of the occupation of Germany, and especially of Berlin – who will occupy which areas and how soon – is also discussed with evident uneasiness.

---

20 May 1945

DANGER OF SEPARATE OCCUPATION ZONES
Delaying Austria's recovery

In Austria, 19 May

Austria has not been ravaged by war to anything like the same extent as Germany. But for a moment, the chaos is even greater, and the scenes accompanying the final round-up of the German Army are all the more fantastic because they occur against a background of snow-streaked mountains, unblitzed villages, and meadows filled with wild flowers.

In some places a newcomer must get the impression that Austria is being occupied not by the Allies but by the Germans.

The Germans are everywhere at every village inn, that knot of grey or green uniforms clustering round the porch, and half the traffic one passes on the roads has the characteristic wavy camouflage markings.

The toll of prisoners has been so enormous that in some cases it has been necessary to deal with them by simply depriving them of arms and then marking off an area on the map within which they are to remain. The other day I drove through an area south of Salzburg where it was estimated that there were 100,000 Germans, though to my eye the number seemed a good deal larger.

Save for its weapons, it was a complete army, seemingly well disciplined and in good shape. For mile after mile I drove past fields full of men sunbathing or laundering in the streams and past tens of thousands of neatly parked vehicles and hundreds of corpses, cavalry chargers, and little piebald Cossack ponies. There were German military policemen directing the traffic at every crossroad.

Hitch-hiking home

Even more fantastic were the encampments of the Displaced Persons, some of them sharing barracks with derelict German soldiers, while others have seized railway trains and are living in the carriages. Every now and again some enterprising Displaced Person manages to get a locomotive running in the hope that, if the points are right, it may take him nearer to his homeland.

Then there are the camps of Allied prisoners of war now liberated and living under American care, and there are plenty of other prisoners who have grown sick of waiting and are trying to hitch-hike home.

At the moment, what with the glorious summer weather and the general relief that the war is ended, all this chaos seems almost funny, but it is widely realised that the underlying situation is not good. The task of feeding the civilian population and the Displaced Persons was a headache even before the Allies found themselves with several million extra prisoners on their hands, and one has only to glance at the mountainous landscape to see that Austria, even more than Western Germany, cannot be self-supporting in food.

Parachute news

By means of parachutes the Shaef [Supreme Headquarters Allied Expeditionary Forces] authorities are now distributing newspapers and leaflets in four languages, warning prisoners and Displaced Persons that it is in their own best interest to remain where they are, but not unnaturally there are signs of restiveness here and there, and in the rapidly changing situation the weaknesses inherent in Military Government are coming to light.

Military government was designed simply to keep order and facilitate rapid movement in the rear of fighting armies.

Indeed, Military Government has, from a short-term viewpoint, been strikingly successful. The speed with which a bomb-wrecked city can be restored to some kind of order is often surprising, but Military Government has suffered from a serious handicap in having no long-term objectives.

Not to have a political policy – except of course the policy of not employing known Nazis – has been a matter almost of pride among officers. When asked any question that appears to touch on politics the stock reply is 'I wouldn't know'.

To give just one example, I encountered one Military Government officer of the rank of captain who 'wouldn't know' the difference between a Social Democrat and a Christian Socialist. Obviously this kind of thing can lead to trouble when political parties and movements begin to revive. In fact it is already happening. Two new Bavarian political parties have made their appearance, and the struggles now going on in various European countries appear to be raising echoes among the appropriate sections of Displaced Persons.

In an indirect way the administration of Germany and Austria is made harder by ignorant public opinion in Britain and the United States.

It often happens that some step which is an obvious military necessity on the spot would cause misunderstanding if revealed at home, and this works against the thorough thrashing out of major problems. But much the worst feature of the present situation is the arbitrary division of these countries into separate zones of occupation. There is very little contact between the Russians and the Western Allies, the armies being usually separated either by a river or a belt of No Man's Land, and the meagre reports that come in suggest that the Russians are following a different policy, at any rate in the treatment of prisoners, from that followed by the Anglo-Americans.

If the present rigid division continues it must set back the economic recovery of these countries and it must lead to a competition for the allegiance of the German and Austrian peoples. This has already started, and the new Austrian Government set up by the Russians in Vienna, but unrecognised in western Austria, is one symptom of it.

Separation desired

At present there cannot be much doubt about the state of popular feeling. The Russians are feared and hated – and the Vienna Government does not seem to evoke much enthusiasm, though the desire for separation from Germany is evidently strong.

But it would be very rash to assume that this frame of mind will be permanent. If it comes to a political struggle the Russians have several factors not obvious at present working on their side. While the feeling against them is partly a hangover of Nazi propaganda, it is difficult to believe that the administration of Austria and Germany can ever be successful unless it is a generally joint administration. And every day that this is delayed will make the final solution harder.

But the first indispensable necessity is that the United States and British Governments shall decide what they mean to do with the defeated countries and state their purpose clearly.

When that has happened certain dangerous misconceptions under which the Germans and Austrians now labour can be removed and the ordinary military commander or Military Government officer will have a clean line to go upon when he has to deal with problems which are every day more nakedly political.

---

27 May 1945

OBSTACLES TO JOINT RULE IN GERMANY

I T is too early to say that a genuinely joint occupation of Germany and Austria is impossible, but it has become obvious in recent weeks that powerful influences are working against it.

This is a disaster, but its worst results may be averted if the facts are faced and the necessary inferences drawn without delay.

Joint occupation, to be real, would imply four things:

First, delegation of as much authority as possible to German and Austrian Governments selected or approved by all the major Allies.

Secondly, an inter-Allied controlling body in permanent session.

Thirdly, a clear agreement as to Germany's future development: political, military and economic.

Fourthly, no 'zones' – that is, free circulation throughout the occupied countries, and as much intermingling as possible by the troops of the occupying Powers.

At present none of these conditions has been realised, and it is probably fair to say that most of the opposition has come from the Russian side. In the circumstances, the Western Allies have only two courses between which to choose. One – which obviously they will not choose – is simply to move out and leave Germany and Austria to undivided Russian control.

The other is to accept the political challenge implied in the present situation and to try to make sure that the mass of the German people looks West and not East for guidance.

It should be realised that the competition for the allegiance of the German people has already started, and had started before the fighting came to an end.

Watertight 'zones'

The division of the country into watertight 'zones' was simply an expression of it: for if the Allies really had a joint policy, what was to prevent them from administering it jointly? And in addition it should be realised that at present most of the cards are in Anglo-American hands.

The majority of Germans dislike very much the prospect of being under Russian control, and have shown it in unmistakable ways. But the comparative popularity of Anglo-America rests on very shaky foundations. To begin with, the food situation is likely to be catastrophic in the coming winter, if not earlier, and it may turn out to be worse in Western Europe than in the mainly agricultural areas controlled by the Russians.

Secondly, the Russians can and probably will introduce much needed reforms such as the splitting up of the East Prussian estates between landless peasants, which it would be difficult for the Western Allies to imitate even if they wanted to. Thirdly, the propaganda problems of the Russians are greatly eased by their exclusion of independent journalists and observers.

At present we have no real knowledge of what is happening in the Russian zone, and when discontent begins to accumulate in the Anglo-American zone the inevitably rosy reports issuing from the other side will have their influence.

At this moment, if the Western Allies chose to imitate the example of the Russians in Vienna and set up a German Government by unilateral action, they could get overwhelming support for it.

Not, of course, a government of Doenitz and Schacht,* but any moderately decent government sponsored by the United States and Britain could be firmly established without any need to fake plebiscites, and the knowledge that it existed would have an immediate influence in the Russian zone. Presumably the governments of Britain and the United States will not take this drastic step, but what they could do, and indeed must do, is to make a prompt and clear declaration of policy.

Enormous questions

Up to date the most enormous questions have been left unanswered. Is German industry to be dismantled or is it to be restored? Are the Ruhr and the Rhineland to be annexed, or are they not? Will the war prisoners be retained as forced labourers or will they be released as quickly as possible?

Which categories of Germans are to be treated as war criminals? There is no one of these questions to which the inquiring German can get a secure answer. And certain dangerous illusions – for instance, the widespread idea that the USSR and the Western Powers will be at war in the near future – have sprung up and need to be contradicted by the highest authorities.

It is also necessary to make the German people realise how bad the prospective food situation is, and how much effort on their own part is needed to retrieve it.

Given some such declaration of policy, the political struggle which has already started would be happening in the open and the average German would know what to expect. At present the evident danger is that he will hope too much from the Western Powers and then, in disappointment, transfer his allegiance to the Russians.

Moreover, we are unlikely to come to a good understanding with the Russians unless we take up their challenge boldly. The present piecemeal occupation of Germany and Austria is exhausting and unsatisfactory to them as much as to us, but they may hope to elbow us out of these countries altogether if they oppose clear policies to feeble or divided ones.

On the other hand, if Anglo-America also produced a plan, and a workable plan, the Russian mood may change and it may be possible to work out the common policy without which this huge problem can hardly be solved.

* Karl Doenitz: German head of state after Hitler's suicide; Hjalmar Schacht: President of the German Reichsbank under Hitler. Later inmate of Dachau Concentration Camp, found not guilty of crimes against humanity at Nuremberg.

---

10 June 1945

UNCERTAIN FATE OF DISPLACED PERSONS

FACTS relating to the problem of the Displaced Persons – that is the foreign forced labourers imported by the Germans during the war – continue to trickle in, but there has been no comprehensive statement and, apparently, no official ruling on one or two very important points.

It is very much to be hoped that the relevant facts will be published in the fairly near future. Otherwise, a valuable sociological opportunity may be missed, and decisions may be taken which public opinion in the United States and Britain would not tolerate if it knew the facts.

UNRRA [United Nations Relief and Rehabilitation Administration] is now at work in 230 camps in Western Germany and the military authorities in a further number of camps unspecified, on the registration of these uprooted people. They are known to number some 4,500,000 in Germany alone. According to present registrations the bulk of this figure is made up of 1,500,000 Russians, 1,200,000 Frenchmen, and 600,000 Poles. There were about 100,000 Belgians – now nearly all repatriated – and there are some 100,000 Dutchmen, with smaller groups of Jugoslavs, Czechs, Scandinavians and Greeks. By last week 1,500,000 had been registered, medically examined and repatriated.

Of the rest, the majority are living under the care of the Military Government, which feeds them as best it can and in some cases employs them at road-mending and similar jobs. Great numbers, however, have refused to be rounded up and have endeavoured to walk home, or have simply lived on the countryside by begging and stealing. Others, though probably not many, have remained on the farms where they were working before the Allied invasion.

Rations reduced

At the beginning most of the Displaced Persons welcomed their liberators with enormous enthusiasm, but this has been somewhat damped by the unavoidable delays in repatriation and the growing food shortage. It had been laid down in advance that in the matter of food supply: the Army came first, the Displaced Persons second and the Germans third; but in practice it is impossible to allow the Germans to starve, and in some areas the point has already been reached where it is necessary to reduce the rations of the Displaced Persons in order to keep those of the Germans up to subsistence level.

It is easy to imagine the ill-feeling that this causes, and in American-controlled areas it is not made better by the wasting of food which anyone in contact with the troops can observe for himself.

Meanwhile, various extremely interesting facts about the Displaced Persons have come to light. To begin with, the term 'slave labour', habitually used in the British Press, is misleading. Some of these people – it might even be possible to determine the number with reasonable accuracy – were volunteers, and the rest, though they could be described as slaves in the sense that they were deported against their will, do not seem, in most cases, to have been badly treated.

Want to stay

Those employed on factory work lived in encampments in semi-prison conditions, but those employed on the land, usually on small farms where all the younger menfolk were away at the war, seem to have fared reasonably well. In many cases they were not only paid wages but were enrolled in the German workers' insurance scheme, and all observers agree that as a whole the Displaced Persons have been well fed.

We can make only the vaguest guess as to how many of these people changed sides on ideological grounds, how many were mere adventurers, and how many were ignorant peasants to whom serving in one army was very like serving in another. Clearly this whole subject needs investigating for the sake of the light it may cast on the changes now occurring in the structure of nationalism. But the investigation must be made within the next few months or the data will have vanished.

One point that does not seem to have been decided – or at least, no authoritative pronouncement has been made – is whether a Displaced Person who does not wish to go home is obliged to do so. The people most affected here are the Poles. It is known that great numbers of Poles, especially from eastern Poland, want to remain abroad. If the Government of the USSR decides that those of them who are now technically Soviet citizens must return, will the British and American Governments feel obliged to repatriate them? Quite obviously this question should not be decided without letting the British and American peoples understand what is happening. Moreover, if the Poles and others who prefer to remain abroad are allowed to do so, what exactly is their status to be?

24 June 1945

MORRISON AND BRACKEN FACE STIFF FIGHTS: HEAVY POLL EXPECTED

I N all of the half-dozen London constituencies that I have visited up to date it is expected that a high percentage of the registered electorate will vote, otherwise considerable uncertainty reigns and there are several areas where leading members of the various parties are by no means sure of their seats.

In Lewisham East, for example, Mr Herbert Morrison has chosen to attack a constituency which had a 7,000 Tory majority in 1935, and the result is likely to be a close thing. In Paddington North, Mr Brendan Bracken is having a tough fight against General Mason-Macfarlane, the

Labour candidate. Partly owing to the bombing, the Paddington area has changed its social composition since the last election, and if Mr Brendan Bracken wins it will quite likely be because Mr C. Groves, the Socialist Party of Great Britain candidate (this is the sole constituency the SPGB is contesting) has split the Labour vote.

In Marylebone, Captain Cunningham-Reid is fighting against the official Conservative candidate, thus for the first time giving Labour some kind of chance in this strongly Conservative area. In Mile End, it is sure to be a close finish between Mr Dan Frankel, the Labour candidate, and the very energetic and popular Communist candidate, Mr Phil Piratin.

The situation is similar in Hackney South, where Mr William Rust, editor of the *Daily Worker*, faces Mr H. W. Butler, a Labour candidate, who is a well-known local figure. The only constituency I have visited where the result seemed to me a foregone conclusion is Limehouse, Mr Attlee's seat, but even here the youthful Conservative candidate, Mr Peter Woodard, is putting up a lively fight and is surprisingly confident about his chances.

Many votes 'lost'

Part of the present uncertainty arises from the shift of the population and the bad state of the electoral roll. Because of the bombing in several East End constituencies the electorate has shrunk from about 40,000 to about 16,000. Moreover many votes are 'lost'. Some people have returned to their London homes to find that they are registered in that place to which they were evacuated and would have to make a special journey if they wanted to vote. Others have been registered as living in premises which have been demolished in recent clearance schemes and it is sometimes impossible to discover their whereabouts. A certain number of workers in special categories have not been registered at all because they still have the old identity cards, and considerable numbers of Service men abroad have failed to register. Hackney, for instance, has 5,000 potential Service voters, of whom only 2,000 have applied for papers.

Except in areas like Stepney, where the entire population is working class, the mechanical difficulties of the election probably operate in the Conservative interest. The 'lost' votes are mostly working-class votes, and the fact that there is now almost no unemployment makes things harder for the Left-wing parties. Canvassing and other organisational work used to be done largely by unemployed men, but it is now very difficult in working-class areas to find anyone who has spare time on his hands before six in the evening.

The election is only just 'warming up', and I have not yet overheard a spontaneous remark about it in the street nor have I seen a single person stopping to look at an election poster. On the other hand, the indoor meetings of all parties, though usually not large (the blitzing of many public buildings has had its effect here) are well-attended and lively, and even when there is rowdiness the questions and interruptions are generally to the point. Both speakers and audiences seem anxious to deal with the real issues – that is, nationalisation of industry and the continuance of Mr Churchill in office – and to disregard irrelevancies. The anti-Laski campaign, for instance, seems to have made very little impression, and even Communist speakers put somewhat more emphasis on housing, old age pensions, etc. than on recriminations about the past. On the other hand, there seems to be little interest in the war against Japan and no feeling that this is an electoral issue.

Professional hecklers

No one can doubt that in London, at any rate, the political current is still running strongly Leftward and the Conservative meetings are usually the rowdiest. But the violence of feeling varies a good deal from constituency to constituency.

In Lewisham, for instance, the fighting is clean, whereas in Paddington it is distinctly dirty. On Thursday night there were concerted efforts to shout down Mr Brendan Bracken, who, however, won in the end because he had a loudspeaker and his interrupters had not. And in Mile End on Friday, the Communist speaker was subjected to a certain amount of interruption which had the appearance of being organised. A few Party agents have told me that in their opinion gangs of professional hecklers are being sent from meeting to meeting, but even among the Conservatives – the worst sufferers from interruption – this view is not general.

Many observers also believe that rowdiness tends to defeat its own purpose in the long run – or even in the short run – for a foolish interruption gives a quick speaker the chance to score a cheap laugh. Within the next week we shall be able to see whether the big public has grasped the momentousness of this election or whether the political apathy produced by a ten-years' Parliament is something that has come to stay. But up to date, among the section of the public that has entered into the struggle, the prevailing attitude is serious and democratic and gives evidence of a great advance in political intelligence.

---

1 July 1945

LIBERAL INTERVENTION AIDS LABOUR
'Puzzle' blocks of voters

E LECTION feeling in London has not 'hotted up' to the extent that had been expected and the reactions of large blocks of the people are still unpredictable. The most one can say is that, among those who are articulate, the Labour Party is still gaining ground. It also seems to be agreed that the intervention of the Liberals splits the Conservative and not the Labour vote, especially in middle-class areas. But the agents of all parties refuse to make detailed forecasts.

At Wandsworth Central, Mr Ernest Bevin is fighting a hard and doubtful battle against his Conservative opponent, Brigadier General Smyth, VC. Mr Bevin was returned to his seat unopposed during the war, but the Labour majority at the previous election was less than 500, and since then the electorate has dropped by 6,000 and altered in composition. Islington East is also anybody's fight. Mrs Cazalet Keir, the outgoing Conservative member, had a majority of 4,000 at the last election and has won renown as the champion of equal pay for women teachers; on the other hand, her attitude on old age pensions is considered locally to be unsatisfactory, and Dr Eric Fletcher, her Labour opponent, evidently has a good chance.

At Holborn, Captain Max Aitken seems likely to win in a straight fight against Miss Marchuse, the Labour candidate. But even here there is considerable uncertainty because of the difficulty of canvassing in this area, with its mixed and shifting population.

Above the belt

At Hammersmith South, a Conservative win by a small majority seems likely. In this constituency it is a straight fight between Labour and Conservative, and most of the blows are landed above the belt. It is distinctly different in Hammersmith North, a penny bus ride away, where the official Labour candidate, Mr W. H. Church, is contending not only against the Conservative, Major L. Caplan, but against the outgoing member Mr D. N. Pritt. This is probably the most interesting as well as the most acrimonious contest now happening in the London area.

Mr D. N. Pritt has held the seat for a number of years, but was expelled from the Labour Party in 1940. His posters have not made it altogether clear that he is not the Labour candidate, and Mr Church has been obliged to spend much energy in establishing this point. Locally Mr Pritt has a good record and he probably started off with a big advantage, but Mr Church seems to have been gaining ground during the past week. The situation is a curious one. If Mr Church and Mr Pritt run neck and neck, Major Caplan is quite likely to win, since the Labour majority in the last election was only 1,600. But the spirit in which the election has been fought has compelled Major Caplan to turn most of the guns against Mr Pritt, and on Wednesday night he announced at a large and stormy meeting that he was issuing a writ for alleged libel. If his efforts to demolish Mr Pritt succeed, the result will probably be a win for Mr Church. Mr Pritt and Major Caplan are both barristers and are close neighbours in the Temple.

There is a somewhat similar situation in Putney, where there are five candidates – Mr H. N. Linstead, the outgoing Conservative Member, Mr P. Stewart, the Labour candidate, Sir Richard Acland for Common Wealth, a Liberal, and an Independent who represents the Never Again Association [an anti-racism movement]. Putney has always been strongly Tory, and Sir Richard Acland appears to have chosen this unpromising constituency under the impression that Labour was not contesting it. The Liberal and the Independent will capture some Conservative votes, but effectively the struggle is three-sided. Labour is thought to have a block vote of about a quarter of the electorate in the local factories, but Sir Richard Acland seems to be making good progress, and once again the effect of inter-Left rivalry may be to ensure a Conservative victory.

Wasted efforts

Except for Hammersmith North and possibly Wandsworth Central, I have not yet seen a Labour seat which I thought the Conservative Party could win. But almost all observers of all parties agree on the impossibility of knowing what the big masses are thinking. Indoor meetings get good audiences, and in spite of some organised rowdiness the level of questions and discussion compares well with the mud-slinging in sections of the Press, but here only minorities are involved, and outdoor meetings, at any rate, in the more thickly populated parts of London, do not seem to be having much success.

More than once I have seen a loudspeaker wasting its efforts on an audience composed entirely of small boys and dogs. Just once during this week I have overheard a spontaneous comment on the election – from a Scotswoman whose sympathies appeared to be with Labour. Direct questioning sometimes elicits this disconcerting answer: 'Well, you see, I don't know anything about politics.' Canvassers in some areas report that 'I haven't made up my mind yet' is a frequent answer. But when the time comes these seemingly uninterested masses will most of them cast their votes and there is still the possibility that they will be swayed by some last-minute appeal.

The Laski campaign has now definitely failed, and some Conservative agents say frankly that they regard Lord Beaverbrook as a liability. The thing that is likeliest to influence the doubtful votes at the last moment is alarm at the thought of dropping Mr Churchill, and it is a swing of this kind, possibly precipitated by events abroad, that Labour Party organisers are most afraid of.

PROFILE: ANEURIN BEVAN

THIS week's debate on Housing will certainly bring a major speech from the new Minister of Health.

For several of the war years Aneurin Bevan – 'that architect of disloyalty' as Mr Churchill once called him in a heated moment – was known as the most turbulent MP on the Opposition benches and it is only sixteen months since his own party came near to expelling him for voting against the Government on a major issue. His weekly paper *Tribune*, whose editorship-in-chief he had inherited from Sir Stafford Cripps, also criticised the conduct of the war, and British foreign policy, with a freedom that sometimes bordered on irresponsibility. These activities have tended to stamp him in the public mind as the naughty boy of the Labour Party and to obscure the solid achievements that actually lie behind him. Yet in the job of rehousing Britain his experience in local government and in trade union administration may be as important as the restless energy of his temperament.

Aneurin Bevan was born in 1897, the son of a coalminer. He himself left school at thirteen and went to work in the pit. In spite of his powerful physique he was a shy, bookish boy, left-handed and troubled by a severe stammer, which still has a slight tendency to return in moments when he is overtired. In such spare time as he could get he read voraciously, making a speciality of books on philosophy. He had the chance to educate himself, he says, quite largely because the Tredegar public library happened to be an exceptionally good one and the librarian took a personal interest in him. As for his stammer and his nervousness, he got rid of them by deliberately involving himself in street-corner meetings and other situations where he knew he would be compelled to speak extempore.

Some years later he was able to leave the pit and study at the Central Labour College. He was only nineteen when he was chairman of the largest miners' lodge in South Wales and was still a very young man when he became a member of the local Urban District Council. He was a miners' dispute agent in 1926 and has held the Ebbw-Vale seat since

1929. With this background, his natural affinity might seem to be with the trade union end of the Labour Party, but in fact he has until lately been looked on with some suspicion by the chiefs of the TUC.

His following outside his own constituency has been chiefly among the 'intellectuals' of the Party branches and the growing body of middle-class people whose sympathies have turned Leftward during the past five or ten years. He was the close associate of Sir Stafford Cripps until Cripps joined the Churchill Government, and he has many foreign refugee Socialists among his friends and advisers. He is more of an extremist and more of an internationalist than the average Labour MP, and it is the combination of this with his working-class origin that makes him an interesting and unusual figure.

On any issue of domestic policy – on housing, social security, education, public health – Bevan thinks and feels as a working man. He knows how the scales are weighted against anyone with less than £5 a week and during the war he has defended the right of the workers to strike, even at moments when strikes did or could seriously hamper the war effort. But he is remarkably free – some of his adversaries would say dangerously free – from any feeling of personal grievance against society. He shows no sign of ordinary class consciousness. He seems equally at home in all kinds of company. It is difficult to imagine anyone less impressed by social status or less inclined to put on airs with subordinates. Everyone who has more than a nodding acquaintance with him calls him by his nickname of 'Nye'. He has the temperament that used to be called 'mercurial' – a temperament capable of sudden low spirits but not of settled pessimism. His boisterous manner sometimes gives casual observers the impression that he is not serious and his warmest admirers do not claim that punctuality is his strong point. But in fact he has a huge capacity for work and manages to put in a great deal of time at his rather inaccessible constituency.

Some of Bevan's qualities may be traceable to his Welsh blood. Though only tepidly interested in Welsh Nationalism, he has not lost touch with his origins and retains traces of his Welsh accent. His infrequent holidays are always devoted to climbing in his native hills. He is a typical Celt not only in his quickness of speech and abrupt alternations of mood but in his respect for the intellect. He does not have the suspicion of 'cleverness' and anaesthesia to the arts which are generally regarded as the mark of a practical man. Those who have worked with him in a journalistic capacity have remarked with pleasure and astonishment that here at last is a politician who knows that literature exists and will even hold up work for five minutes to discuss a point of style.

Bevan's campaign against Churchill in Parliament and in the Press was very bitter, and sometimes undignified. There were moments when Bevan seemed to be actuated by personal dislike and Churchill, too, was more easily 'drawn' by Bevan than by any other opponent. Some observers have remarked that the two men are natural antagonists 'because they are so alike'. In fact, there are points of resemblance. Both men are naturally genial but capable of sudden anger and rough speech, both of them have been held back in their careers by the 'cleverness' which did not commend itself to more stolid colleagues. Whether Bevan is fully Churchill's equal in obstinacy remains to be seen.

The post he now holds, a post in which he is responsible not only for public health but for rehousing, is a thankless and difficult one. In the matter of houses the public expects miracles and is certain to be disappointed at not getting them. Bevan is well aware of this and knows all about the fight with local authorities, with the building trade and with the BMA that lies ahead of him. He has clear ideas about what is desirable and what is possible in the matter of housing. His own private preference is for a house and not a flat and he holds it as a principle that everyone should have the right to choose between the two. But he also realises that if people are to live in big conglomerations they must spread themselves vertically, and he would like, if he can, to popularise the idea of the small town which is a single building – the 'skyscraper in open country'.

He sought out his present job because he feels strongly about slum clearance, about the effects of the housing shortage on the birth-rate, and about the need to put the practice of medicine on a non-commercial basis. Those who know him believe that he can make decisions boldly, will get results, and will soon return to the headlines as a quite different figure from the fiery debater of the last five years.

MARX AND RUSSIA

T HE word 'Communism', unlike 'Fascism', has never degenerated into a meaningless term of abuse. Nevertheless, a certain ambiguity does cling to it, and at the least it means two different things only rather tenuously connected: a political theory and a political movement which is not in any noticeable way putting the theory into practice. On the face of it the deeds of the Cominform might seem more important than the prophecies of Marx, but, as Mr John Plamenatz reminds us in his recently published booklet [*What is Communism?*, 1947], the original vision of Communism must never be forgotten, since it is still the dynamo which supplies millions of adherents with faith and hence with the power to act.

Disciples

Originally, 'Communism' meant a free and just society based on the principle of 'to each according to his needs'. Marx gave this vision probability by making it part of a seemingly inevitable historical process. Society was to dwindle down to a tiny class of possessors and an enormous class of dispossessed, and one day, almost automatically, the dispossessed were to take over. Only a few decades after Marx's death the Russian Revolution broke out, and the men who guided its course proclaimed themselves, and believed themselves, to be Marx's most faithful disciples. But their success really depended on throwing a good deal of their master's teaching overboard.

Marx had foretold that revolution would happen first in the highly industrialised countries. It is now clear that this was an error, but he was right in this sense, that the kind of revolution that he foresaw could not happen in a backward country like Russia, where the industrial workers were a minority. Marx had envisaged an overwhelmingly powerful proletariat sweeping aside a small group of opponents, and then governing democratically through elected representatives. What actually happened, in Russia, was the seizure of power by a small body of classless professional revolutionaries, who claimed to represent the common people but were not chosen by them nor genuinely answerable to them.

From Lenin's point of view this was unavoidable. He and his group had to stay in power since they alone were the true inheritors of the Marxist doctrine, and it was obvious that they could not stay in power democratically. The 'dictatorship of the proletariat' had to mean the dictatorship of a handful of intellectuals ruling through terrorism. The Revolution was saved, but from then onwards the Russian Communist Party developed in a direction of which Lenin would probably have disapproved if he had lived longer.

Placed as they were, the Russian Communists necessarily developed into a permanent ruling caste or oligarchy, recruited not by birth but by adoption. Since they could not risk the growth of opposition, they could not permit genuine criticism and since they silenced criticism they often made avoidable mistakes; then, because they could not admit that the mistakes were their own, they had to find scapegoats, sometimes on an enormous scale.

The upshot is that the dictatorship has grown tighter as the regime has grown more secure, and that Russia is perhaps farther from egalitarian Socialism to-day than she was eighty years ago. But, as Mr Plamenatz rightly warns us: never for one moment should we imagine that the original fervour has faded. The Communists may have perverted their aims, but they have not lost their mystique. The belief that they and they alone are the saviours of humanity is as unquestioning as ever. In the years 1935–39 and 1941–44 it was easy to believe that the USSR had abandoned the idea of world revolution, but it is now clear that this was not the case. The idea has never been dropped: it has merely been modified, 'revolution' tending more and more to mean 'conquest'.

The future

No doubt unavoidably in so short a book, Mr Plamenatz confines himself to one facet of his subject, and says very little about the role and character of the Communist parties outside the USSR. He also rarely touches on the question of whether the Russian regime will, or indeed can, grow more liberal of its own accord. This last question is all-important, but for lack of precedents one can only guess at the answer.

Meanwhile, we are faced with a world-wide political movement which threatens the very existence of Western civilisation, and which has lost none of its vigour because it has become in a sense corrupt. Mr Plamenatz concludes bleakly that, though the USSR will not necessarily precipitate an aggressive war against the West, its rulers regard a struggle to the death as inevitable and will never come to any real agreement with those whom they regard as their natural enemies. Evidently, as Commander Stephen King-Hall says in his Introduction, if we want to combat Communism we must start by understanding it. But beyond understanding there lies the yet more difficult task of being understood and – a problem that few people seem to have seriously considered as yet – of finding some way of making our point of view known to the Russian people.

---

9 May 1948

WILDE'S UTOPIA

O SCAR Wilde's work is being much revived now on stage and screen, and it is well to be reminded that Salome and Lady Windermere were not his only creations. Wilde's 'The Soul of Man under Socialism', for example, first published nearly sixty years ago, has worn remarkably well. Its author was not in any active sense a Socialist himself, but he was a sympathetic and intelligent observer; although his prophecies have not been fulfilled, they have not been made simply irrelevant by the passage of time.

Wilde's vision of Socialism, which at that date was probably shared by many people less articulate than himself, is Utopian and anarchistic. The abolition of private property, he says, will make possible the full development of the individual and set us free from 'the sordid necessity of living for others'. In the Socialist future there will not only be no want and no insecurity, there will also be no drudgery, no disease, no ugliness, no wastage of the human spirit in futile enmities and rivalries.

Free choice

Pain will cease to be important; indeed, for the first time in his history, Man will be able to realise his personality through joy instead of through suffering. Crime will disappear, since there will be no economic reason for it. The State will cease to govern and will survive merely as an agency for the distribution of necessary commodities. All the disagreeable jobs will be done by machinery, and everyone will be completely free to choose his own work and his own manner of life. In effect, the world will be populated by artists, each striving after perfection in the way that seems best to him.

To-day these optimistic forecasts make rather painful reading. Wilde realised, of course, that there were authoritarian tendencies in the Socialist movement, but he did not believe they would prevail, and with a sort of prophetic irony he wrote: 'I hardly think that any Socialist nowadays would seriously propose that an inspector should call every morning at each house to see that each citizen rose up and did manual labour for eight hours' – which, unfortunately, is just the kind of thing that countless modern Socialists would propose. Evidently something has gone wrong. Socialism in the sense of economic collectivism is conquering the earth at a speed that would hardly have seemed possible sixty years ago, and yet Utopia, at any rate Wilde's Utopia, is no nearer. Where, then, does the fallacy lie?

If one looks more closely one sees that Wilde makes two common but unjustified assumptions. One is that the world is immensely rich and is suffering chiefly from maldistribution. Even things out between the millionaire and the crossing-sweeper, he seems to say, and there will be plenty of everything for everybody. Until the Russian Revolution this belief was very widely held – 'starving in the midst of plenty' was a favourite phrase – but it was quite false, and it survived only because Socialists thought always of the highly developed Western countries and ignored the fearful poverty of Asia and Africa. Actually, the problem for the world as a whole is not how to distribute such wealth as exists but how to increase production, without which economic equality merely means common misery.

Secondly, Wilde assumes that it is a simple matter to arrange that all the unpleasant kinds of work shall be done by machinery. The machines, he says, are our new race of slaves: a tempting metaphor, but a misleading one, since there is a vast range of jobs – roughly speaking, any job needing great flexibility – that no machine is able to do. In practice, even in the most highly mechanised countries, an enormous amount of dull and exhausting work has to be done by unwilling human muscles. But this at once implies direction of labour, fixed working hours, differential wage rates, and all the regimentation that Wilde abhors. Wilde's version of Socialism could only be realised in a world not only far richer but also technically far more advanced than the present one. The abolition of private property does not of itself put food into anyone's mouth. It is merely the first step in a transitional period that is bound to be laborious, uncomfortable and long.

Brotherhood

But that is not to say that Wilde is altogether wrong. The trouble with transitional periods is that the harsh outlook which they generate tends to become permanent. To all appearances this is what has happened in Soviet Russia. A dictatorship supposedly established for a limited purpose has dug itself in and Socialism comes to be thought of as meaning concentration camps and secret police forces. Wilde's pamphlet and other kindred writings – *News from Nowhere*, for instance [William Morris, 1890] – consequently have their value. They may demand the impossible and they may – since a Utopia necessarily reflects the aesthetic ideas of its own period – sometimes seem 'dated' and ridiculous, but they do at least look beyond the era of food queues and party squabbles and remind the Socialist movement of its original half-forgotten objective of human brotherhood.

PROFILE: KRISHNA MENON

ONE man to whom the Exhibition of Indian Art, just open at Burlington House, will bring quiet pride is Mr V. K. Krishna Menon, High Commissioner in London for the Dominion of India. His new post and the Exhibition are both tokens of a sympathetic intercourse between Britain and India which in earlier life he can scarcely have expected. People here are used to think of Mr Menon as the arch-rebel, working in their midst against the British Raj. For years they watched him conducting his political activities from 165 Strand, the old office of the India League.

Menon came to this country in 1924, a young man of twenty-six. From Mrs Annie Besant, his political guru, he had heard much about Britain; his study of Burke, Mill and Shakespeare had given him a great wish to see the strange land which had such titles to fame and could yet keep millions of his own people in subjugation. His intention, then, was to return to India in six months. Instead, he stayed on and has been here ever since, rarely visiting India and then only for short periods.

This tall, severe-looking man with classical features is by nature an ascetic: he neither drinks nor smokes, has never married, and is a strict vegetarian. Before moving a few months ago into that magnificent edifice in Aldwych called India House, he used to live in a small bed-and-breakfast room in one of the side-streets of Camden Town. From 1934 up to his recent appointment he sat for Labour on the St Pancras Borough Council. He had been active in the Labour movement even earlier, working closely with Ellen Wilkinson in the grim 'hunger-march' days.

In 1939 he was chosen as parliamentary Labour candidate for Dundee, but resigned from the Party over its India policy during the war years. Then, as always with him, India came first. He rejoined in 1945, after the Labour Party conference had passed its famous 'Independence for India' resolution against the advice of the executive.

Even as a boy, wandering in the streets of Calicut, the land of black pepper and coconuts, where trains pass through gardens and gardens touch the sea, Menon dreamt of freedom for India. Defiance runs in his family. His father, a lawyer, had little respect for British-made laws; his eldest sister fought her way against sex discrimination into a secondary school hitherto reserved for boys.

Soon after graduating from the Presidency College, Madras, Menon was drawn into Mrs Besant's 'Home Rule' agitation, and she promptly chose him as one of her young volunteers. For five years he lived and worked in the Besant community, leaving only to come to England.

His first job here was teaching history at St Christopher's School, Letchworth. At the same time he took evening classes at the London School of Economics, graduating with first-class honours and also gaining the London University Diploma in Education. After a period of research in the psychological laboratory of University College, which brought him his MA, he returned to the LSE, where he became one of Professor Laski's favourite pupils and added the MSc (Economics) to his remarkable bag of academic distinctions.

His inclination, however, was towards an independent profession rather than a teaching post; his next step was to qualify as a barrister of the Inner Temple. He practised at the Bar, but was not a great success; perhaps because law is a jealous mistress, and his first love has always been politics. A fluent speaker, he soon became known in Labour circles as an authority on India. In 1929 he was elected General Secretary of the India League, then not much more than a club where Left-wing sympathisers such as Lansbury, Lee Smith, and Pethick-Lawrence met to discuss Indian problems with earnest young Indians. Menon made the League a political force; before long the Congress leaders recognised it as their chief mouthpiece in Europe.

In 1935 Pandit Nehru came to London; he was impressed by Menon's work, and the friendship then formed between the two men has never waned. It was certain that as Nehru's star rose Menon's would rise with it. When last year Nehru became Vice-President of the Indian Interim Government he at once made Menon his personal envoy in Europe, and later sent him to the United Nations General Assembly as a member of the Indian delegation. Finally, when Nehru became Prime Minister, Menon was appointed to represent his country at the Court of St James's.

However, it would be quite wrong to think of Menon as merely a client of Nehru. He is a self-made man with an arresting personality who would in any event have carved out a notable career for himself, very possibly in Parliament. He writes English as well as he speaks it, is the author of several books and innumerable pamphlets, and was the first editor of the Pelican Series and the Twentieth Century Library, a most unusual distinction for an Indian.

In personal life Menon is difficult to know. He has an immense range of acquaintances, but not many friends. People either admire or condemn him; they rarely get an opportunity to break through his armour of reserve. He is sensitive to the reactions of others and tries to take them into his confidence, but he is seldom able to lower his guard. Only with children does he find it easy to unbend.

To his subordinates Menon often seems a hard taskmaster: he has an almost Curzonian passion for detail and likes to keep the strings of authority in his own hands. Tireless himself, he is often at his desk by 8 a.m., and is apt to work eighteen hours a day. But he has seen enough of the ups and downs of life to appreciate the difficulties of others; his judgements are more generous than his manner usually allows him to show. Very few have ever suffered at his hands, though more than a few have tried to damage his reputation.

Because of his critical role in the past many people imagine that Menon does not like the British. Nothing could be further from truth. In fact, it is inconceivable that he would ever feel at home now in any other country. He has lived with the British so long and has known them so well that he has grown genuinely fond of them. With Lord and Lady Mountbatten he has established lately a firm friendship; for his character and integrity they have a high regard. We can be sure that the former rebel will do his utmost to strengthen the new alliance – the free alliance he has always wanted – between his country and ours.

THE REVIEWS

1942–49

AN AMERICAN CRITIC

The Wound and the Bow, by Edmund Wilson
(Secker and Warburg, 15s.)

ALTHOUGH in this new book of critical essays Mr Edmund Wilson ranges from Sophocles to Hemingway via Casanova and Edith Wharton, it is chiefly valuable for two long studies of Dickens and Kipling, both of which incorporate a certain amount of original research, or, at any rate, of little-known information. Writing in 1940 or 1941, after the publication of Miss Gladys Storey's memoir, Mr Wilson is able to make use of biographical details which earlier critics of Dickens had regarded as either irrelevant or as a disgraceful secret to be hushed up at all costs. The contrast between Dickens's literary personality – his literary emanation, as one might say – and his private life is even more baffling than is usual with creative writers, and if Mr Wilson reaches no very definite conclusion he does at least throw brilliant flashes of light on some very dark places.

Dickens's last surviving daughter, Mrs Perugini, wrote a memoir of her father, which she destroyed because it gave 'only half the truth', but afterwards conveyed the substance of it verbally to Miss Gladys Storey. It brought out the facts about Ellen Lawless Ternan, who is enigmatically mentioned in Dickens's will and who in fact was his mistress during the later years of his life. Mr Wilson makes the very interesting observation that this girl's name appears in quasi-anagrammatic form in his last three novels (Estella Provis, Bella Wilfer, and Helena Landless). What is remarkable is not that Dickens should have indulged in a mistress but that he evidently behaved with abominable cruelty towards his wife, and at least very tyrannically towards his children.

> 'I loved my father,' said Mrs Perugini, 'better than any man in the world – in a different way of course... I loved him for his faults.' And she added, as she rose and walked to the door: 'my father was a wicked man – a very wicked man.'

It is a strange epitaph for the author of *Pickwick Papers*. If one judges Dickens by his literary personality, the only part of him that now matters, it is clear that he was not a wicked man. The outstanding thing about his work is a certain native goodness, and in the few passages where his moral sense fails him one feels the contrasts immediately. Yet the last person who remembered him remembered him as wicked. One is forced to believe in a sort of split personality, in which David Copperfield rather than Charles Dickens is the real man. Mr Wilson indeed hints at a definite criminal strain in Dickens, and the essay tails off into a discussion of the meaning of Edwin Drood, about which Mr Wilson has a new and rather sensational theory.

Dickens was a writer-with-a-purpose, and all serious critics of him have noted this, but they have differed between themselves as to whether his 'purpose' was moral or political. At the one extreme there is Chesterton, who very nearly succeeded in turning Dickens into a Catholic medievalist, and at the other there is Mr T. A. Jackson, who presented Dickens not only as an all-but-perfect Marxist but – an even harder feat – as an extreme naturalist. Mr Wilson is somewhere between the two, but inclines more towards the Jackson school. He is undoubtedly right in pointing out that the themes of Dickens's novels reflect first his belief in and then his disillusionment with the commercial middle class and he makes the interesting point that in his last completed novel, *Our Mutual Friend*, Dickens shows a sympathy he had not shown before with the petty aristocracy (Wrayburn, Twemlow) and the proletariat (Lizzie Hexam). But he does not add that in *Our Mutual Friend* Dickens's thoughts have come full circle and he has returned to his early notion of individual benevolence as the cure for everything, having apparently despaired of any political solution. Perhaps also he overstresses the element of symbolism in Dickens's work and understresses the mechanical side of commercial story-writing. But this side is the best essay on Dickens that has appeared for some time.

If the essay on Kipling is less satisfying it is probably because Kipling is nearer to our own time and therefore more capable of arousing anti-British feeling. I do not know whether Mr Wilson is one of those Americans who avoid visiting England lest their hatred for it should evaporate, but at times that is the impression he gives. But the Kipling essay contains some very interesting biographical material. Kipling spent several years in the United States, and ended by involving himself in a quarrel in which he behaved in an extremely undignified way, the whole incident probably casting light on his peculiar role as a sedentary apostle of violence. It is a pity that for the rest Mr Wilson occupies himself principally with Kipling's later stories, those he wrote after 1918. Whatever psychological interest these may possess, something had gone out of Kipling by that time, and the stories are synthetic. Mr Wilson hardly mentions Kipling's verse, evidently agreeing with the accepted view that Kipling is primarily a prose-writer.

The other essays in the book are slighter, but they include an interesting elucidation of Joyce's *Finnegans Wake*. Mr Wilson at times writes clumsily, even vulgarly, but he is one of the few literary critics of our day who give the impression of being grown up, and of having digested Marx's teachings instead of merely rejecting them or swallowing them whole.

---

2 August 1942

PORTRAIT OF THE GENERAL

Charles de Gaulle, by Philippe Barrès
(Hutchinson, 9s. 6d. net.)

M R Philippe Barrès's book may be taken as the 'official' biography of General de Gaulle, and it probably gives as full and frank an account of the Free French movement as was possible at the time when it was written – that is, some time during the summer of 1941. Necessarily silent on certain points, such as the Syrian campaign and the unsuccessful Dakar expedition, it gives much valuable detail about the circumstances of the French collapse, and it has the merit of quoting most of the relevant documents in full.

As is now widely known, General de Gaulle's views on mechanised warfare, ignored by his own countrymen, were taken up and acted upon by the Germans, who seem actually to have built up their armoured divisions for the Polish campaign on the specifications set forth in de Gaulle's book, published five years earlier. In the years between Hitler's rise to power and the outbreak of war de Gaulle had agitated as best he could, chiefly through Paul Reynaud, for a more modern conception of war than was implied in the Maginot line and a five-million conscript army, and Chapter V of Mr Barrès's book gives the text of the memorandum which he submitted to the High Command in January of 1940, after five months of 'phony' war. In general terms this document foretold exactly what did happen a few months later.

Needless to say, his warnings went unheeded. De Gaulle languished in obscurity till the Battle of France, when for a brief period he held an important command and won some minor success with the inadequate forces at his disposal. It was fortunate that in these few weeks he earned sufficient renown to make him the natural rallying-point of those Frenchmen who wanted to go on fighting. But why had no one, outside Germany, listened to his teachings earlier? If one thinks simply, in technical terms, this is easy enough to understand. The two wars were only twenty-one years apart, and the generals who had won the war of 1914, or thought they had, were still in command. It was their instinct to see that nothing was changed, just as the Duke of Wellington struggled to keep the British Army the same in the 1850s as it had been at Waterloo. There was also the pacifism of public opinion, disillusioned by victory and only too ready for an inert defensive policy, as in England. But Mr Barrès barely touches on the deeper political and economic causes of the French collapse. A book of this kind, written while events are still in the making, is bound to avoid certain issues. The delicacy of the situation lies in the fact that whereas in France the 'collaborators' are the politicians of the Right, the Free French are of literally all political colours. General de Gaulle himself, denounced daily over the radio as a Jewish Marxist and freemason, is a Catholic of provincial aristocracy and perhaps of royalist antecedents. Mr Barrès is naturally rather anxious to avoid tying a political programme on to the Free French movement, though since the book was written some steps in that direction have been taken. In his pages de Gaulle appears simply as the personification of 'la patrie', of the simple instinct which makes decent men of all shades of opinion unite against a foreign conqueror. On that level this book is a worthy tribute. The American translation could be improved upon.

PORTRAIT OF AN ADDICT

A Modern de Quincey, by Captain H. R. Robinson
(Harrap, 8s. 6d.)

U NJUSTIFIED in other ways, the title of this book does have the excuse that its author, like de Quincey, is very much interested in his own reactions as an opium-smoker. An officer of the Indian Army, seconded to the Burma Military Police, he was axed in 1923 and settled down for a couple of years in Mandalay, where he devoted himself almost exclusively to smoking opium, through he did have a brief interlude as a Buddhist monk and made unsuccessful efforts to float a gold mine and run a car-hiring business. After a short visit to England, during which he tried quite vainly to cure himself of the opium habit, he returned to Mandalay, and on being arrested for debt attempted suicide – a ghastly failure, for instead of blowing out his brains as he had intended he merely blew out both eyeballs, blinding himself for life.

This bald outline of the facts does not do injustice to Captain Robinson's book, which in spite of the long passages devoted to the delights of opium, leaves a great deal unexplained. Those who knew the author in Mandalay in 1923 were completely unable to understand why a young, healthy and apparently happy man should give himself up to such a debilitating and – in a European – unusual vice, and on this point the book throws no further light. Captain Robinson merely explains that one night in Mandalay he happened to see some Chinese smoking their opium, decided to try what it was like, and thereafter became a habitual opium-smoker. Some other reason for wanting to escape from real life there must have been. It is never mentioned, but the clue is possibly to be found in the earlier part of the book, which describes Captain Robinson's adventures as a frontier magistrate among the little-known tribes in the north-east corner of Burma.

What are the pleasures of opium? Like other pleasures, they are, unfortunately, indescribable. It is easier to describe the miseries which the smoker suffers when deprived of his drug; he is seized with feverish restlessness, then with violent fits of yawning, and finally howls like a dog, a noise so distressing that when an opium-smoker is imprisoned in an Indian gaol he is usually, quite illegally, given diminishing doses to keep him quiet. Like many other smokers, Captain Robinson felt himself, while under the influence of the drug, to be possessed of almost divine wisdom. He was aware that he not only knew the secret of the Universe, but had reduced this secret to a single sentence, which he was unfortunately never able to recall when he woke up. One night, so as to make sure of remembering it, he took a pad and pencil when he lay down to smoke. The sentence in which all wisdom was contained turned out to be: 'the banana is great, but the skin is greater'.

This book is a small but not valueless contribution to the literature of opium. It is amateurishly written, but its facts are truthful. The description of the attempted suicide is worth the rest of the book put together. It is profoundly interesting to know what the mind can still contain in the face of apparently certain death; interesting to know, for instance, that a man can be ready to blow his brains out but anxious to avoid a disfiguring wound. Those who knew Captain Robinson in those days will be glad to receive evidence of his continued existence and to see the photograph of him at the beginning of the book, completely cured of the opium habit and apparently well-adjusted and happy, in spite of his blindness.

---

12 September 1943

PARIS IS NOT FRANCE

France is a Democracy, by Louis Lévy
(Gollancz, 5s.)

EVEN if Mr Louis Lévy's book had no other quality it would perform a useful service in reminding the average English reader that Paris is not France. To our grandfathers France meant cheap champagne, Sunday theatres, and the novels of Paul de Koch. That legend has almost passed away, but in recent years there has been an equally dangerous tendency to notice nothing in France except the antics of a few Paris politicians. In the pre-war years, even after Munich, most observers in this country took the *Front Populaire* at its face value and ignored the strong pacifist tendencies inside the Labour movement; in 1940 and even later, on the other hand, the belief was almost general in this country that the whole of France was ready to 'collaborate'. France was supposed to be ripe for either Communism or Fascism, and the strong democratic traditions of the mass of people were forgotten. It is to correct this mistaken view and bring the provinces back into the Englishman's picture of France that Mr Lévy's book is written.

Nearly half the book is a sort of topographical survey which runs over the French departments one by one and indicates the political colour of their inhabitants. Although the main object of this is to show that radicalism and republicanism have deep roots nearly everywhere, it has the added value of reminding English readers that France is a big country with considerable regional variations; Mr Lévy does not even mind turning aside from time to time to throw in a few notes on the local wines and cheeses. But he is concerned above all to give a background to his chapters on political history and thus to show why France fell so easily, and why the overthrow of French democracy cannot possibly be permanent.

France was defeated in a military sense, but it is admitted that the treachery of the ruling classes played its part, and there can be little doubt that the attitude of the common people made their treachery easier. Pacifism of a sort was extremely widespread, and its effect was to make both preparation for war and a firm system of alliances almost impossible. The small French birth-rate, and the terrible losses suffered by France in the last war, made it nearly inevitable that war should seem the worst of all evils to a people who had quite obviously gained no benefit from their victory of 1918. The industrial workers, for instance, were anti-Fascist, but they were also traditionally anti-military; the school teachers were anti-Fascist, but inclined towards 'pure' pacifism; the peasants were republican, but they knew that war does not pay – and besides, so many of their fathers and uncles had been killed at Verdun.

Thus at every point at which the Fascist advance might have been stopped, even when the Popular Front was in power, it was possible to damp down the enthusiasm of the common people by the threat that a firm attitude 'might mean war'. When war actually came the Government could show no good reason for standing firm after a long series of retreats, and in addition the Communist Party, particularly powerful in the Paris area, had by this time changed sides owing to the Russo-German pact.

Having shown just why the French peasant, the factory worker, the petty functionary, and the shopkeeper allowed themselves to be pushed into a suicidal policy by their natural enemies, Mr Lévy draws on the background he has established earlier to show what kind of revulsion is bound to occur in each case. There is no popular basis for any regime that either Pétain or the Germans could set up. Respect for the individual and for democratic processes are ineradicable, for, as Herriot said, 'Liberty cannot die in the country in which it was born.'

Mr Lévy does not profess to know with certainty what regime will follow the German collapse. Of course, it will be a Socialist regime; partly because no other will work, partly because the rich have discredited themselves by 'collaborating', and the systematic plundering carried out by the Germans will have simplified the task of nationalising industry. He also hopes that it will be a democratic regime, but has his fears about the possibilities of interference from outside. He is not an uncritical follower of General de Gaulle, and is not happy to see men like Charles Vallin, the ex-Fascist, in the general's camp. 'Frenchmen,' he says, 'have endorsed political "Gaullism" because it had been presented to them as a democratic movement, but they are suspicious. All the more so, as they particularly fear military dictatorships and political generals.'

Various quotations from the underground Press show that the forces of resistance inside France, while willing to accept General de Gaulle as an interim leader until a constitutional government can be set up, are not struggling against one dictatorship in order to set up another. And Mr Lévy places near the end of his book the significant warning:

Anyone who tries to force upon French democracy a
Government not in accordance with its wishes will find that he
has let loose the bloodiest and most terrible of civil wars.

The point is hammered home by Professor Laski, who contributes a brilliant introduction and voices his doubts about the political complexion of the Gaullist movement a good deal more forcibly than does Mr Lévy.

REVOLT IN THE URBAN DESERT

Reflections on the Revolution of Our Time,
by Harold J. Laski
(Gee, Allen and Unwin, 15s.)

T HIS book is an impressive and courageous attempt to disentangle the intellectual muddle in which we are now living. In defining what is meant by Socialism and Fascism, and in proclaiming the ends we ought to aim at and the dangers that lie ahead, Professor Laski avoids mere propaganda as completely, and states unpopular views as boldly, as anyone who is personally involved in politics could well do. He has the advantage that his roots lie deeper than those of the majority of Left-wing thinkers; he does not ignore the past, and he does not despise his own countrymen. But the position of someone who is a Socialist by allegiance and a Liberal by temperament is not easy and, though he never states it in those words, Professor Laski's book really revolves round this problem.

This is most apparent in his chapter on the Russian Revolution, and in the long chapter towards the end entitled 'The Threat of Counter-revolution'. Professor Laski is rightly concerned with the danger that totalitarianism may soon extend itself to the countries which now call themselves democracies. He sees clearly enough that the war has made no structural change in Britain or the USA, that the old economic problems will recur in more pressing forms the moment that the fighting stops, and that the inroads on privilege that might have been accepted in the moment of national danger will be resisted when there is no enemy at the gate. He is probably right, therefore, in saying that if we do not put through the necessary reforms during the war, when general consent is at any rate thinkable, we shall soon have them imposed on us by violence and at the cost of a long period of dictatorship. Professor Laski knows pretty well what reforms he wants, and few thinking men will disagree with him: he wants centralised ownership, planned production, social equality and the 'positive state'. Much too readily, however – indeed with an almost nineteenth-century optimism – he assumes that these things not only can but certainly will be combined with democracy and freedom of thought.

All through his book there is apparent an unwillingness to admit that Socialism has totalitarian possibilities. He dismisses Fascism as simply monopoly capitalism in its last phase. This is the habitual Left-wing diagnosis, but it seems to have been adopted on the principle of *extra ecclesiam nulla salus* [lit. 'outside the church there is no salvation'], and a false inference has followed from it. Since Fascism was evidently not Socialism, it followed that it must be a form of capitalism. But capitalism, by definition, cannot 'work', therefore Fascism cannot 'work' – or at best it can only, like any capitalist economy, solve the problem of surplus production by going to war.

Fascist States, it has been assumed, are inherently and inevitably warlike. Professor Laski repeats this over and over again – 'the counter-revolution', he says 'is bound to make war'. In reality one has only to look at the map to see that most counter-revolutions don't make war and avoid it at almost any cost. Germany, Italy, and Japan bear out Professor Laski's thesis; for the rest, one country after another, in Europe and America, has gone through a counter-revolutionary process and adopted a Fascist economy, without engaging in foreign war. Does General Franco want war, for instance, or Marshal Pétain, or Dr Salazar, or half a dozen petty South American dictators? It would seem that the essential point about Fascism is not that it solves its problems by war but that it solves them non-democratically and without abolishing private property. The assumption that every totalitarian system must finally wreck itself in meaningless wars is therefore unjustified.

Needless to say, Professor Laski is very unwilling to admit a resemblance between the German and Russian systems. There is much in the Soviet regime that he does not like, and he says so with a boldness that will get him into serious trouble with the Left. He is, perhaps, even too hard on the 'oriental' worship accorded to Marshal Stalin – for, after all, Stalin is not praised more slavishly than a king or a millionaire. But he does defend the purges, the GPU [a forerunner of the KGB], and the crushing of intellectual liberty by saying that they result from the USSR's backwardness and insecurity. Let Russia be really safe from foreign aggression, he says, and the dictatorship will relax. This is a poor answer because the Russian dictatorship has evidently grown tighter as the USSR grew stronger, militarily and economically.

What the Soviet regime has demonstrated is what the Fascist States have demonstrated in a different fashion: that the 'contradictions' of capitalism can be got rid of non-democratically and without any increase in individual liberty. Economic insecurity can be abolished at the price of handing society over to a new race of oligarchs. This is not in itself an argument against the Soviet system, for it may well be that the Western conceptions of liberty and democracy are worthless. But if they are not worthless, then certain features in Russian policy are not defensible. One cannot have it both ways. Professor Laski does show signs of wanting to have it both ways, and therein is the chief weakness of his book.

Clearly his own instincts are all for liberty, and even for an old-fashioned version of liberty. His remarks on education point to an individualist outlook hardly compatible with any kind of 'positive state'. All the more ought he to realise that Socialism, if it means only centralised ownership and planned production, is not of its nature either democratic or equalitarian. A hierarchical version of Socialism (Hilaire Belloc's 'Servile State') is probably just as workable as the other, and at this moment is much likelier to arrive. Times beyond number Professor Laski repeats that victory in the present war will achieve nothing if it leaves us with the old economic problems unsolved, and without doubt he is right. But it is a pity he did not say more forcibly that to solve our economic problems will settle nothing either, since that, like the defeat of Hitler, is only one step towards the society of free and equal human beings which he himself so obviously desires.

OUT OF STEP

Lest We Regret, by Douglas Reed
(Cape, 12s. 6d.)

I Sit and I Think and I Wonder, by Sidney Dark
(Gollancz, 5s. 6d.)

IT seems strange to look back five years and remember Mr Douglas Reed as a Cassandra figure warning a heedless world that the Nazis were dangerous. And it is even stranger to think of the enthusiasm with which 'Insanity Fair' was greeted in the Left-wing Press. 'Anti-Fascist' was the term generally applied to it – for, in those days, anyone who opposed Chamberlain's policy was held to be anti-Fascist. The ancient truth that 'he who fights too long against dragons becomes a dragon himself' had been forgotten for the time being.

Readers of an earlier book will remember Mr Reed's admiration for Otto Strasser, the 'black' Nazi, Hitler's Trotsky. Strasser's programme, set forth by Mr Reed without much sign of disapproval, was simply a modification of Hitler's. Nazism was to be more or less retained, the Jews were to be persecuted, but a little less viciously, and Britain and Germany were to gang up for an attack on the USSR. In his present book Mr Reed does not mention Strasser, but spends his time in maundering about Britain's post-war policy, the dominant notes being back to the land, more emigration, down with the Reds and – above all – down with the Jews.

Much of what Mr Reed says about the evils of private property in land, and the monstrous crime committed against the English people by the enclosure of the commons, would be impressive if it did not remind one all the time of the articles that used to appear in Mosley's *British Union*; and also if it were accompanied by any comprehensive economic programme, or even any intelligible agricultural policy. But though an enemy of landlords Mr Reed does not seem to be an enemy of private property. His chief quarrel with the Enclosures is apparently that they have made things difficult for hikers; and he opposes the electrification of the Highlands on the ground that it would spoil the scenery. Mixed up with this are complaints about the victimisation of the middle classes (even the tyres of their laid-up motor-cars are taken away from them!) and tirades against bureaucrats and 'aliens'.

Mr Reed objects equally strongly to 'aliens' being given jobs and to Fascist sympathisers being interned under 18B. And, above all, he objects to the notion that the German Jews somehow merit our sympathy. For the Jews, it appears, have never been persecuted in Germany, or not to speak of. Everybody else has been persecuted, but not the Jews: all the stories about pogroms and so forth are just 'propaganda'.

Now, the general pattern of Mr Reed's thought is a familiar one. The ex-officers who formed an important part of Mosley's following believed just the same things about Jews, Reds, aliens, bureaucrats, agriculture, and the need for more emigration. On top of this, however, Mr Reed is notable for a very marked dislike of his own country. The climate, the manners, the social customs, the politics of England, all repel him. He has lived long in Central Europe, and where it is possible to compare the British and the German way of doing things he makes no disguise of preferring the German way. Nevertheless, Mr Reed is as certain as ever that Britain must defeat Germany, and in alliance with the USSR must dominate the Continent. The desire to see Britain beat Germany is the one thing in which he has never wavered. Even when he backed Otto Strasser he made the reservation that he himself did not wish to see Germany again become a great military Power.

It is here that the psychological puzzle comes in. For one is obliged to ask, if Britain is the Jew-haunted plutocracy that Mr Reed believes, what is it that makes him wish to see Britain victorious? This question is not answered by the familiar pacifist claim that war induces a Fascist mentality. But it is worth thinking over, for Mr Reed is a persuasive writer, with an easy journalistic style, and capable of doing a lot of harm among the large public for which he caters.

Mr Sidney Dark, the vehement pamphleteer and (till recently) editor of the *Church Times*, is a change from Mr Reed. His politics are almost exactly those of the Popular Front, and he is worth the attention of Left-wingers who have failed to notice the political tendencies of the Anglo-Catholic movement and lightheartedly assumed that every religious believer is a reactionary. In a way, in spite of his allegiance to the Church, he is almost too ready to bow to Left-wing orthodoxy and to accept over-simple solutions to difficult questions – the Palestine question, for instance. Also it is a pity that Mr Dark deals in literary judgements as well as political ones. It will distress some of his colleagues of the *Church Times* to see him walloping his co-religionist, Mr T. S. Eliot, with great violence but with no apparent understanding of what Mr Eliot is after. But there is no rancour in Mr Dark: he can like people even when he disagrees with them, and at his most Marxist moments he never loses touch with the fundamental Christian belief that every human being is an individual and capable of salvation.

---

28 November 1943

HIDDEN SPAIN

Spain in Eclipse, 1937–1943, by E. Allison Peers
(Methuen, 15s.)

Behind the Spanish Mask, by Lawrence Dundas
(Robert Hale, 6s.)

THE titles of both of these books are symptomatic of the fact that we know very little of what has been happening in Spain since the end of the Civil War. There have been hunger and pestilence, great numbers of people are in gaol, and the regime has been markedly friendly to the Axis – that is about as far as common knowledge extends. Opinions on anything else are likely to be coloured by the political sympathies of the writer, and one must keep it in mind that Mr Dundas is vigorously pro-Republic, while Professor Peers should rather be described as mildly and regretfully pro-Franco.

Professor Peers devotes part of his book to the Civil War; but his best chapters are those dealing with the last four years. He considers that the Franco regime for a while enjoyed majority support; that its political persecutions have probably been exaggerated, and that it has not in fact given much solid aid to the Nazis. He does not, however, believe that it will last much longer, and though he himself hopes for some kind of Liberal monarchist regime, he thinks that a swing to the extreme Left is not impossible.

It is noticeable that Professor Peers seems surprised as well as pained that the 'non-belligerent' Spanish Government has been so consistently unfriendly to ourselves. He lists the endless provocations, and the inspired campaigns of libel in the Spanish Press, as though these in some way contradicted Franco's earlier record. But, in fact, there was never very much doubt as to where the sympathies of Franco and his more influential followers lay, and the time when it might have been useful to point out that Franco was the friend of our enemies was in 1936. At that time Professor Peers did nothing of the kind. No one would accuse him of falsifying facts, but the tone of the books he was then writing did, there is little doubt, tend to make the Nationalist cause more respectable in British eyes. In so far as books influence events, Professor Peers must be held to have done something towards establishing Franco's regime, and he ought not now to be astonished because Franco has behaved in very much the manner that every supporter of the Republic foretold at the time.

Mr Dundas's book is written round the speculative but interesting thesis that a quite different kind of rebellion – a Conservative but not Fascist rebellion – had been planned in the beginning, and that events only took the course they did because of Sanjurjo's death* and because the Nationalists, having failed in their first coup, had to apply for help to the Germans and Italians, who imposed their own terms. The importance of this is that the regime which has actually been set up is, as Mr Dundas says, 'not Spanish'. It is a regime modelled on foreign lines and intolerable from the point of view of an ordinary Spaniard, even an aristocrat: it might therefore turn out to be brittle in a moment of emergency. The book contains some interesting details about Civil War events in Majorca. But Mr Dundas is surely wrong in suggesting that Franco will fight for the Axis if the Allies invade Europe. Fidelity is not the strong point of the minor dictators.

* Sanjurjo led the rebel forces at the outbreak of the Spanish Civil War in July 1936. His death enabled Franco to assume leadership and proclaim himself chief of state.

WANDERING STAR

Collected Poems of W. H. Davies
(Cape, 10s. 6d.)

SEEN in bulk, W. H. Davies's work gives a somewhat different impression from that given by the handful of poems that have found their way into so many anthologies. So far as manner goes, indeed, almost any of his poems is representative. His great fault is lack of variation – a quality that one might, perhaps, call wateriness, since it gives one the feeling of drinking draught after draught of spring water, wonderfully pure and refreshing, but somehow turning one's mind in the direction of whisky after the first pint or two. On the other hand – and it is here that the anthologies have probably misrepresented him – his subject-matter is remarkably variegated. Not only did his years of vagabondage in common lodging-houses supply a large part of it, but he shows a distinct tinge of morbidity. Behind the lambs and the wild flowers there is an almost Baudelairean background of harlots, drunkenness, and corpses, and in poems like 'The Rat' and 'Down Underground' he does not flinch from the most horrible subjects that any writer could deal with. Yet his manner never varies, or barely varies: the clouds in the April sky and the dead girl rotting in her grave are spoken of in almost the same tone of voice.

One thing that emerges from this collection of over 600 poems is the perfection of Davies's taste. If he lacks vitality, at least he has a sort of natural good breeding. None of his poems is perfect, there is not one in which one cannot find an unnecessary word or an annoyingly bad rhyme, and yet nothing is vulgar either. More than this, however empty he may seem, there is nothing that one can put one's finger on and say that it is silly. Like Blake, he appears to avoid silliness by not being afraid of it; and perhaps (like Blake again) this appearance is partly deceptive, and he is less artless than he seems. Davies's best qualities, as well as some of his faults, can be seen in the justly celebrated poem, 'The Two Children':

'Ah, little boy: I see
  You have a wooden spade,
Into this sand you dig
  So deep – for what?' I said.
'There's more rich gold,' said he,
  'Down under where I stand,
Than twenty elephants
  Could move across the land.'

'Ah, little girl with wool:–
  What are you making now?'
'Some stockings for a bird,
  To keep his legs from snow.'
And there those children are,
  So happy, small and proud:
The boy that digs his grave.
  The girl that knits her shroud.

How near this comes to folly and sentimentality! But the point is that it doesn't get there. Whether Davies is being deliberately cunning it would be hard to say. The almost namby-pamby language in which the poem starts may or may not be intended to give force to the two magnificent lines at the end. But at any rate, whether it is consciously or not, Davies always does avoid the stillness and vulgarity which so often seem to be in wait for him.

On the blurb of this book Sir John Squire is quoted as preferring Davies to 'the fashionable poets of to-day' (at the time of writing this probably meant Mr T. S. Eliot) and Mr Basil de Selincourt as seeing in Davies an upholder of 'our English tradition'. Davies has had much praise of this kind, and has been used as a stick to beat many another contemporary, basically because he does not force anyone to think. Not to be made to think – and therefore, if possible, to prevent literature from developing – is often the aim of the academic critic. But Davies is not, as Sir John Squire and Mr de Selincourt seem to claim, the restorer of an ancient tradition. Indeed, if there is one thing that he is not, it is traditional. He belongs in no line of descent; he does not derive from his immediate predecessors, and he has had no influence on his successors.

According to his own account, he was brought up by a pious grandmother whose only books were *Paradise Lost, The Pilgrim's Progress,* Young's *Night Thoughts* and (presumably) the Bible. He read Shelley, Marlowe and Shakespeare on the sly, as another boy might read Sexton Blake. At the age of thirty-four, when still living in a common lodging-house and never having seen even the fringes of the literary world, he began to write poems. He gives the impression of having imitated chiefly the poets of the seventeenth century; there are frequent echoes, though probably no plagiarisms. Having completed his first batch of poems, Davies attempted to sell them from door to door at threepence a copy – needless to say, without success.

Sir Osbert Sitwell contributes a pleasant and informative introduction. It is interesting to learn that when Davies was a child his grandmother once warned him, between blows, that if he did not turn over a new leaf he would end by being no better than his cousin who had 'brought disgrace upon the family'. This cousin was Sir Henry Irving. These poems are well edited and excellent value for the money. With its agreeable cover, good print, and – by current standards – very good paper, the book would make an attractive as well as a cheap Christmas present.

---

2 January 1944

IN THE FIRING LINE

Armies and the Art of Revolution, by K. C. Chorley
(Faber, 12s. 6d.)

IN the last resort, society as we know it rests upon force and moreover we live in an age in which naked physical power tends more and more to grow in importance as against financial power. The structure and political outlook of armies, navies and airforces is therefore a subject of the most vital importance, whether one looks at it from a revolutionary or a reactionary point of view. As Captain Liddell Hart says in his foreword to this book, the relation of the armed forces to society has not received as much study as it might. Mrs Chorley's book, though it has some gaps in it, is a stimulating introduction.

Two important facts emerge from every revolution or civil war that she examines. The first is that in the modern world a popular insurrection cannot succeed against a regular army which is really exerting its strength. In every case that seems to contradict this there has either been foreign intervention or sympathy with the rebels on the part of the armed forces, or else some hidden factor which may not be strictly military but which is part of the strategic situation. A good example is the Irish Civil War, which Mrs Chorley examines at some length. The hidden factor here was English (and American) public opinion. The strategy of the Irish nationalists was not to engage in real warfare in which they must have been defeated, but to make it morally impossible for the British to strike back at them. They used guerrilla tactics (assassinations, sudden attacks on unarmed soldiers by men dressed as civilians, etc.) which could only have been countered by a policy of brutal reprisals. The British were unequal to this, not probably from any excess of humanity but because English opinion was largely sympathetic to the Irish and world opinion could not be disregarded. Similar guerrilla tactics have made little impression on the Japanese, who exclude foreigners from their dominions and do not have a Nonconformist conscience to contend with. Since the invention of the machine-gun, straightforward rebellions have always failed, unless they are either made by the armed forces, or the armed forces are disintegrating as a result of defeat in foreign war.

The second point brought out by Mrs Chorley is that for political purposes 'the army' nearly always means the officers. Except when they have been defeated, or at the end of a long war, the lower ranks tend to be politically apathetic, especially in long-service professional armies. The officers, on the other hand, better educated, more conscious and more homogeneous socially, tend to regard themselves not as the servants of the State but of a particular political party. Instances of governments being blackmailed into this or that action because 'the army', meaning the officers, threatened mutiny are innumerable. Mrs Chorley concludes that an army whose officers are drawn from the higher ranks of society can never be trusted to support a 'Left' government.

This raises the very difficult question of how it is possible, if at all, for an army to be democratised. Any government, and especially a 'Left' government, must have officers who are politically reliable, but the trouble is that they must also be militarily efficient. As an example of an army which is genuinely democratic in structure, and which could not possibly make a reactionary *coup d'état*, Mrs Chorley points to the Swiss Army. This army, however, is unlikely ever to have to go to war, and its structure is conditioned by that fact. Britain, for instance, or the USSR, could not possibly make do with a citizens' militia in which even an officer served only 400 days in his whole lifetime. And the prolonged training and mind discipline needed in modern mechanised forces are probably anti-democratic in tendency. Mrs Chorley's remarks on the French and Russian revolutions and the Spanish Civil War show how even in revolutionary armies the tendency is always away from egalitarianism. An army can only be kept democratic by means of soldiers' committees and political delegates, and both of these are a bar to efficiency.

Mrs Chorley suggests that the important thing, from the point of view of a democratic government, is to make sure that the corps of officers is not drawn from reactionary strata of the population. This may be so, but it may also be that a professional officer's social origin is almost irrelevant to his political outlook. Modern military methods and the discipline they demand may be producing an 'officer type' whose outlook will be much the same whether he is the son of a duke or of a factory worker. It is here that the chief omission in Mrs Chorley's book makes itself felt – namely that, after saying a good deal about the Red Army during the revolution and the civil war, she says little or nothing about its subsequent development.

There are some other omissions. It seems a pity – though perhaps it would have needed another book – to exclude all mention of South America, which must have provided at least one test-tube demonstration of every conceivable revolutionary situation. But this is a valuable book and, though admittedly written from a 'Left' angle, about as objective as is possible in these days.

16 January 1944

TAPPING THE WHEELS

Democracy and the Individual, by C. K. Allen
(Oxford, 3s. 6d.)

Disraeli and the New Age, by Sir R. George Stapledon
(Faber, 10s. 6d.)

MARXISM may possibly be a mistaken theory, but it is a useful instrument for testing other systems of thought, rather like one of those long-handled hammers with which they tap the wheels of locomotives. Tap! Is this wheel cracked? Tap! Is this writer a bourgeois? A crude question, ignoring much based on the principle of *cui bono* and assuming in advance that you know what is meant by *bono*: and yet it is surprising how often a pretentious book will seem suddenly hollow if you apply to it the simple question: Does this writer, or does he not, take account of the economic basis of society?

By this test both these books – the one by an old-fashioned Liberal, the other by an old-style Tory repainted and brought up to date – fail, or partly fail. Mr Allen's able and quite extensive inquiry into the working of democracy gives one all the time a feeling of unreality, because he never seems ready to admit that economic inequality makes democracy impossible. It is not of much value to discuss methods of making Parliaments more representative, or private citizens more public-spirited, or laws more just, or liberty more secure, unless one starts by asking where the real seat of power lies. If the economic structure of any society is unjust, its laws and its political system will necessarily perpetuate that injustice. No tinkering with juridical forms, nor even that panacea, 'education', will ever make much difference.

Though dismayed by certain features in our society, Mr Allen seems to assume that Britain is a democracy. He is partly right, but he persistently underrates the power of money and privilege. It is staggering, for instance, to be told – and told immediately after an admission that rich men can and do buy up all the best lawyers – that we are all more or less equal before the law. On the other hand, Mr Allen is quite right in emphasising the relative *decency* of British society, the lack of official corruption, the absence of a gendarmerie, the tolerance of minorities, the freedom of speech and – in theory – the Press. If democracy means popular rule, it is absurd to call Britain democratic. It is a plutocracy haunted by the ghost of a caste system. But if democracy means a society in which you can safely go into the nearest pub and utter your true opinion of the Government, then Britain is democratic. In any country two things are of fundamental importance: its economic structure and its history. Mr Allen at any rate does not ignore the second when he is dealing with Britain. But if he would take a leaf out of Marx's book he might come to feel that such questions as the plural vote or the exact limits of individual liberty are hardly of first-rate importance while 5 per cent of the population own everything that matters.

In a way, Sir George Stapledon's incoherent book – it is not so much a book on Disraeli as a commentary on modern life with texts from Disraeli as starting-points – shows a better grasp of the nature of society than Mr Allen's. His agricultural bias gives him something real to cling to, and he knows more or less what kind of world he wants to live in, and is aware that the spirit matters more than the forms. But he, too, seems to think it possible to effect a social change without any radical economic change. He wants a simpler, less hedonistic, more agricultural society than our own, a society with the emphasis on duty and loyalty rather than on 'rights' and the cash nexus. Much of what he says, especially when he speaks of a favourite subject, the decay of English agriculture, is acute and stimulating. But he nowhere makes it clear how drastically, if at all, he would be willing to redistribute property. He does not even make clear, while mentioning agriculture on almost every page, what are his feelings about the private ownership of land. And though he rightly deplores the way in which the English people have deserted the soil, when it comes to showing *why* they have deserted the soil, he can only give superficial reasons.

Disraeli's name is much in the air at this moment, because of a widespread recognition that hedonism and the profit motive will not keep society healthy. Disraeli had a sense of *noblesse oblige*. He did not think in terms of 'enlightened self-interest' and devil take the hindmost. But he did think in terms of hereditary privilege, and was able to combine this with very enlightened views on many subjects because, as a foreigner, he had an unjustified admiration for the British aristocracy. The society he wished for was a kind of moralised feudalism, a society neither plutocratic nor equalitarian. Herein lies his attraction for the neo-Tories, who are aware that *laissez-faire* capitalism is finished, but are frightened of the real alternatives. They want more charity, but not more justice – a redistribution of income, for instance, but not a redistribution of property. In other words, they want a better world with the same people at the top. But unfortunately the world is what it is just because those people are at the top, and it is sad to see anyone as sympathetic as Sir George Stapledon chasing an *ignis fatuus* [will-o'-the-wisp].

---

30 January 1944

CHOSEN PEOPLE

The Devil and the Jews, by Joshua Trachtenberg
(Oxford University Press, 23s. 6d.)

Why I am a Jew, by Edmond Fleg
Translated by Victor Gollancz
(Gollancz, 2s. 6d.)

I T is time that Mass Observation or some similar body made a full inquiry into the prevalence of anti-Semitism, delicate though this subject is in the context of the present war. Popular prejudice against Jews is certainly widespread, and may be growing. But it is very important to determine how far this is true anti-Semitism, an essentially magical doctrine, and how far it is mere xenophobia and rationalisation of economic grievances.

Explanations of anti-Semitism generally fall into two schools which might be called the 'traditional' and the 'economic'. Neither is fully satisfying. Left-wing thinkers nearly always accept the second explanation, seeing the Jew as simply a convenient scapegoat whom the rulers of society can make responsible for their own misdeeds. When crops fail or unemployment increases, blame it on the Jews – that is the formula, roughly. The trouble is that it is not clear why the Jews, rather than some other minority group, should always be picked on, why anti-Semitism also flourishes among people who have no strong economic grievance, or why it should be mixed up with irrelevant magical beliefs. But the other theory, which sees anti-Semitism as chiefly a heritage from the Middle Ages, does not cover all the facts either, as these two books show.

Edmond Fleg, in his touching little book – it describes his return to the faith of his forefathers after many years of scepticism – suggests that the Jews are persecuted simply 'because they are Jews', that is, because they have clung to their religious and cultural identity in an alien environment. But so have many other small groups all over the world, and it is very doubtful whether modern Europe cares enough for doctrinal questions to want to persecute people merely because they are not Christians.

Mr Trachtenberg thinks that anti-Semitism is a medieval hangover which the modern world has somehow forgotten to get rid of. With immense wealth of instances and copious illustrations he traces the persecution of the Jews from the early Middle Ages onward. They were lynched, burned, broken on the wheel, expelled from one country after another; they were accused of poisoning, sodomy, communicating with the Devil, practising ritual murder, drinking the blood of children, seducing Christian maidens, emitting a distinctive and disgusting smell, desecrating the Host, riding on broomsticks, giving birth to young pigs – pretty well everything, in fact. Although 'infidels', they were also, somewhat illogically, regarded as 'heretics' and the worst persecution of the Jews more or less coincides with the period of heresy-hunting – that is, from about the twelfth century onwards. The Reformation did them little good, for they were equally heretics from the Protestant point of view, Martin Luther being an exceptionally bitter anti-Semite.

Mr Trachtenberg has no difficulty in showing the irrational nature of the medieval attitude towards the Jews. There was no clear basis for it except the charge that the Jews were usurers and, as he points out, Christian competition invaded this field as soon as moneylending became really profitable. Had he extended his survey to modern times, he might have added that contemporary ideas about the Jews are often equally irrational – for instance, the characteristic Fascist belief that the Jew somehow contrives to be a capitalist and a Communist simultaneously, or that the poverty-stricken Jewish working class are all secretly millionaires.

But two things remain unexplained. One is why the persecution of Jews, which is, after all, a pre-Christian thing, ever started. The other is why – if Mr Trachtenberg's thesis is correct – this particular medieval superstition should have survived when so many others have perished. Very few people now believe in witchcraft, belief in which, according to Mr Trachtenberg, led to a hundred thousand executions between 1450 and 1550 in Germany alone. Why are so many people still ready to believe that Jews 'smell', or that they caused the war, or that they are plotting to conquer the world, or that they are responsible for slumps, revolutions and venereal disease? The whole subject needs cold-blooded investigation. And the fact that we should probably find that anti-Semitism of various kinds is alarmingly common, and that educated people are not in the least immune from it, ought not to deter us.

---

27 February 1944

UTMOST EDGE

The Edge of the Abyss, by Alfred Noyes
(John Murray, 5s.)

INCOHERENT and, in places, silly though it is, this book raises a real problem and will set its readers thinking, even if their thinking only starts to be useful at about the place where Mr Noyes leaves off. His thesis is that Western civilisation is in danger of actual destruction, and that it has been brought to this pass not by economic maladjustments but by the decay of the belief in absolute good and evil. The rules of behaviour on which any stable society has to rest are dissolving:

> What promise can we trust, what firm agreement can ever be made again in a world where millions upon millions have been educated to believe that, if it seems in their interest to violate it, no pact or pledge, however solemnly drawn up, need be regarded by 'realistic' minds, or 'cold statesmanship' as more than a 'scrap of paper', even though its violation involve the murder by night of sleeping and innocent millions?

There is much force in this question, which Mr Noyes repeats over and over again in various forms. In the chaos in which we are living, even the prudential reasons for common decency are being forgotten. Politics, internal or international, are probably no more immoral than they have always been, but what is new is the growing acquiescence of ordinary people in the doctrines of expediency, the callousness of public opinion in the face of the most atrocious crimes and sufferings, and the black-out memory which allows blood-stained murderers to turn into public benefactors overnight if 'military necessity' demands it. Quite new, too, is the doubt cast by the various totalitarian systems on the very existence of objective truth, and the consequent large-scale falsification of history. Mr Noyes is quite right to cry out against all this and he probably even under-emphasises the harm done to ordinary common sense by the cult of 'realism', with its inherent tendency to assume that the dishonest course is always the profitable one. The loss of moral standards does, indeed, seem to undermine the sense of probability. Mr Noyes is also within his rights in saying that the intelligentsia are more infected by totalitarian ideas than the common people, and are partly to blame for the mess we are now in. But his diagnosis of the reasons for this is very shallow, and his suggested remedies are doubtful, even from the point of view of practicability.

To begin with, it will not do to suggest, as Mr Noyes does throughout, that a decent society can only be founded on Christian principles. It amounts to saying that a good life can only be lived on the fringes of the Atlantic. About a quarter of the population of the world is nominally Christian, and the proportion is constantly diminishing. The vast block of Asia is not Christian, and without some unforeseeable miracle it never will be. Are we to say that a decent society cannot be established in Asia? If so, it cannot be established anywhere, and the whole attempt to regenerate society might as well be given up in advance. And Mr Noyes is probably wrong in imagining that the Christian faith, as it existed in the past, can be restored even in Europe. The real problem of our time is to restore the sense of absolute right and wrong when the belief that it used to rest on – that is, the belief in personal immortality – has been destroyed. This demands faith which is a different thing from credulity. It seems doubtful whether Mr Noyes has fully grasped the distinction.

Then there is the question of the amount of blame attaching to 'the highbrows' ('our pseudo-intellectuals' is Mr Noyes's favourite name for them) for the breakdown of moral standards. Mr Noyes writes on this subject in rather the same strain as the *London Mercury* of twenty years ago. 'The highbrows' are gloomy, they are obscene, they attack religion, patriotism, the family, etc., etc. But they are also, it appears, in some way responsible for the rise of Hitler. Now this contradicts the facts. During the crucial years it was precisely the 'pseudo-intellectuals' whom Mr Noyes detests who cried out against the horrors of Fascism, while the Tory and clerical Press did its best to hush them up. Mr Noyes condemns the policy of appeasement, but what was the attitude of his own Church and its Press on that subject?

On the other hand, the intellectuals whom he *does* approve of are only very doubtfully on the side of the angels. One, of course, is Carlyle, who was one of the founders of the modern worship of power and success, and who applauded the third German war of aggression as vociferously as Pound did the fifth. The other is Kipling. Kipling was not totalitarian, but his moral outlook is equivocal at best. Mr Noyes remarks, at the beginning of his book, that one cannot cast out devils with the aid of Beelzebub, but he is also extremely angry because anti-British books can still be published in England and praised in British newspapers. Does it not occur to him that if we stopped doing this kind of thing the main difference between ourselves and our enemies would have disappeared?

12 March 1944

WAVELL ON HELICON

Other Men's Flowers,
Selected and Annotated by A. P. Wavell
(Cape, 10s. 6d.)

MOST of the poems in Lord Wavell's anthology are probably to be found in other anthologies, but that is nothing to complain about at a time when libraries are bombed or shut for the duration and almost any book is liable to be out of print. Picking almost at random among the two hundred or more poems that the book contains, here are some of the things that one comes upon:

'High Tide on the Coast of Lincolnshire' (Jean Ingelow), 'The Mary Gloster' (Rudyard Kipling), 'I've been in Debt, in Love, and in Drink' (Alexander Brome), the *Rubaiyat of Omar Khayyam*, 'I have a Rendezvous with Death' (Alan Seegar), 'The Owl and the Pussy-Cat' (Edward Lear), 'Auguries of Innocence' (Blake), 'Bishop Blougram's Apology' (Browning), 'She was Poor but She was Honest' (Anon.), 'The Hound of Heaven' (Francis Thompson), 'To his Coy Mistress' (Marvell), 'How we Beat the Favourite' (Adam Lindsay Gordon), 'An Irish Airman Foresees his Fate' (W. B. Yeats), 'Cynara' (Ernest Dowson), 'Dream Pedlary' (Thomas Lovell Beddoes).

Even to put one's hand on all of these one would have to be better provided with books than most people are nowadays, and Lord Wavell's choice ranges more widely than this list indicates. But it is, he says, 'a purely personal anthology', consisting of 'the poems I could repeat, entire or in great part'. Like many other people, he likes to repeat verse to himself when driving a car or riding a horse (but not when walking, he adds), and he admits a preference for verse that can be declaimed. This perhaps accounts for his having included in his collection some distinctly 'phony' battle-pieces by G. K. Chesterton. Quoting a poem written about London during the blitz, Lord Wavell adds this footnote:

I read these verses in an Egyptian newspaper while flying from Cairo to Barce in Cyrenaica at the beginning of April 1941, to try to deal with Rommel's counter-attack. I was uncomfortable in body – for the bomber was cramped and draughty – and in mind, for I knew I had been caught with insufficient strength to meet a heavy counter-attack: reading this poem and committing it to memory did something to relieve my discomfort of body and mind.

It so happens that the poem in question is a very bad one, but these lines could only have been written by a true lover of poetry. It is a peculiarity of poetry that it always makes its strongest impact at odd and unsuitable moments (when one is dodging the traffic in Oxford Circus, for instance), and though we have not all got Lord Wavell's prodigious memory, no one can ever be truly said to 'care about' a poem unless he has made at least an effort to learn it by heart.

To review an anthology is inevitably to find fault, and some serious charges can be made against this one. One could forgive Lord Wavell for allowing too much space to Browning and Kipling, but in too many cases he has represented a poet by only one poem and then chosen the wrong one. For instance, if Suckling is to appear only once it was a pity to put in the hackneyed 'Why so pale and wan, fond lover?' and not the less-known and immensely superior 'Ballad upon a Wedding'. Or again, with only one piece from the 'Ingoldsby Legends', why pick on 'The Lay of St Cuthbert', instead of, say, 'The Lay of St Dunstan', or 'Bloudie Jacke of Shrewsberrie'. Thackeray is represented by 'The Chronicle of the Drum' and 'The King of Brentford': 'The Ballad of the Bouillabaisse' would have been better. Gerard Manley Hopkins, who is none too accessible and needs all the reprinting he can get, is only represented by four rather colourless lines. It was also a pity to quote only a tiny fragment of Hilaire Belloc's brilliant early poem, 'The Modern Traveller', which is now seemingly almost unprocurable.

One could extend this list of complaints – though of course such complaints add up in the end to the statement that the only perfect anthology is the one you have compiled for yourself. At least there will be something in this book to please everyone who cares for poetry at all, and though some readers may squirm when they come across 'Lepanto' or Newbolt's 'Drake's Drum' (why not the comparatively sympathetic 'Vitaï Lampada' if Newbolt was to appear at all?), still, they must admire the catholic taste which can find enjoyment in this kind of thing along with Shakespeare's Sonnets, 'Sir Patrick Spens' and 'La Belle Dame Sans Merci'.

Lord Wavell has arranged his chosen pieces according to their subject-matter and added notes which, he says, were demanded by the publisher and should not be taken too seriously. They are, nevertheless, well worth reading, especially his remarks on war poetry. He has little enjoyment in any modern verse – anything subsequent to 1919, that is – but with unusual humility admits he may be wrong. When a poem lacks a title he gives it one himself, sometimes with happy results. It was a neat touch to reprint the passage from *Henry IV*, in which Hotspur complains of the 'popinjay' who came to claim the prisoners and head it 'The Staff Officer'. This is not a perfect anthology, but it is quite good enough to make one feel a certain regret that the man who compiled it should be wasting his talents on the most thankless job in the world.*

* From 1943 to 1947 Lord Wavell was Viceroy of India.

---

26 March 1944

OLD MASTER

Tolstoy: His Life and Work, by Derrick Leon
(Routledge, 25s.)

Tolstoy's adult life – it starts with a brilliant, worldly, rather dissolute young aristocrat and ends with a tormented old man who had renounced everything, or come as near renouncing it as his family would let him – is dramatic enough, but finally it is less interesting than his work, and the most valuable part of Mr Leon's biography is the careful exposition that he gives of each of Tolstoy's books in turn, showing just how it is related to Tolstoy's spiritual development.

Tolstoy's creed, gradually developed over a period of about fifty years, could be described as Christian Anarchism. All material aims, all violence, all revolutions in the last analysis, all laws and governments, are evil; there is no happiness except in self-abnegation: man has no rights, only duties, being on earth solely to do the will of God. All this is derived from his reading of the Gospels, but before his beliefs were fully formulated he had adopted two doctrines which are only doubtfully Christian. One is a strict determinism. A man's actions, Tolstoy holds, are all predetermined, his sole freedom consisting in the knowledge of necessity. The other is a conviction of the essential misery of earthly life, and the wickedness of physical pleasures, which goes far beyond anything the churches have ever countenanced.

Mr Leon writes as a disciple and he does not seriously answer, though he does mention, the charge many people have made – that Tolstoy's later work is largely the projection of his own egoism. In stretching self-abnegation to mean practically a refusal of the process of life – in saying for instance that marriage is of its nature 'misery and slavery' – it is doubtful whether he is saying much more than that he is unhappy himself and would like to make others unhappy as well. Tolstoy was, of course, extremely conscious of the dangers of egoism, indeed his life was in some sense a continuous struggle against it, but he does not seem to have seen that the form it took in himself was not a desire for money or success, but simply a taste for intellectual bullying: his essay on Shakespeare is an outstanding example of this.

Nevertheless his life-story is inspiring as well as tragic, and we should feel him to be a remarkable man even if he had written nothing except his pamphlets. Directly, his influence on the life of our time has not been very great because he abjured all the methods by which anything can actually be achieved. But indirectly, through individuals, it must have been enormous. No one can read Tolstoy and come away with quite the same feeling about war, violence, success, government, and 'great' men – though, somewhat ironically, the special thing that he has to say is said most effectively in the novels of his middle period, *Anna Karenina*, and *War and Peace*, which he afterwards came to look on as almost reprehensible.

It is a pity that throughout his narrative Mr Leon shows such an implacable hostility for the wretched Countess Tolstoy, for by assuming that in every disagreement the Countess must have been in the wrong he avoids discussion of one of the most difficult problems of a writer's life – the conflict between the literary and the private personality or, to put it differently, between love of humanity and ordinary decency. Otherwise this is an outstanding book, and though one cannot advise people to buy books costing twenty-five shillings, at least everyone who can borrow a copy should read it.

GROUNDS FOR DISMAY

The Road to Serfdom, by F. A. Hayek
(Routledge, 10s. 6d.)

The Mirror of the Past, by K. Zilliacus
(Gollancz, 7s. 6d.)

T AKEN together, these two books give grounds for dismay. The first of them is an eloquent defence of *laissez-faire* capitalism, the other is an even more vehement denunciation of it. They cover to some extent the same ground, they frequently quote the same authorities, and they even start out with the same premise, since each of them assumes that Western civilisation depends on the sanctity of the individual. Yet each writer is convinced that the other's policy leads directly to slavery and the alarming thing is that they may both be right.

Of the two, Professor Hayek's book is perhaps the more valuable because the views it puts forward are less fashionable at the moment than those of Mr Zilliacus. Shortly, Professor Hayek's thesis is that Socialism inevitably leads to despotism, and that in Germany the Nazis were able to succeed because the Socialists had already done most of their work for them, especially the intellectual work of weakening the desire for liberty. By bringing the whole of life under the control of the State, Socialism necessarily gives power to an inner ring of bureaucrats, who in almost every case will be men who want power for its own sake and will stick at nothing in order to retain it. Britain, he says, is now going the same road as Germany, with the Left-wing intelligentsia in the van and the Tory Party a good second. The only salvation lies in returning to an unplanned economy, free competition, and emphasis on liberty rather than on security.

In the negative part of Professor Hayek's thesis there is a great deal of truth. It cannot be said too often – at any rate, it is not being said nearly often enough – that collectivism is not inherently democratic, but, on the contrary, gives to a tyrannical minority such powers as the Spanish Inquisitors never dreamed of.

Professor Hayek is also probably right in saying that in this country the intellectuals are more totalitarian-minded than the common people. But he does not see, or will not admit, that a return to 'free' competition means for the great mass of people a tyranny probably worse, because more irresponsible, than that of the State. The trouble with competitions is that somebody wins them. Professor Hayek denies that free capitalism necessarily leads to monopoly, but in practice that is where it has led, and since the vast majority of people would far rather have State regimentation than slumps and unemployment, the drift towards collectivism is bound to continue if popular opinion has any say in the matter.

Mr Zilliacus's able and well-documented attack on imperialism and power politics consists largely of an exposure of the events leading up to the two world wars. Unfortunately the enthusiasm with which he debunks the war of 1914 makes one wonder on what grounds he is supporting this one. After re-telling the sordid story of the secret treaties and commercial rivalries which led up to 1914, he concludes that our declared war aims were lies and that we declared war on Germany 'because if she won her war against France and Russia she would become master of all Europe and strong enough to help herself to British colonies'. Why else did we go to war this time? It seems that it was equally wicked to oppose Germany in the decade before 1914 and to appease her in the 1930s, and that we ought to have made a compromise peace in 1917, whereas it would be treachery to make one now. It was even wicked, in 1915, to agree to Germany being partitioned and Poland being regarded as 'an internal affair of Russia': so do the same actions change their moral colour with the passage of time.

The thing Mr Zilliacus leaves out of account is that wars have results, irrespective of the motives of those who precipitate them. No one can question the dirtiness of international politics from 1879 onwards; it does not follow that it would have been a good thing to allow the German Army to rule Europe. It is just possible that some rather sordid transactions are going on behind the scenes now, and that current propaganda 'against Nazism' (cf. 'against Prussian militarism') will look pretty thin in 1970, but Europe will certainly be a better place if Hitler and his followers are removed from it.

Between them these two books sum up our present predicament. Capitalism leads to dole queues, the scramble for markets, and war. Collectivism leads to concentration camps, leader-worship, and war.

There is no way out of this unless a planned economy can be somehow combined with the freedom of the intellect, which can only happen if the concept of right and wrong is restored to politics.

Both of these writers are aware of this, more or less; but since they can show no practicable way of bringing it about, the combined effect of their books is a depressing one.

---

23 April 1944

POWER HOUSE

The Poisoned Crown, by Hugh Kingsmill
(Eyre and Spottiswode, 9s.)

TOTALITARIANISM is generally considered to be traceable to the wickedness of a few ambitious individuals or else is explained away as a last effort to prop up a collapsing economic system. However, there is another school of thought, of which Mr F. A. Voigt is the best-known exponent, which holds that any attempt to set up a materialistic Utopia must inevitably lead to despotism. Mr Hugh Kingsmill belongs to this school, and in this brilliant book he illustrates his thesis by four short biographies of Queen Elizabeth, Cromwell, Napoleon and Abraham Lincoln.

As Mr Kingsmill sees it, all of these illustrate 'the barrenness of action and the corrupting effects of power'. They are nevertheless not very easy to fit into a single pattern, and of the four of them only Cromwell bears a close resemblance to the dictators of our own day. It is especially difficult to see why Mr Kingsmill included Elizabeth, who was absorbed from early youth with the problem of remaining alive and on the throne, and who by the standards of her own day was neither bigoted nor cruel. Her unhappy sister Mary, who burned her subjects alive because she loved them so much, would probably have been a better example. Lincoln, on the other hand, does not seem to have been much corrupted by power, and Mr Kingsmill has to press his case rather hard to show that Lincoln's achievement was valueless.

Nevertheless the section dealing with Lincoln is probably the best thing in the book. Lincoln's one great concession to expediency, Mr

Kingsmill thinks, was his declaration that slavery would be abolished if the Confederate states were defeated. He had not wanted to make this declaration (in its origins the war was only indirectly concerned with the issue of slavery), partly because he saw that the country as a whole was not ready for it and the slaves would not benefit by emancipation, partly because he did not wish to give the war the character of a crusade, with all the self-righteousness and vindictiveness that that implies. He was driven into making the declaration by the necessity of winning the war. By proclaiming slavery to be the issue he cut the moral ground from beneath Britain and France, who might otherwise have intervened on the side of the South. But in doing so he was also surrendering to the extremists among his followers who were not, as one might expect, high-minded Abolitionists but hard-faced business men determined to break the economic power of the Southern states.

The complete victory won by the North left the business men in control, and the moral atmosphere of the United States deteriorated accordingly. Lincoln had sacrificed everything, including a fragment of his conscience, to winning the war, and the result was a country where there could be no more Lincolns – that at least is Mr Kingsmill's picture. Incidentally he suggests that the obscure lunatic who murdered Lincoln was employed not by Southerners but by Lincoln's own rivals among the Republicans.

One frequently has the feeling that Mr Kingsmill is being unfair, not, perhaps, to Lincoln himself but to his achievement and therefore to the United States. Was it not, after all, a step forward that the slaves should be freed, even though they were merely converted into wage-slaves? And one even has the feeling that he is unfair to Napoleon, who was a crook but may have been a necessary instrument of history. Without Napoleon, or at least somebody like Napoleon, revolutionary France would probably have been crushed round about 1800 and the peasants would not have kept the land. Napoleon, though his motives were totally selfish, did stave off defeat long enough to make it impossible for the *Ancien Régime* to be restored. On the other hand, Mr Kingsmill's debunking of Cromwell, though probably it is not fair either, is a good antidote to the usual middle-class worship of this prototype of all the modern dictators, who perpetrated massacres which make the German exploits at Lidice look like a schoolgirls' romp.

Mr Kingsmill's book begins with a chapter entitled 'The Genealogy of Hitler'. The line of descent is traced from Napoleon and Byron through Dostoevsky, Nietzsche and H. G. Wells to Hitler and Charlie Chaplin. (Chaplin, says Mr Kingsmill, is the Little Man's version of Byron, Hitler his version of Napoleon.) There are many quarrels, big and small, that one could pick with Mr Kingsmill. Like all thinkers of his school, he assumes that reformers want to make the world perfect, whereas in general they only want to make it better, and he frequently writes as though progress, even material progress, were of its nature impossible, which implies that we are still in the Stone Age. But this is an outstanding book, and a felling blow at every form of tyranny, not excluding the ones which it is now fashionable to admire.

---

7 May 1944

ALL CHANGE HERE

This Changing World, edited by J. R. M. Brumwell
(Routledge, 12s. 6d.)

On Living in a Revolution, by Julian Huxley
(Chatto and Windus, 12s. 6d.)

Reshaping Man's Heritage, by various authors
(Allen and Unwin, 5s.)

WE may be sure that when Noah was building the Ark someone was writing a book called *This Changing World*, and though the manuscript will have perished in the Deluge it is possible to make a good guess at what it was like. It pointed with approval to recent scientific discoveries, denounced superstition and obscurantism, urged the need for radical educational reform and greater equality of the sexes and probably had a chapter on the meaning of modern poetry. Its central thesis was that nothing is permanent but that everything is all for the best. The phrases 'this is an age of transition' and 'we live amid rapid and startling changes' occurred on almost every page, and perhaps the author remembered them with a certain bitterness as he went bubbling down into the dark waters.

The book now edited by Mr Brumwell conforms to much the same pattern. In an introductory chapter Mr Herbert Read notes that this is a changing world, and at the end, summing up the conclusions of the other contributors, he adds that the world is changing. In between are essays by C. H. Waddington, Karl Mannheim, J. D. Bernal, Franz Borkenau, Thomas Balogh, John Macmurray, Lewis Mumford and others. Of course, this list is a sufficient guarantee of the book's readability, at any rate in places, but it is astonishing how few of the contributors give the impression of writing about the actual world in which we are now living. Only Mr Balogh, who insists on the impossibility of internal reforms while the world as a whole remains chaotic, and Dr Borkenau, who traces the connection between democracy and totalitarianism, seem to have their feet anywhere near the ground. From very few of the others would you gather that the actual existence of civilisation is in danger.

Professor Bernal, for instance, writes on recent developments in science and the necessity for making the general public more scientific in outlook. He does not seem to see, or at least does not mention, that science itself is threatened by the world-wide trend towards dictatorship. Mr Lewis Mumford does see this danger, but appears to think that it will right itself of its own accord. Dr Darlington has some stimulating ideas on education, but hardly faces up to the question 'education by whom and for what?'. Mr John Summerson defends glass and concrete against 'traditional' architecture. Dr Macmurray thinks that the Christian religion will survive, but that in order to do so it will have to change: unfortunately he omits to say in what way it will change and what its new doctrines will be, if any. Miss Kathleen Raine weighs in with an essay on contemporary literature and supplies a list of thirty-five outstanding modern writers in which she includes herself while leaving out Shaw, Wells, Dreiser, Belloc, Pound, Koestler, and a few dozen others.

As you look at this book, with its vaguely modernistic jacket, its shiny photographs, its perky but inaccurate bibliography, and its general air of complacent progressiveness, it is hard to remember the atrocious reversal of history that is actually going on. The mass slaughter that has been happening for the past ten or fifteen years does not perhaps matter very much. All it means is that we happen to possess better weapons than our ancestors. The truly sinister phenomena of our time are the atomisation of the world, the increasing power of nationalism, the worship of leaders who are credited with divine powers, the crushing, not only of freedom of thought but of the concept of objective truth, and the tendency towards oligarchical rule based on forced labour. That is the direction in which the world is changing, and it is the failure to discuss these subjects that makes it hard to take this book seriously.

Two other books which were probably in preparation when the waters of the Flood were gathering were *On Living in a Revolution* and *Reshaping Man's Heritage*. It should hardly be necessary to say in detail what the principal essay in Professor Huxley's book is about, since most of us have heard it rather often already. The 'revolution' is the transition to a centralised economy, and Professor Huxley hopes that we shall achieve it democratically. Unfortunately, he does not explain with any precision how we are to set about this and it is evident that, like the contributors to *This Changing World*, he has not reckoned – perhaps is frightened to reckon – with the terrible power of the psychological forces now working against democracy, against rationalism, and against the individual. However, the book contains a good essay debunking racialism, and others on animal pests and Hebridean birds, subjects which are near to Professor Huxley's own heart, and on which he is eminently readable.

Reshaping Man's Heritage is a collection of reprinted broadcasts by H. G. Wells, J. B. S. Haldane, J. C. Drummond, and others, and is concerned partly with food and agriculture, partly with medicine. There is a good talk on anaesthetics by L. J. Witts, and some useful information about rats by James Fisher. But the book as a whole has the sort of timid chirpiness that books of collected broadcasts seldom avoid.

VESSEL OF WRATH

*'42 to '44. A Contemporary Memoir upon Human Behaviour
During the Crisis of the World Revolution,* by H. G. Wells
(Secker and Warburg, 42s.)

T HE chief difficulty of writing a book nowadays is that pots of paste
are usually sold without brushes. But if you can get hold of a brush
(sometimes procurable at Woolworth's), and a pair of scissors and a
good-sized blank book, you have everything you need. It is not necessary
to do any actual writing. Any collection of scraps – reprinted newspaper
articles, private letters, fragments of diaries, even 'radio discussions'
ground out by wretched hacks to be broadcast by celebrities – can be sold
to the amusement-starved public. And even the paper shortage can be
neutralised by – as in this case – issuing your book in a limited edition
and selling it at an artificial price.

This seems to be the principle that Mr Wells has followed. His book
has gilt edges, which costs the reader an extra thirty shillings, but its
contents are simply a sprawl. Quite largely it consists of a series of
attacks on people who have shown insufficient enthusiasm for the
document which Mr Wells calls the 'Universal Rights of Man'. Other
attacks (on the Catholic Church, for instance, the War Office, the
Admiralty, and the Communist Party) do not seem to be occasioned by
anything but bad temper. But in so far as the book has a unifying
principle, it is the by now familiar idea that mankind must either develop
a World State or perish.

What is very striking is that except in certain books in which he invoked
a miracle, Mr Wells has never once suggested how the World State is to be
brought into being. This is to say that he has never bothered to wonder
who the actual rulers of the world are, how and why they are able to hold
on to power, and by what means they are to be evicted. In formulating the
'Rights of Man', he does not even drop a hint as to how such a document
could be disseminated in, say, Russia or China. Hitler he dismisses as
simply a lunatic: that settles Hitler. He does not seriously inquire *why*
millions of people are ready to lay down their lives for a lunatic, and what

this probably betokens for human society. And in between his threats that *homo sapiens* must mend his ways or be destroyed he continues to repeat the slogans of 1900 as though they were self-evident truths.

For instance, it is startling to be told in 1944 that 'the world is now one'. One might as well say that the world is now flat. The most obvious fact about the contemporary world is that it is *not* one and is becoming less and less of a unit every year, physically as well as psychologically.

In spite of some momentary misgivings, Mr Wells is not ready to admit that his declaration of the 'Rights of Man' is a purely Western document. Almost any Indian, for instance, would reject it at a glance. (One gathers from some angry 'asides' that a number of Indians have rejected it already.) What is more serious, he is not ready to admit that even among scientists and thinkers generally the intellectual basis for world unity does not exist. He has not seen the red light of phrases like 'Aryan chess' and 'capitalistic astronomy'. He still talks of the need for a world encyclopaedia, ignoring the fact that there are whole branches of knowledge upon which no sort of agreement exists or is at present possible. As for the increase in human equality which Mr Wells also considers imperatively necessary, there is no sign that that is happening either.

Intermittently, of course, Mr Wells does realise all this, but only as a nurse notices the unaccountable naughtiness of a child. And his response is the same as the nurse's – 'Now, you'll take your nice medicine or the bogey-man'll come and eat you up.' *Homo sapiens* must do what he is told or he will become extinct. 'Knowledge or extinction. There is no other chance for man,' says Mr Wells. It is, however, very unlikely that man will become extinct except through some unforeseeable cosmic disaster. He has about doubled his numbers in the last century and is still probably on the increase, and no competing species is in sight. The ants, Mr Wells's favourites, can hardly be taken seriously. Nor is there any reason to think that man or even in the technical sense civilisation will be destroyed by war. Wars do a great deal of local destruction, but probably lead to a net increase in the world's industrial plant. The picture that Mr Wells drew long ago in 'The War in the Air', of the world being plunged back in the Dark Ages by a few tons of bombs has turned out to be completely false. The machine culture thrives on bombs. The danger seemingly ahead of us is *not* extinction; it is a slave civilisation which, so far from being chaotic, might be horribly stable.

It is perhaps unnecessary to add that incoherent and – in places – annoying though it is, this book contains brilliant and imaginative passages. One expects that of Mr Wells. More than any other writer, perhaps, he has altered the landscape of the contemporary mind. Because of him the moon seems nearer and the Stone Age more imaginable, and for that we are immeasurably in his debt. So perhaps we can forgive a few scrappy books, even at forty-two shillings a time, from the author of *The Time Machine, The Island of Dr Moreau, Love and Mr Lewisham*, and about a dozen others.

---

11 June 1944

BEHIND THE RANGES

Burma Surgeon, by Gordon S. Seagrave
(Gollancz, 9s.)

India Since Cripps, by Horace Alexander
(Penguin Special, 9d.)

UP to date the Burma campaign of 1942 has not been well documented. Sensational and inaccurate books have been published by American journalists, while better-informed manuscripts from British and Burmese sources have failed to find publishers, because it is felt that the public is not interested in Burma except as a land of snakes, tigers, elephants, and pagodas. The political background of the campaign has been largely ignored or misrepresented. Dr Seagrave's book is valuable because the events it describes begin in 1922 and the Japanese invasion is placed in its proper setting. Moreover, being written by a missionary, and a medical missionary at that, it is exceptionally free from political partisanship. Dr Seagrave's experiences have not given him any reason for idealising either the Burmese, the British, the Indians, the Chinese, or the wild tribes, and though his manner of writing is often tiresome his book deserves to be read.

Dr Seagrave was born into a family of missionaries and spoke Karen from his earliest childhood onwards. When, however, after being educated in the United States, he returned to Burma, it was as a medical and not a religious missionary. With almost no money, with a set of worn-out instruments and with, at first, no trained assistance, he set up his hospital at Namkham, in the wild country where the Burma road was later to be built. Life for years after that was an unending struggle not only against disease but against filth, ignorance, and poverty. Malaria flourished in its most deadly form, goitre was common, venereal diseases almost equally common. There were also periodical outbreaks of plague. Dr Seagrave had to build his hospital and his nurses' quarters with stones procured from the nearest river bed, and he had to raise money wherever he could find it, from the British Government, from the Shan chieftains, and even from the primitive villagers whom he attended. A twenty-mile ride over roadless mountains, followed by three hours' work on a difficult childbirth, might be rewarded by a fee of one rupee. It was, he says

> surgery with waste-basket instruments. Orthopaedic surgery without an X-ray. Urological surgery without a cystoscope. Surgery without any actual cautery except a stray soldering-iron. Surgery without electricity. Medicine without a laboratory, and without medicines often.

He did, however, have in his favour the incredible insensitiveness to pain of the Mongolian peoples which allowed him to use rough-and-ready methods and effect some surprising cures which were useful in winning him a reputation.

But Dr Seagrave's greatest achievement was in the training of nurses. Such nurses as then existed in Burma were mostly drawn from among the Christian Karens, but Dr Seagrave drew his recruits from all races, including the almost savage Kachins who inhabit the mountain ranges in the north of Burma. He had to give them their entire training from the rudiments upwards, and to do this in three or four different languages, teaching himself Burmese in the process. After years of work he had a brilliant team of nurses, trained to take responsibility and to refuse no matter what job, however dirty, and so used to working together that even experienced observers could not tell to which race each girl belonged.

Throughout most of the Burma campaign they were attached to General Stilwell's Chinese Army, and won golden opinions for themselves. 'Seagrave's Burmese nurses' as they were inaccurately called

– actually there was only one Burmese among them – were known throughout the British, Chinese, and American forces. All the ambulance units were overwhelmed with work, and Dr Seagrave even found it possible to entrust simple surgical operations to his nurses. Some of them were cut off by the Japanese advance, but the majority retreated into India with the army, their tiny bodies standing the fatigue of the long march surprisingly well.

Dr Seagrave is mainly concerned with medical matters, but such remarks as he makes on the Burmese political situation are probably reliable. His estimate of the Burmese attitude towards the war is much the same as that of some other observers – about 10 per cent actively pro-Japanese, another 10 per cent pro-British, and the rest neutral and primarily anxious to remain alive. He gives evidence of Burmese fifth-column activity – also of a good deal of shooting of fifth columnists by the Chinese – and confirms other accounts of the fearful effects of bombing on the wooden towns of Burma. His book ends with a note that Namkham has been visited by American bombers and his nurses' home presumably destroyed.

Dr Seagrave's chronicle ends in 1942 and to some extent *India Since Cripps* carries on the story. The peculiarly stupid deadlock now existing in India dates from the Burma campaign, and now that the danger of a Japanese invasion of India has obviously receded, a satisfactory settlement might be achieved if the initiative came from this country. Mr Alexander's book is a useful popularly written account of the existing situation. Quite rightly, since he is addressing a British audience, he stresses the Indian rather than the British case and shows that even when Indian politicians have acted foolishly their chronic suspicion of British motives is not unpardonable.

25 June 1944

TEMPERATURE CHART

The Sociology of Literary Taste, by L. L. Schucking
(Kegan Paul, 7s. 6d.)

THIS learned, but rather rambling essay sets out to explain the variation in literary taste from one age to another, and to show why it is that even a writer such as Shakespeare, who is generally in favour, is admired for totally different reasons in different periods.

Literary taste can be explained either as a reflection of current social conditions, or as something created from above, as it were, by writers of outstanding talent. In other words, one can regard either the author or the public as the dominant factor. Dr Schucking, while conceding a great deal to the influence of individual writers, literary cliques and enterprising publishers, takes the second position. Artists, in general, produce what is required of them, and changes in technique may be produced by quite crudely mechanical causes. For example, it seems that the reason – at any rate the immediate reason – why English novels grew shorter at the beginning of the nineties was a decision of the lending libraries. The three-volume novel had become uneconomic and so it had to go. Even such things as shortage or abundance of paper can affect literary form.

Probably the most interesting passages in Dr Schucking's book are those that trace the connection between classicism and an aristocratic society. It is not merely that 'good form' is best appreciated in a small homogeneous society, while half-educated people are nearly always repelled by what seems to them the coldness and emptiness of classicism. It is also that the aristocrat objects to emotional violence, and on the other hand to naturalism, because he knows that they are dangerous to his own kind:

> His life is dominated by tradition, which in his view is bound to
> be powerful because his whole existence is dependent on
> inheritance. Property, which is a further condition of his
> existence, implies a permanent temptation to the enjoyment of
> life, an enjoyment which is refined by the inherited feeling for
> form; form acquires further an extraordinary importance from

the fact that it is the precise means of social differentiation... His characteristic style of living and the external claims based upon it, further, make him anti-individualistic and promote the creation of types. The complete exposure of the life of the emotions, like all that is ruthless in expression, is thus bound to be unattractive to him. It is always revealing things that must at all costs be suppressed.

Dr Schucking probably rather over-stresses the advantage from the writer's point of view, of a middle-class as against an aristocratic society. But it is true that in capitalist society the dependence of the artist on his patrons has been less direct and humiliating than in previous ages. As Dr Schucking points out, the appearance of the commercial publisher was an important turning-point in the history of literature. As soon as books began to be published by subscription, the writer was the servant of a caste rather than an individual, and when they became ordinary commercial speculations he was only answerable to the amorphous big public, which did not know very well what it wanted, and would, or at any rate might, listen respectively to the critics.

One result of this was an improvement in the status of the artist. In previous ages the artist had been simply a rather expensive and superior kind of servant: the poet who appears as a character in *Timon of Athens* is represented as a sponging hanger-on. It was only in the nineteenth century, when the artist had been economically emancipated, that he could begin to take an inflated view of himself, and indulge in such theories as 'art for art's sake'. But what he could or could not write was still partly determined by non-literary considerations, among which Dr Schucking lists the current notion of sexual ethics, the normal size of the family circle, the prevalence or otherwise of the café-going habit, the arbitrary decision of publishers, and also the writer's own flair for publicity. The conclusion seems to be that the artist, at any rate the writer, fares best under old-style capitalism but remains in essence a tradesman, dominated in the last resort by his customers.

In explaining literary fashion Dr Schucking does not, perhaps, allow enough weight to tradition and sheer imitation and he says very little about the effect on any national literature of the structure of its language.

English verse, for instance, must owe some of its characteristics to the fact that the English language lacks rhymes. It was also unfortunate that this book should, apparently, have been written before the rise of Hitler, or at any rate before 1933. Totalitarianism affects the artist, and especially the writer, more intimately than any other class of person. In effect, the 'patron' has come back again, but he is a patron enormously less civilised, less tolerant, less individual and more powerful than in the past.

It is not very pleasant to read about the out-at-elbow poets who had to dance attendance while 'my lord' consumed his morning chocolate, but 'my lord' was probably not a harder master than Dr Goebbels, or even the MOI [Ministry of Information], and his literary taste was probably better. What the position of the artist would be in a democratic Socialist regime is still uncertain and much disputed. We do not, indeed, yet know to what extent freedom of thought is separable from economic independence. Dr Schucking might well follow up his present book with a consideration of that subject.

---

9 July 1944

RETURN JOURNEY

In a Strange Land. Essays by Eric Gill
(Jonathan Cape, 6s.)

Aᴺ uneasy awareness that medievalism is a by-product of industrialism seems to underlie much of Eric Gill's writing. With more grip on reality than Chesterton, who was saying much the same thing in a more flamboyant way, he gave the same impression of constantly nagging away at a half-truth and evading every real criticism that could be brought against him. But it must be allowed to both of them that the half-truth they got hold of was an unpopular one and therefore worthy of emphasis.

In this little book of collected essays and lectures, Gill is presenting his usual thesis: the fundamental evil of industrial society. The good life is well-nigh impossible, and the arts are mostly dead, because we live in an age in which the workman is not master of his own work. He is simply a cog in an enormous machine, performing over and over again some mechanical task of which does not know the meaning and in which he has no interest except the wage he receives for it. His creative instincts have to be satisfied, if at all, outside his working hours, and they are constantly perverted by mass-produced goods that capitalism forces upon him. True civilisation, Gill thinks, can only return when people choose their own work and do it in their own time, and when they are conscious of being free agents while possessing a common body of belief. This much one might accept, even though Gill makes the usual parochial claim that the common belief of humanity must be *Christian* belief, and even though his dislike of factory production is illogically mixed up with ideas about currency reform and the special wickedness of bankers.

But however much one may agree with Gill's indictment he has no real remedy to offer. Naturally his programme is a return to peasant ownership, hand production, and, in general, to an idealised version of the Middle Ages. But there are two insuperable objections to this, neither of which he really meets. One is that the world is so manifestly not going in that direction that to wish for it is like wishing for the moon. Elsewhere in his writings, though not in this book, Gill does admit this and seems to realise that the way to a simpler life must lead through greater complexity. The other objection is that Gill and all similar thinkers have no real notion of what a non-industrial society would be like, nor indeed, much idea of the meaning of work.

Much the best thing in this book is a diary of a trip to Ireland in 1919. As a Catholic convert, slightly Anglophobe and in love with peasant society, Gill is naturally inclined to idealise Ireland, and he does so even to the extent of claiming that the Irish country people are less ugly than the English. But whenever he encounters an Irish working man, for instance a trade union organiser, he notes with dismay that the Irishmen seem to have the same outlook as their English colleagues. That is, they think in terms of mechanisation, efficiency, shorter hours, and higher wages, and are not much interested in the sacredness of private property. 'They appear,' he says, 'to be quite content to promote a co-operative commonwealth in which there shall be no individual ownership or responsibility – i.e. the factory system in public instead of private hands.' Elsewhere in the book he explains this by saying that the working man has taken over his employer's systems of values. What he does not see is that the working man's attitude is founded on hard experience. Middle-class people hardly have the right to question it.

The point is well brought out in a bit of dialogue in Shaw's *Man and Superman* between the sentimental Octavius and the chauffeur 'Enery Straker:

> *Octavius* : I believe in the dignity of labour.
> *Straker*. That's because you never done any, Mr Octavius.

Eric Gill, a sculptor, obviously thinks of manual labour as being of its nature creative labour, and in thinking of the past he tends to forget the lower strata of the population. The world he imagines is a world of craftsmen – owner-farmers, carpenters, handloom weavers, stonemasons, and the like – and it is also a world almost without machinery. But, of course, in a world without machinery the average person is not a craftsman but a serf, or as near it as makes no difference. The job of getting food out of the soil without machinery is so laborious that it necessarily reduces large numbers of people almost to the status of animals, and we forget this aspect of pre-industrial life precisely because the poorest classes were too worn out by drudgery to leave much record behind them. In many primitive countries to-day, the ordinary person is toiling like a slave from the age of about ten onwards, and even his seeming aesthetic superiority is probably only due to lack of opportunity. Nothing could really improve his situation except the machinery, the division of labour, and the centralised economy which Gill so much dislikes.

The book also contains an address delivered to the Peace Pledge Union, an essay on clothes and some remarks on Ruskin and on the painter, David Jones. Gill was a pacifist, at any rate towards the end of his life, and in spite of his theories about land-ownership and cottage industries, he toyed with the idea of Socialism. But the central thing in him was his hatred of the machine. He was right, no doubt, in his denunciations of present-day society, but wrong in looking for a quick way out, and like all people who hanker for the past, he could not altogether escape affectation and pretty-prettiness. Not to be arty and crafty, not to resemble William Morris – naturally, this was his claim. But one does not reject one's own age without paying the penalty, and the price Gill paid can be seen in the carvings outside Broadcasting House, in the woodcuts that adorn this book, and in his over-simplified way of writing.

---

28 July 1944

THE ROMANTIC CASE

Romanticism and the Modern Ego,
by Jacques Barzun
(Secker and Warburg, 18s.)

WHEN one's ears are full of the wailing of sirens and the boom of distant explosions, the news that Rousseau was *not* the father of totalitarianism is apt to seem unexciting. And yet the issues that Mr Barzun is discussing in this learned and polemical book are of great importance, and without making up one's mind upon them one cannot have any clear picture of the post-war world.

Briefly, Mr Barzun's aim is to defend romanticism against the now common charge that by exalting passion as against reason it has led directly to modern power-worship and the Absolute State. He makes out a very strong case, but it suffers by being too narrowly defined. To begin with he treats ideas almost as though they were unconnected with economic conditions, and hardly raises the question of *why* the classical or the romantic outlook should prevail in different epochs. Secondly, the very use of such terms as 'classical' and 'romantic' ties the controversy to the schoolroom, whereas what is at issue is the much wider question of progress and original sin.

He himself does indeed recognise that 'romantic' is a much-abused word. A table of quotations at the end of the book shows over fifty different usages (it is applied, for instance, to Napoleon, to the Middle Ages, to almost any female film star, to royalism, to republicanism, to Catholicism, to Protestantism, to reactionaries, revolutionaries, saints, highwaymen, cosmetics, ruined castles, and what-not). Worse yet, the distinction between classical and romantic art is reliable only within rather narrow limits, roughly 1650 to 1850, and even then there are individuals, Byron for instance, who seem to have a foot in both camps. In our own day the words 'classical' and 'romantic' have changed their meaning, or at least have become very much subtilised. Thus Mr T. S. Eliot ranks as classical while, say, A. E. Housman would be regarded as romantic, but Pope or Dr Johnson would probably have failed to notice the distinction.

On his own ground, that is to say the eighteenth and nineteenth centuries, Mr Barzun certainly has the better of his adversaries. He is able to show that the unfortunate Rousseau preached almost none of the ideas popularly attributed to him, and that the German Romantics and the English poets of the early nineteenth century have been similarly traduced. He rightly insists on the energy and intellectual curiosity of the whole Romantic movement, and on the interconnection between classicism and an aristocratic society. Louis XIV, he points out, was at least as great a tyrant as Napoleon and was worshipped at least as slavishly, and it needs a great deal of juggling to derive modern authoritarianism from the Romantic cult of the individual. On the other hand, he hardly inquires *why* our own age should have seen a revival of the yearning for authority, together with a rejection of the Romantic values. He speaks of the

> prevailing search for a single truth, a single religion, a single allegiance. Whether Marxist or Thomist or Anglican or neo-classicist or Fascist or Falangist, the universal cry seems to be: 'Give us a dogma, give us a leader'. If we add to this the doctrinal scholasticism of these groups, the preciosity and religiosity of its artistic standard-bearers, together with their united drive on romanticism, we have the clearest evidence we could desire for the prophecy that a new classical age is in the making, that we already live and breathe in the classical atmosphere.

This is largely true, though there are enough exceptions to spoil it as a generalisation. Mr Barzun is quite right in denouncing the Marxists, neo-Thomists, and other enemies of freedom of thought, and in pointing out that their own attack on romanticism is a species of bluff. Their real aim is the destruction of liberty, and they consequently argue that any extension of liberty must lead to slavery. But he does not discuss the deeper reasons for their attitude, nor does he set forth his case in plain enough terms. Very broadly, two principles are at work. One is the belief that human beings are by nature fairly decent and that a society founded on justice and liberty could be fairly easily established. The other is the belief that Man can only be trusted to behave himself when he is gagged and handcuffed. Clearly, the second belief prevails at this moment, and equally clearly Mr Barzun is on the other side. But he would be a more effective champion of liberty if he bothered less about defending Rousseau and attacking Boileau.

If one uses the labels 'classical' and 'romantic' to mean authoritarian and libertarian – and this is practically what Mr Barzun does – the many exceptions distract the average reader's attention from the main issue. For example, Voltaire is a classical writer and Carlyle a romantic one. Therefore Carlyle was a friend of liberty and Voltaire its enemy – which is ridiculous. One could think of countless similar objections. Exasperated by rivals who would like to wipe out at one stroke the poems of Wordsworth and the principles of the French Revolution, Mr Barzun has made himself the almost uncritical champion of Romanticism in all its aspects. The result is a certain amount of muddle and, at times, an avoidance of awkward but important questions. But, though this is an unsatisfactory book, much of it is well worth reading.

---

6 August 1944

CHINESE MIRACLES

The Dragon Beards versus the Blue Prints,
by Hsiao Ch'ien
(The Pilot Press, 4s. 6d.)

READERS of Mr Hsiao Ch'ien's earlier book, *Etching of a Tormented Age*, will remember that many of the problems it dealt with were curiously familiar. Chinese intellectuals who have grown up since the Revolution appear to have gone through much the same phases as their contemporaries in Europe, though not necessarily in the same order. In China, as in

England, poets who would not have known which end to milk a cow wrote praises of the country life, others wrote proletarian literature which the proletariat was unable to understand, and the rival claims of propaganda and pure art were savagely disputed. In his present book (most of the essays in it have been delivered as lectures or broadcasts) Mr Hsiao carries on the story, but here he is concerned less exclusively with literature and more with the impact of the machine age on Chinese culture as a whole.

As he points out, the machine came to Asia suddenly and disturbingly. 'The London buses of to-day are a development of your Victorian horse-omnibus, and who knows, perhaps the next development will be air transport over London, with aerial conductresses shouting "Hold tight, we're taking off!" But the motor buses in Hong-kong or Shanghai have no tradition behind them. Your wireless sets are, in a way, the successors of your pianolas and your musical boxes... but the wireless sets in China seem just like miracles dropped from heaven.' There was the additional fact (writing for an English audience, Mr Hsiao is too polite to emphasise this) that for some decades the Chinese experienced the benefits of Western civilisation chiefly in the form of bullets. It was not unnatural that they should go though a period of violent hostility to machinery as such. Earlier than this they had simply despised Western science as the uninteresting product of barbarians. In the seventeenth century –

When a German astrologer, Schell, tried to introduce the Solar calendar into China, he was first rebuked by native scholars, and finally died in prison of a broken heart... A scholar of the time, Yang Kwang-hsien, wrote, 'We would rather live without an accurate calendar, than adopt an alien one. Without an accurate calendar we may miscalculate the cycle of the moon, or miss an eclipse, but the Empire will prosper just the same.'

This attitude was excusable at a time when China was visibly more civilised than the West (at a time, for instance, when Orientals washed themselves and Europeans did not), but far later, when China was already in imminent danger of conquest, Chinese sages were still producing delightful arguments to prove that machines were no good. In the mid-nineteenth century Wang Jen Chiu wrote:

What is a steamship but the clumsiest of ships, and field guns but the clumsiest of cannons? The virtue of a ship lies in its speed, and the best cannons should be easily manoeuvrable. Now, these barbarous ships cannot sail an inch without being fed with coal, and their guns cannot be raised or moved without involving several hands. If one meets a brave soldier in the battlefield who rushes at one with bloody sword, he cannot but be killed.

It might almost be Marshal Pétain debunking the tank. However, the ships and the guns proved all too efficient, and after a period of obstinate conservativism the Chinese changed their attitudes to the machine and began to develop what Mr Hsiao describes as 'blind admiration'. Scientific studies became immensely popular, but the tendency was to concentrate on what was narrowly utilitarian. Young men studied animal husbandry rather than biology, ship-building rather than general engineering. Only comparatively recently was it realised that the Western technical achievements were based on theoretic studies of no immediate value.

Naturally the question that exercises Mr Hsiao Ch'ien is: will the ancient Chinese culture be able to survive China's transformation into a modern mechanised state? It is perhaps an even more pressing question for the rest of the world, for if China should take the same road as Japan the results would hardly bear thinking about. China already manufactures machine-guns, and will no doubt be manufacturing bombing planes before long. Mr Hsiao is convinced, however – and he can quote many statements to support him – that his countrymen have no liking for a merely materialistic civilisation, and that their artistic traditions are too deeply rooted to be destroyed by the machine. Meanwhile China has to exist in the modern world, and does not enjoy being told that pigtails are more picturesque than steel helmets. But she would gladly return to her 'dragon beards' (that is, to Chinese calligraphy, and the leisurely culture that it implies), if she could be reasonably secure from outside interference.

Apart from the essays dealing with the arrival of the machine, there is one dealing with the influence of Ibsen and Bernard Shaw on the Chinese theatre, and another dealing with recent Chinese literature. The

Chinese vernacular theatre seems to have started with direct imitation of European models and in its early days to have been inseparable from propaganda. One author wrote of his own work, 'Although the play is aesthetically immature, I am glad to say that I have touched on matrimony and rural bankruptcy, the two up-to-date social problems confronting us.' Both Ibsen and Bernard Shaw were immensely valued as 'problem playwrights', though *Mrs Warren's Profession* caused a scandal in Shanghai as late as 1921. Later there was a reaction in favour of sentimental love-dramas and later still in favour of 'proletarian' plays. It is interesting to learn that the very first plays to be adapted for the Chinese theatre were *La Dame aux Camélias* and *Uncle Tom's Cabin*. *Uncle Tom's Cabin*, incidentally, had the effect of convincing the Chinese that 'Westerners were not all callous'.

This is a slight book, but well worth the hour or so that it takes to read. It would have been better in places if Mr Hsiao Ch'ien were not over-anxious to avoid giving offence. Europe has not behaved well towards Asia, and in certain contexts it is necessary to say so. The publishers are to be congratulated on the make-up of the book, which is printed on the kind of hand-made paper which most of us have not seen for several years.

---

20 August 1944

PURITAN POET

Milton: Man and Thinker, by Dennis Saurat
(Dent, 15s.) *

T HIS book, with all its learning, does not remove the impression that Milton, considered as anything except a poet, was an uninteresting person. It cannot be said that his life was uneventful; he went blind, he was twice married, and in the period of the Commonwealth he played an important part by answering, more or less officially, the leading pamphleteers of Europe. He also had the courage to continue writing anti-Royalist pamphlets when the Restoration was obviously imminent. And yet somehow Professor Saurat's claim that Milton was a 'profound thinker' as well as a 'marvellous poet' does not seem to be justified.

Milton is remembered by his phraseology, it is difficult to feel that he added anything to our stock of ideas.

Professor Saurat has very little to say about Milton's private life and not a great deal about his political outlook. The main emphasis of the book is religious. Milton's creed, it seems, was a kind of Deism or pantheism, definitely heretical even by Puritan standards. He did not believe in the duality of body and soul, and therefore only doubtfully believed in individual immortality. As he saw it, the Fall and the Atonement were a struggle that took place anew in every human being, and it was a struggle between reason and passion rather than between good and evil. In this scheme of things the doctrine of the Atonement in its Christian form had no place, and Milton does not even mention the Crucifixion in *Paradise Regained*. Implicit in his outlook is the belief that the Kingdom of Heaven will be finally established on this earth, as was also believed by the ancient Hebrews before the doctrine of the immortality of the soul took root.

Professor Saurat accepts Blake's dictum that Milton 'was of the Devil's party without knowing it' but adds that 'he was also of God's party, and what is more important, he knew it'. *Paradise Lost* is a dramatisation of his own struggle, moral and political. The story of the Fall, which is different from the Biblical version, sets forth his own view of sexual ethics, while the relationship between Adam and Eve ('He for God only, she for God in him') emphasises the necessary subjection of Woman. There are indeed passages in *Paradise Lost* in which it is difficult not to feel that Milton is writing 'at' his first wife. Professor Saurat does not say this, but he does say that Milton's subject-matter is in one way or another always himself. His political opinions sprang very directly out of his subjective feelings. Persecution made him a champion of liberty, but on the other hand he was not in favour of toleration for those he seriously disagreed with, such as the Catholics. He believed in democracy until he found that the common people were not of his way of thinking. Professor Saurat admits Milton's egotism and his tendency to base his theories on personal motives, but turns this into a virtue:

> But we may as well think... what a powerful personality was here, a
> personality which, in the exercise of its normal needs, was brought

up against everything that was arbitrary in the laws and customs of the time. This man was under no necessity to think in order to discover the abuses of the social order: all he had to do was to live, and he naturally came to stumble against every prejudice and to trip against every error. He was naively surprised, and wondered why everyone did not think as he did. His egotism and his pride were so deep that they acted as hardly conscious natural forces, as though human nature, trammelled, bound and imprisoned in all other men, had held to its free course in Milton alone.

This is ingenious, but when one remembers, for instance, that Milton only became an advocate of divorce when he wanted to dissolve his own marriage, it hardly seems to hold water.

This is, of course, a book about Milton as a thinker and not as a writer, but one cannot help feeling that a little more should have been made of the fact that Milton was a poet. For his outstanding characteristic, which cannot be left out of any full account of him, is his sheer skill with words. It is fair to call it unique, not only because it has never been successfully imitated, in spite of some well-marked stylistic tricks, but because, far more than in most great poets, it is independent of meaning. Many of Milton's best verbal effects are got by monstrously irrelevant digressions, lists of names, and sheer trivialities, things like –

> *the barren plains*
> *Of Serlcana, where Chineses drive*
> *With sails and wind their cany*
> *wagons light.*

If Milton did a service to the human intellect, it was not by writing pamphlets against Salmasius but by weaving noble words round comparatively simple thoughts. For instance:

> *I did but prompt the age to quit their clogs,*
> *By the known rules of ancient liberty,*
> *When straight a barbarous noise environs me*
> *Of owls and cuckoos, asses, apes and dogs.*

Over a period of 300 years, how many defenders of free speech must have drawn strength from that line, 'By the known rules of ancient liberty'! However, perhaps Professor Saurat will write another book about Milton, considered this time as a poet.

* The first edition of this book was published in French in 1920 and in English in 1925. One section is now published for the first time in English. [Original footnote.]

---

3 September 1944

BACK TO THE LAND

Selections from the Works of Gerrard Winstanley,
edited by Leonard Hamilton,
with an Introduction by Christopher Hill
(Cresset Press, 7s. 6d.)

EVERY successful revolution has its June Purge. A moment always comes when the party which has seized power crushes its own Left wing and then proceeds to disappoint the hopes with which the revolution started out. The dictators of the past, however, lacked modern thoroughness in silencing their opponents, and the defeated minorities of one revolution after another have left behind residues of thought which have gradually coalesced into the modern Socialist movement. Even the poor, humble English Diggers, as these pamphlets show, were able in their few years of activity to disseminate ideas which may have contributed to Spanish Anarchism and may even have remotely influenced such thinkers as Gandhi.

Winstanley, who it seems was not the originator of the Digger movement but was its chief publicist, was born in Wigan in 1609 and was for a while a cloth merchant in London. He was ruined by the Civil War. In 1649 he and twenty or thirty others took over and began cultivating some waste land on St George's Hill, near Cobham, forming themselves into a self-supporting community on what would now be called Communist–Anarchist lines. In this community there was to be no money, no trade, no inequality, no idle persons, no priests, and as far as possible no law. As Winstanley saw it, the land of England had once belonged to the common people and had been unjustly taken from them and the best way to get it back was for bodies of landless men to form colonies which would act as an example to the mass of the nation. At the beginning he was simple enough to imagine that even the landlords could ultimately be won over to this Anarchist programme. But ideas similar to his own were evidently widespread as other colonies of Diggers were started in various parts of the country at about the same time.

Needless to say, the Diggers were swiftly crushed. The parvenu gentry who had won the Civil War were willing enough to divide the lands of the Royalists among themselves, but they had no intention of setting up an egalitarian society, and they saw the danger of allowing such experiments as Winstanley's to succeed. The Diggers were beaten up, their crops were trampled on, their stock was taken away from them by means of law suits in which packed juries imposed impossible damages. Troops of soldiers sent to deal with them tended to be sympathetic – this was the period of the revolt of the Levellers in the army – but the gentry won and the Digger movement was effectively finished by 1652. Winstanley vanishes from history about 1660.

It is clear from these pamphlets that, though a visionary, Winstanley was by no means a fool. He did not expect his ideas to be accepted immediately and he was ready to modify them at need. After his experiment had failed, he submitted to Cromwell a quite detailed and practical programme from which the earlier extravagances had been eliminated. This makes provision for laws, magistrates and foreign trade, even, in spite of his pacifist tinge, for a standing army and the death penalty for certain offences. But the central idea is still the same – a society founded on brotherhood and co-operation, with no profit-making and, for internal purposes, no money. 'Everyone shall put to their hands to till the earth and bring up cattle, and the blessing of the earth shall be common to all when a man hath need of any corn or cattle, take from the next store-house he meets with. *Acts iv: 32.**'

Winstanley's thought links up with Anarchism rather than Socialism because he thinks in terms of a purely agricultural community living at a low level of comfort, lower than was even then strictly necessary. Not foreseeing the machine, he states that a man cannot be rich except by exploiting others, but it is evident that, like Mr Gandhi, he also values simplicity for its own sake. Moreover, he clings to a belief which seems to haunt all thinkers of the Anarchist type – the belief that the wished-for Utopia has already existed in the past. The land did once belong to the common people, but has been taken away from them. According to Winstanley, this happened at the Norman Conquest, which in his eyes is the cardinal fact in English history. The essential struggle is the struggle of the Saxon common people against the Frenchified upper class. In every pamphlet, almost in every paragraph, he refers to the defeated Royalists as 'Normans'. But alas he could see only too clearly that the victors of the Civil War were themselves developing 'Norman' characteristics.

> And you, zealous preachers and professors of the City of London, and you great officers and soldiers of the army, where are all your victories over the Cavaliers, that you made such a blaze in the land, in giving God thanks for, and which you begged in your fasting days and morning exercises? Are they all sunk into the Norman power again, and must the old prerogative laws stand? What freedom did you then give thanks for? Surely that you had killed him that rode upon you, that you may get up into his saddle to ride upon others. Oh, thou City, thou hypocritical City! Thou blindfold, drowsy England, that sleeps and snorts in the bed of covetousness, awake, awake! The enemy is upon thy back, he is ready to scale the walls and enter possession and wilt not look out?

If only our modern Trotskyists and Anarchists – who in effect are saying the same thing – could write prose like that! This is not a book that can be read through at one sitting, but it is a book to buy and keep. Mr Hill's short introduction is useful and interesting.

* Acts iv 32: 'Now the multitude of those who believed were of one heart and one soul; neither did anyone say that any of the things he possessed was his own, but they had all things in common.'

NEW WORLD

The American Problem, by D. W. Brogan
(Hamish Hamilton, 10s. 6d.)

IT is uncertain what Professor Brogan intended to achieve by this book, which seems to fall mid-way between being a popular history of the United States and a forecast of American behaviour in the post-war world. His book, *The English People*, written a year or two ago, had a clear enough purpose. It was obviously written 'at' America, with the object of explaining the British social system and allaying anti-British prejudice, and its – on the whole – too favourable tone was therefore understandable. But the present book, presumably written to enlighten British readers, also gives the impression that Professor Brogan had an American rather than a British public in mind. The issues that are soft-pedalled are the ones that American opinion is sensitive about; and though the British reader will carry away many picturesque facts, he gets no clear answer to the questions that he is likeliest to ask about the United States at this moment.

The main emphasis of the book is historical. Professor Brogan rightly lays great stress upon the enormous achievement, quite unparalleled in human history, of colonising the North American continent, and on the 'frontier' habit of mind which persisted after the frontier had ceased to exist. He also has some penetrating things to say about the position of American women, their civilising influence in the early days when the West was opened up, and the effects on American industry of their struggle for emancipation. He is also good on regional differences, and on the American climate and its effects on character, architecture and much else. But on the whole it is either marginal things of this kind that he is discussing, or else very large and vague issues: the immediate concrete problems are only mentioned in passing, if at all.

For instance, in discussing the American governmental machine, Professor Brogan gives a lot of details about the working of Congress, and utters some wide generalisations about the American love of oratory, but he hardly answers the question which almost any Englishman would ask – namely, what sections of the population, and what economic interests, do the two main parties represent? Again, though he has some good passages on American agriculture and the position of the farmer, he says very little about the economic structure of American society, the distribution of wealth, the trade unions, the ownership of the Press, and the popularity or otherwise of collectivist theories. Nor does he definitely say whether class distinctions are increasing or decreasing. The Negro problem is very lightly skated over. Professor Brogan does give a few pages to the Negroes, but only in connection with the backwardness of the South as a whole, and it is only in a couple of parentheses that he mentions that millions of Negroes are both half-starved and disenfranchised.

The thing, of course, that Professor Brogan is talking about and about is American isolationism. Will the Americans, or will they not, give the world the moral lead it is waiting for and play their part in building a sane society? No doubt he is right to leave the answer open, but not, surely, to imply that it is merely a question of the Americans becoming less fixated on internal affairs and more aware that the outside world exists and is dangerous. The ignorant isolationism of the American mother who does not want 'our boys' killed in foreign wars is not the main danger. The United States, now the greatest world power, will presumably have an active foreign policy after the war: the question is whether it will be an enlightened and unselfish policy. There are symptoms and tendencies which may help to give an answer, but Professor Brogan does not mention them or barely mentions them.

For example, he says almost nothing about American imperialism, actual or potential. Nor does he discuss the meaning of the swing towards the Republican Party which appears to have been going on during the past year or two. Nor – this indeed is a question which involves Britain as much as the United States, but which obviously should not have been left out of account – does he say anything about the problems of migration, and especially the migration of the coloured peoples. And he is exceedingly cautious on the subject all-important from our point of view of anti-British feeling. Even when he mentions it, he is content to give the well-worn historical explanation and does not point to the fact that different sections of American society are anti-British for different and incompatible reasons. Professor Brogan seems to hint that the less we interfere in American affairs the better... and there he is probably right.

But it is still important to us to know what the Americans think about us, and to what extent traditional and cultural hostilities are a cover for something else. Professor Brogan's witty manner of writing and his ability to drag in recondite illustrations for nearly everything that he says do not compensate for his avoidance of essentials.

In general this is a 'get together' book. Though it is full of digressions, its main aim seems to be to convince the British public that the United States is a powerful and important country whose faults are those of youth, and with whom we should do well not to quarrel. This was hardly worth saying. Britain cannot afford to quarrel with America and there is very little popular anti-American feeling. On the other hand, we could do with some expert information about American policy internal and external: Professor Brogan is probably qualified to give it, but the fact that he always has at least one eye on a possible American reader prevents him from doing so.

---

1 October 1944

BURMA ROADS

Burma Pamphlets:
1 – Burma Background, by V. R. Pearn; *2 – Burma Setting,* by O. H. K. Spate; *3 – Buddhism in Burma,* by G. Appleton
(Longmans, 1s. each.)

Burma, by Ma Mya Sein
(Oxford University Press, 1s.)

Wings Over Burma, by Kenneth Hemingway
(Quality Press, 15s.)

Wingate's Raiders, by Charles J. Rolo
(Harrap, 8s. 6d.)

UNTIL very recently Burma has been so badly publicised in this country that it has been difficult even for the most thoughtful newspaper readers to form any opinion about it. The campaign of 1942 was inadequately reported, there has been as nearly as possible no information about what is happening under Japanese rule, and nothing has been divulged about Britain's post-war intentions towards Burma. Nor has there been much reliable information about Burma's background problems and its relations with China and India. The newly published Burma Pamphlets – they appear to have been printed and perhaps planned in India – are therefore a useful departure, and may help public opinion to exert itself in favour of a reasonable settlement when the Japanese have been evicted.

Of the three that have so far appeared, *Burma Background* – a brief history of the country from the eleventh century onwards – is probably the most useful, but *Burma Setting* fills up a number of gaps by giving a picture of the day-to-day life of the country and describing its climatic conditions and natural resources. *Buddhism in Burma*, which gives the appearance of having been written by a Christian missionary, is less useful from the point of view of the average reader, as it concentrates on the doctrinal side of Buddhism and does not say enough about the extremely important political and social activities of the Burmese priesthood.

Ma Mya Sein's pamphlet (what a novelty, by the way, to find something about Burma written by a Burmese!) overlaps to some extent with the other three. The author has had a distinguished public career in Burma and is, one gathers, a very moderate Nationalist. She gives a general survey of the country, with as much reference as is necessary to its past history, and is at pains to emphasise that in spite of its numerous races Burma is a natural unit and capable of full nationhood. Unlike the writers in the other series, she touches on present-day politics and adds the warning that 'any attempt to reconstruct Burma after the war can only succeed if it gets full nationalist sympathy behind it'.

The other two books are not concerned with political problems, though *Wingate's Raiders* does throw some indirect light upon them. *Wings Over Burma* – an account of the heroic effort of the small goup of RAF, and the AVG [American Volunteer Group], to fight off the Japanese invasion – is a tale of continued battles against odds, ending triumphantly some time in 1943, when the Allies began to gain mastery in the air, and the unfortunate Burma towns, already partly destroyed by the Japanese, began to get their second dose of bombing and machine-gunning from the skies. It is full of technical slang, but vivid and readable. *Wingate's*

Raiders is a more school-boyish type of book, obviously written with the object of building round Brigadier-General Wingate the same kind of legend as surrounds Gordon and T. E. Lawrence; but its detailed account of Wingate's methods should be valuable to students of guerrilla warfare.

The book does not deal with Wingate's part in the successful operations against Myitkyina in 1944, in which he met his death. It is chiefly concerned with his preliminary raid into Japanese-occupied territory a year earlier. Lord Wavell, who remembered Wingate's achievements in Palestine and Abyssinia, brought him to Burma in 1942, when the campaign was already lost, but while there was still time to study the Japanese tactics in jungle warfare.

Wingate saw that the British and Indians, apart from being outnumbered and ill-supported in the air, were hopelessly hampered by being tied to mechanised transport. The more lightly equipped Japanese could move round them and cut their communications at will. He set himself to produce an even more mobile force, which would use the game-tracks where the Japanese used the cart-tracks, and which could be supplied entirely by air, and therefore be quite independent of lines of communication. Any man who was medically fit, he said, could be made into a good jungle fighter. And in the event his mixed force of British, Indians, and Burmese – the British were mostly second-line troops who had seen no fighting before – penetrated hundreds of miles into strongly occupied territory, did an immense amount of damage, and got out again, having suffered terribly from hunger and hardship, but with comparatively few battle casualties.

As Lord Wavell says in his foreword, this expedition had no strategic aim except the secondary one of taking the pressure off the Kachin levies who were still beleaguered at Fort Hertz; but it was invaluable experience and prepared the way for Wingate's airborne descent into the Japanese rear at Katha a year later. Wingate's originality of mind is apparent in his every action.

It is interesting to notice that the column seems to have been received almost everywhere in friendly fashion by the Burmese villagers – a sign, perhaps, that after a year of occupation the Japanese promises were already wearing thin.

INDIAN INK

Verdict on India, by Beverley Nichols
(Jonathan Cape, 12s. 6d.)

I T is fair to say that this book does not read as though it were intended to make mischief, but that is the effect it will probably have. Mr Nichols spent about a year in India – as an unofficial visitor, he insists – travelling all over the country and interviewing Indians of every description, from maharajahs to naked mendicants. When he got there the menace of a Japanese invasion still loomed large and the 'Quit India' campaign was in full swing. A little later there was the Bengal famine, of which he records some horrifying details. In a slapdash way he has obviously tried very hard to get at the truth, and his willingness to disclose scandals, together with frank, even violent, partisanship in Indian internal affairs, will cause much offence among Indians. It would not even be surprising if this book, like *Mother India* [by Katherine Mayo: London, 1927], provoked a whole series of counterblasts.

Mr Nichols's essential quarrel is with Hinduism. He detests the Hindu religion itself – its cow-worship, the obscene carvings in the temples, its caste system, and the endless superstitions which war against science and enlightenment – but above all he is politically anti-Hindu. He is an advocate of Pakistan, which he believes will certainly be established by one means or another, and his favourite Indian politician is Mr Jinnah. Much of what he says is true, but his way of saying it, and the things he leaves out, may mislead some people and will certainly antagonise countless others.

The thing Mr Nichols never really gets round to admitting is that India's major grievance against Britain is justified. The British are still in India long after the Indians have ceased to want them there. If one keeps that in mind, much of Mr Nichols's indictment of the Congress politicians can be accepted. India's immediate problems will not be solved by the disappearance of the British, and the Nationalist propaganda which declares every existing evil to be a direct result of British rule is dishonest as well as hysterical. As Mr Nichols is aware – indeed, too much aware –

this propaganda is lapped up by well-meaning Liberals in this country and America who are all the readier to accept what Indian apologists tell them because they have no real interest in Indian problems. Many of Mr Nichols's points would have been well worth making if only he could have made them in a better-tempered way.

It is quite true that Hindu–Moslem antagonism is played down in Nationalist propaganda and that the Moslem end of the case seldom gets a fair hearing outside India. Again, it is true that the Congress Party is not the idealistic Left-wing organisation which Western Liberals imagine it to be, but has considerable resemblances to the Nazi Party and is backed by sinister business men with pro-Japanese leanings. Again, it is true that pro-Indian and anti-British propaganda habitually skates over huge problems such as Untouchability and ignores or misrepresents the positive achievements of the British in India. One could make a whole list of similar points on which Mr Nichols is probably in the right. But he does not see that the appalling atmosphere of Indian politics, the hysteria, the lies, the pathological hatred, suspicion and credulity, is itself the result of wounded national pride. He observes with some acuteness the mentality of a subject people, but talks of it as though it were innate or simply the product of the Hindu religion.

For instance, he has an undisguised contempt for the army of half-educated youths, picking up a precarious living from journalism and litigation, who are the noise-makers of the Nationalist movement. He barely admits that the existence of this huge unemployed intelligentsia is a commentary on British educational methods, or that these people might develop a more grown-up mentality if they had real responsibilities to face.

A more serious mistake is that he repeatedly attacks Mr Gandhi, for whom he has an unconquerable aversion. Mr Gandhi is an enigmatic character, but he is obviously not a plain crook, which is what Mr Nichols seems to imply, and even his endless self-contradictions may be simply a form of sincerity. Throughout nearly the whole of Mr Nichols's book, indeed, there is an air of prejudice and irritation which weakens even his justified criticisms.

Mr Nichols is not unwilling to admit that the British in India have faults, especially social faults (he says, exaggerating slightly, that no European ever says 'Thank you' to an Indian), and towards the end he makes some constructive suggestions. The British, he considers, both should and will quit India in the fairly near future. It would have created a very much better impression if he had said this on the first page of the book. Morally, he says, there is no case for our remaining there after the war is won, though it was, as he rightly emphasises, an absurdity to ask Britain simply to hand India over to the Japanese. His formula is 'Divide and Quit' – that is, we are to recognise Indian independence, but make sure that Pakistan is established first. This is perhaps a thinkable solution and, if the Moslem League has the following that Mr Nichols claims for it, it might help to avert civil war after the British power is withdrawn.

---

12 November 1944

POET AND PRIEST

Gerard Manley Hopkins, by W. H. Gardner

(Secker and Warburg, 25s.)

I T is a hundred years since the birth of Gerard Manley Hopkins, and also since the birth of his friend Robert Bridges, who outlived him by forty years and edited the *Poems* that appeared in 1918. It is at least possible that if it had not been for Bridges we should never have heard Hopkins's name, and the current notion – shared intermittently by Mr Gardner – that Bridges behaved throughout the whole affair like an ignorant philistine seems quite unjustified. His admiration for Hopkins was qualified, but he had had the acuteness to see as early as the seventies that Hopkins had first-rate talents, and by holding up the publication of the *Poems* till 1918 he probably did his reputation a great service. For by that time public taste, educated by Pound, Eliot, the renewed vogue of Donne, and also by certain poems of Bridges's own, was ready for Hopkins. Mr Gardner fills a whole chapter with extracts from reviews and criticisms, and the striking thing about them, with very few exceptions, is how respectful they are. Mr Gardner appears to feel that Hopkins has been underpraised, but one has only to think of the streams of abuse that greeted Joyce and Lawrence to realise that Hopkins, ignored during his lifetime, has not done so badly after death.

Mr Gardner, writing as a disciple rather than a critic, is apt to be on the defensive when he speaks either of Hopkins's vocabulary or his religious beliefs. Underlying this is a question always present when Hopkins is discussed, though not often brought out into the open: Did the fact that Hopkins was a Jesuit priest damage him as a poet?

Mr Gardner evidently thinks that it did not, and almost certainly he is right. The most severe discipline, if it does not entail actual dishonesty, is not necessarily damaging to a poet, and in Hopkins's case his life as a priest *was* his subject-matter. Art arises out of suffering, and it is clear that Hopkins was unhappy, and not merely because he was of poor health, neglected as a poet, and condemned to unsympathetic work in dreary places. He was also unhappy because although his faith was secure, to live up to it was not easy. He was in the position of a soldier fighting in a war which he believes to be just but which he does not pretend to enjoy. Intellectually and emotionally he was full of anomalies. He was intensely an Englishman, preferring England to other countries, and yet a Catholic convert, a devout Christian and yet full of an almost pantheistic love of Nature which made him feel a certain kinship with Whitman. One may guess that he could embrace poverty and chastity a good deal more easily than obedience, and that he was never able to efface his own individuality so completely as he would have wished.

There is no reason to suppose that he would have been a better poet if he had been an unbeliever. Probably he would have been a less original poet, giving less evidence of strain, and less tortured in his language.

Everyone has felt that there is some connection between Hopkins's religious struggles and his strange diction, and it is hard not to feel that over and above the endless search for exact meanings there is also at work an unconscious desire to be unusual. He was completely subordinated in one world, that of the Church, and he may have wanted to compensate himself by being a rebel in another, that of poetry. Needless to say, Mr Gardner will not hear of this interpretation. He comes near to claiming that Hopkins's language is entirely free from affectation, and adds that Hopkins always strove 'to put *meaning* before mere suggestion and sound'. It is true, of course, that one gets used to Hopkins's diction (for instance, his trick of dropping relative pronouns), and that much that seems arbitrary is justified if one looks more closely.

But it is also true that one cannot read far in his work without coming upon some word that appears to have been pushed in either because it is strange or because the sound of some nearby word has called it up. And similar tendencies – inversion of words and phrases, for instance – appear in his prose.

Mr Gardner is right in proclaiming Hopkins a great poet, but not in asking readers – as in effect he does – to lay aside their critical faculties. In no single instance does he admit that an adverse criticism of Hopkins is justified, and he sometimes hints that such criticisms are not honest either. One ought to be able to say of Hopkins, as one can of any other poet, that some of his work is good and some bad. One ought to be able to say that 'Felix Randal' is probably the best short poem in the English language, and at the same time that one objects to a phrase like 'very-violet-sweet' and agrees with Bridges that to rhyme 'communion' with 'boon he on' is 'hideous'. Mr Gardner's attitude is 'Take it or leave it'. This is a book that anyone interested in Hopkins ought to read, but the second volume which Mr Gardner promises will be more valuable if he remembers that criticism and hagiography are different things.

---

26 November 1944

SINGING MEN

A Critical History of English Poetry,
by Herbert J. C. Grierson and J. C. Smith
(Chatto and Windus, 21s.)

A book of 521 pages, which starts with *Beowulf* and ends with Mr Henry Treece, necessarily lays the emphasis on history rather than on criticism. This book, which deals at varying lengths with something over 300 English poets, is primarily a work of reference, and as such it will be extremely useful in these days when libraries are scattered and minor classics often unprocurable.

The authors trace the development of English poetry from the Dark Ages onwards, following more or less the usual methods of classification. A few major poets get a chapter to themselves, and Irish and Scottish poetry are given their due share of attention. Poetic drama is adequately dealt with, and even hymns are not despised. But in so inclusive a book it seems a pity that there is almost no mention of comic verse, which till recently often contrived to be a species of poetry, and a species in which the races of the British Isles were pre-eminent. There is no reference to Barham, Thackeray, or Lewis Carroll, for instance, and Calverley only just makes the grade. Mr Belloc is dismissed with the remark that 'some of his sonnets, epigrams and "cautionary" rhymes are not yet forgotten', which is, to put it mildly, an understatement. Nor is there any mention of the English nursery rhymes – a pity, not only because some of them are true poems, but because the authors could have done a public service by pointing out the disgraceful fact that no full collection of nursery rhymes has ever been printed.

The purpose for which the average reader consults a book of this kind is to be told something about the lesser-known poets (the fifteenth-century ones, for instance), or about such works as *The Faerie Queene*, which he knows he ought to admire but feels disinclined to read. Necessarily he has to take a good deal on trust. But there is one way in which the critical judgements in such a book can be tested – that is, by seeing what it says about contemporary poetry, on which no established body of opinion yet exists. It is astonishing how badly many anthologies and works of academic criticism emerge from this test. *The Oxford Book of English Verse* is an example. It is a good selection up to the point at which the compiler had to begin using his own judgement, after which it deteriorates noticeably.

Professor Grierson and Dr Smith, however, have kept well in touch with recent developments, and perhaps even give contemporary verse more space than it deserves. There is, indeed, much in their judgement that one might quarrel with. They confess to a preference for the Georgians (we are told of Mr Ralph Hodgson, for instance, that 'almost all he has written is memorable'), they only mention Hopkins very shortly, and though they give Mr Eliot a page or two they do not mention the Sweeney poems, and make only a slighting reference to 'Prufrock'. Pound is excluded from mention on what appear to be political grounds, and Joyce is not spoken of as a verse-writer, although he wrote the only successful villanelle in English. But still, the authors do not share the delusion, only too common with the possessors of great learning, that literature stopped about forty years ago. They are willing to take seriously not merely Auden and MacNeice but even Dylan Thomas and the Apocalyptics. The ordinary reader who is not a scholar can therefore accept what they tell him about (say) Henryson or Traherne or Shenstone with some confidence.

The book's greatest weakness – perhaps, however, it could not have been avoided without making the book much longer – is that it says only the minimum about the social background of literature. Changes of form, subject-matter, and language are recorded, but only very briefly explained. After the English language has settled into more or less its modern shape – at about the beginning of the sixteenth century, say – the striking thing about English poetry is its diversity and the ebb and flow of certain moods. In one age almost anyone seems capable of writing a passable lyric poem, while in another, perhaps less than a hundred years later, the lyric seems almost to have vanished. Throughout the greater part of the eighteenth century the heroic couplet is almost the only mode, Shakespeare is only doubtfully admired, and Pope's rewriting of Chaucer is looked upon as an improvement; then, quite suddenly, the classical style of writing seems stilted and even ridiculous, and poetry is governed for more than a hundred years by the wildest romanticism.

Professor Grierson and Dr Smith do make some attempt to relate such changes as these to major historical events, but on the whole they treat the history of poetry as the history of individuals or of 'schools' centring on individuals. This was, perhaps, unavoidable if they were to mention so many poets as they contrive to do, but frequently as one reads one finds oneself wishing for more background information – more explanation of *why* the English were once the most musical people in Europe and then fell from that position, or *why* one age should ignore Nature, another worship it and another find it slightly horrifying. However, the authors no doubt narrowed their field intentionally, and what they set out to do they have done successfully. It is an informative book and anyone who buys it is likely to keep it.

SPANISH PRISON

An Interlude in Spain, by Charles d'Ydewalle
Translated by Eric Sutton
(Macmillan, 8s. 6d.)

U NWILLING witnesses are generally accounted the most reliable, and
Mr Charles d'Ydewalle is at least partly an unwilling witness
against Franco's Spain. He is a Belgian journalist (evidently a devout
Catholic), and during the Spanish Civil War he was a warm partisan of
General Franco, in whose territory he appears to have spent some
months. When his own country was subjugated by the Germans and he
set out on the roundabout journey to England, he was quite confident
that Nationalist Spain, whose 'crusade' he had supported as best he
could, would offer no obstacle. It was therefore with some surprise that
he found himself arrested and flung into gaol almost as soon as he had
set foot on Spanish soil.

This was towards the end of 1941. He was not released until eight
months later, and at no time did he discover what offence, if any, he was
charged with. Presumably he had been arrested because his flight to
England indicated Allied sympathies. He was incarcerated first of all in
the Model Prison in Barcelona, which had been built to hold 700
prisoners and at this time was holding 8,000. Later he was placed in a
concentration camp among refugees of many different nationalities.
Here the conditions were comparatively sympathetic; it was possible to
buy small luxuries; one could choose one's hut mates; and there was
international rivalry in the matter of digging tunnels under the barbed
wire. It was the Model Prison that opened or partially opened Mr
d'Ydewalle's eyes to the nature of the regime.

At the end of 1941, nearly three years after the ending of the Civil
War, people were still being shot, in this prison alone, at the rate of five
or six a week. In addition there was torture, presumably for the purpose
of extracting confessions, and on occasion the torturer 'went too far'.
Political prisoners and ordinary criminals were more or less mixed up
together, but the majority of the prisoners were left-overs from the Civil

War, usually serving sentences of thirty years. In many cases, Mr d'Ydewalle noted, this would take them to the ripe age of ninety-five or so. The shootings were carried out with the maximum of cruelty. No one knew, until the morning of execution, whether he was to be shot or not.

Early every morning there would be a trampling [sic] of boots and a clanking of bayonets along the corridor, and suddenly this door or that would be thrown open and a name called out. Later in the day the dead man's mattress would be seen lying outside the cell door. Sometimes a man was reprieved and then shot a day or two later for some different offence. But there were no shootings on Sundays or holidays. The display of religiosity with which the life of the prison was conducted stuck in Mr d'Ydewalle's gizzard almost more than the cruelty.

Mr d'Ydewalle spent only a day or two in Spain as a free man, but in the concentration camp he noted that the wretched Spanish soldiers who guarded them were glad to beg scraps of food from the better-off internees. He does not record things like this with any satisfaction, and is reluctant to draw their full moral. To the end, indeed, he seems to have remained convinced that in the Civil War Franco was in the right, and that it was only afterwards that things went wrong. In prison he sometimes comforted himself with the thought that the wretched victims round about him had been doing the same thing to Nationalist sympathisers only a few years before. He reiterates his belief in 'red atrocities', and shows more than a trace of anti-Semitism.

The main impression that the book conveys is one of bewilderment. Why had he been locked up? How could the 'glorious crusade' have led to this kind of thing? He even expresses astonishment that a regime calling itself Catholic could lend its support to Hitler and Mussolini, which does seem to be carrying simplicity rather far, since General Franco can hardly be accused of having concealed his political affiliations.

Naturally it is not easy for someone who in good faith supported the Nationalist cause at the time of the Civil War to admit that the horrors of the Model Prison were implicit in the Nationalist regime from the beginning. But Mr d'Ydewalle also had the handicap of coming from a comparatively orderly and well-governed country and therefore not having any preliminary understanding of totalitarianism.

The essential fact about a totalitarian regime is that it has no laws. People are not punished for specific offences, but because they are considered to be politically or intellectually undesirable. What they have done or not done is irrelevant. It took Mr d'Ydewalle some time to get used to this idea and, as he observed, there were other Western European prisoners who had difficulty in grasping it as well. When he had been several months in gaol some British soldiers, escaped from France, came to join him. He told them about the shootings. At the beginning they flatly disbelieved him and only gradually, as mattress after mattress appeared outside this cell or that, came to realise that what he said was true: whereupon they commented, not inaptly: 'Well, give me England every time.'

This book is a useful footnote to history. The author's simplicity of outlook is an advantage to him as a narrator. But if one may make a guess, the next variant of General Franco who appears will not have Mr d'Ydewalle's support.

---

31 December 1944

POET IN DARKNESS

Flower of Evil: A Life of Charles Baudelaire,
by Edwin Morgan
(Sheed and Ward, 7s. 6d.)

THE general outline of Baudelaire's life, his debts, his drug-taking, his Negro mistress, his almost infantile attachment to his mother and hatred of his blimpish stepfather, is well known. Except for his brief visit to Mauritius he never travelled further than Belgium, and in a physical sense his life was not adventurous. The two main factors in it were the morass of debts from which he never escaped, and his dependence, both financial and emotional, on his mother. To the last he continued writing to her, discussing all his projects, sending copies of his poems, boasting of future successes, and never once, apparently, arousing in her a flicker of interest in his work or any other reaction than a desire that he should 'try to be like other people'. He died in her arms, a worn-out, white-haired old paralytic, at the age of forty-six.

It is impossible to feel that even with the best of luck Baudelaire's life could have been in the ordinary sense successful. He wrote his own history in the famous line *'Ses ailes de géant l'empêchent de marcher'*, and if he had been capable even for a moment of respectability or common sense we should probably never have heard his name. He is the poet of squalor, of perversity, of self-disgust, and of ennui, which Mr Morgan inadequately translates as 'boredom'. (There is no exact English equivalent of this word in the sense in which Baudelaire uses it. Perhaps *taedium vitae* would be a correct translation.) And it hardly seems worth re-telling his story unless one is willing to recognise the considerable element of moral revolt which his work contains.

Unfortunately Mr Morgan's book is an attempt to build Baudelaire up into a good Catholic – or, at any rate, a 'true' Catholic. The grounds for this are Baudelaire's alleged return to the Church during his last year of life, and the claim that Baudelaire's writings are essentially Christian, even when, as is often the case, he chooses to turn the Christian ethical code upside down. This claim has been made – and refuted – before. Even the concrete evidence by which Mr Morgan seeks to prove Baudelaire's orthodoxy is very unsatisfactory.

The ultimate conversion seems to rest on the testimony of only two or three people. Did Baudelaire ever make any definite submission to the Church, and if so, was he sane when he made it? He lost the power of speech about a year before his death and does not seem ever to have regained it completely. This is only a short book and does not claim to be an exhaustive biography: still, it calls itself a 'life', and what is one to think of a 'life' of Baudelaire which never once mentions that Baudelaire was syphilitic? Possibly Mr Morgan does not believe that this was so – for it has been disputed – but he should at least have mentioned it and produced some other reason for Baudelaire's death as a paralytic at forty-six. This is not merely a piece of scandal: it is a point upon which any biographer of Baudelaire must make up his mind. For the nature of the disease has a bearing not only on the poet's mental condition during his last year but on his whole attitude to life.

Mr Morgan's implied claim throughout the book is that in writing of vice, folly, and their after-effects, Baudelaire is displaying a Christian understanding of the vanity of human happiness. He claims Baudelaire, in effect, as a Christian pessimist, and traces his known dislike of liberalism, democracy, and the idea of progress to other-worldliness. But how can anyone who is suffering from such a disease as Baudelaire's be a disinterested witness on the question of whether earthly happiness is possible? Nor is it easy, on the evidence of Baudelaire's writings, to feel that he was a Catholic in any other than a cultural or, as one might say, anthropological sense. He sometimes toyed with Satanism, but Satanism is not, as it is often declared to be, the mirror image of Christian belief.

This book gives the impression of having been written as propaganda rather than as either biography or criticism. The literal translations which accompany the many quotations from *Les Fleurs du Mal* show remarkable insensitivity. They are everywhere inadequate and in places doubtfully correct, and once or twice Mr Morgan simply omits a phrase without indicating that anything has been left out. He does, however, give due praise to Miss Enid Starkie's biography; and if that book is brought to the attention of a few new readers, his efforts will not have been wasted.

---

14 January 1945

GOING DOWN

The Unquiet Grave: A Word Cycle, by Palinurus
(Horizon Publications, 15s.)

'PALINURUS' is the easily penetrable pseudonym of a well-known literary critic [Cyril Connolly], but even without knowing his identity, one could infer that the writer of this book is about forty, is inclined to stoutness, has lived much in Continental Europe, and has never done any real work. His book is a kind of diary, or rather journal, interspersed with quotations from Pascal, Lao-Tze, La Rochefoucauld, and others, and having as its dominant note, a refined, rather pessimistic, hedonism. In his previous incarnations, the author says, he was 'a melon, a lobster, a lemur, a bottle of wine, Aristippus', and the periods in which he lived were the Augustan age in Rome and 'then in Paris and London from 1660 to 1740, and lastly from 1770 to 1850... Afternoons at Holland House, dinners chez Magny'.

With his background of classical culture, religious scepticism, travel, leisure, country houses and civilised meals, 'Palinurus' naturally contemplates the modern world without enthusiasm and even, at moments, with sheer aristocratic disdain: but also – and this is the peculiar mark of our age – with self-accusation and the consciousness of being an end-product, a mere ghost, like the cultivated pagans of AD 400. On almost every page this book exhibits that queer product of capitalist democracy, an inferiority complex resulting from a private income. The author wants his comforts and privileges, and is ashamed of wanting them: he feels that he has a right to them, and yet feels certain that they are doomed to disappear. Before very long the mob will rise and destroy its exploiters, but in doing so it will also destroy civilisation:

> The English masses are loveable: they are kind, decent, tolerant, practical, and not stupid. The tragedy is that there are too many of them, and that they are aimless, having outgrown the servile functions for which they were encouraged to multiply. One day these huge crowds will have to seize power because there will be nothing else for them to do, and yet they neither demand power nor are ready to make use of it; they will only learn to be bored in a new way. Sooner or later the population of England will turn Communist and then it will take over. Some form of Communism is the only effective religion for the working class; its coming is therefore as inevitable as was that of Christianity. The Liberal Die-hard then comes to occupy historically the same position as the 'good pagan': he is doomed to extinction.

Throughout the book this is repeated over and over again, in varying forms. The Beehive State is upon us, the individual will be stamped out of existence, the future is with the holiday camp, the doodle-bug, and the secret police. Palinurus, however, differs from most of his similarly placed contemporaries in not acquiescing in the process. He refuses to desert the sinking ship of individualism. To the statement that man 'will find fulfilment only through participation in the communal life of an organised group' he answers 'No' seven times over. Yet he sees no escape from the Beehive future. He sees, or thinks he sees, ways in which order and liberty, reason and myth, might be combined, but he does not believe that is the turn civilisation will take. Finally, he has no resource except a sort of lonely defiance, as of the last mammoth, or, like Faustus, trying to forget damnation in the embraces of Helen.

This outlook, product of totalitarianism and the perversion of science, is probably gaining ground, and if only for that reason this rather fragmentary book is a valuable document. It is a cry of despair from the rentier who feels that he has no right to exist, but also feels that he is a finer animal than the proletarian. Its error lies in assuming that a collectivist society would destroy human individuality. The ordinary English Communist or 'fellow-traveller' makes the same assumption, and yields up his intellectual integrity in a frenzy of masochism. 'Palinurus' refuses to yield, but just as blindly as the others he takes 'Communism' at its own valuation.

The mechanism is the same in both cases. They are *told* that the aim of Socialism or Communism is to make men resemble insects: they are conscious that they are privileged people, and that if they resist Socialism their motives must be doubtful; therefore, they look no deeper. It does not occur to them that the so-called collectivist systems now existing only try to wipe out the individual because they are *not* really collectivist and certainly not egalitarian – because, in fact, they are a sham covering a new form of class privilege. If one can see this, one can defy the insect-men with a good conscience. But certainly it is a lot harder to see it, or at any rate to say it aloud, if one is carrying the burden of an unearned income.

---

28 January 1945

PEN AND SWORD

Visions and Memories, by H. W. Nevinson
(Oxford University Press, 10s. 6d.)

IN his introduction to this book – it is a collection of occasional essays written over a period of about thirty years – Professor Gilbert Murray suggests that H. W. Nevinson was an outstanding journalist partly because he did not possess the qualities that usually make for success in that profession. 'He was too gentle, too passionately revolted by scenes of violence and cruelty, to be mixed up in such things as wars or great oppressions; yet in whatever part of the world such things occurred there was always a cry for Nevinson.' He adds that Nevinson was 'a sensitive scholar' and a champion of lost causes: and indeed these two qualities, together with that other one of always happening to be there when the guns are firing, are apparent in nearly every essay in this book.

Most of them are on literary subjects, but it is interesting to see how even in his most violent adventures Nevinson preserves the outlook of a civilised man. In 1897 we find him volunteering to fight for the Greeks against the Turks and suffering fearful hardships in the passes of the Pindus Mountains, but observing his comrades, the Greek irregulars, with a disillusioned eye, and never forgetting the classical associations of the land he is crossing. When, after a three-days march, he staggers to the top of the pass and looks down towards the sea, he thinks promptly of the Battle of Actium and the Empress Theodora. Three years later we find him riding into Pretoria with Roberts's victorious army, which he had followed from Bloemfontein to Johannesburg 'guided by the stench of dead horses and the flights of vultures'. In Pretoria he watches the Union Jack being hoisted and the troops marching past the Commander-in-Chief, and then he notes that in a house nearby 'someone of the defeated race was playing Beethoven'. He reflects that the music will be remembered when the victory and the defeat are both forgotten. In Central Africa –

> A wild native shot one of my few carriers with a cube of copper through the hand, and the other carriers called on me to execute the criminal. I object to capital punishment, but I set the man in the middle of the circle, and raised my rifle, aiming at his heart, while his black face turned a kind of green with terror. Suddenly three of the carriers rushed upon me, knocked up the rifle, and implored me not to shoot. I was immensely relieved, all the more because I knew the rifle was hopelessly jammed and would rather fly than fire.

Nevinson likes to put in little touches, like that of the jammed rifle, which make him appear a slightly ineffectual person. But it was the combination of 'objecting to capital punishment', and yet habitually getting into the kind of situation where it is sometimes necessary to kill people, that lifted him above the ordinary run of journalists.

Nevinson's thoughts were never absent very long from classical antiquity, and the two modern writers who meant most to him seem to have been Goethe and Matthew Arnold. The best thing in this book is the description of an encounter, presumably imaginary, between Marcus Aurelius and a Christian saint. But he also had some rather unexpected enthusiasms. The book contains an excellent reminiscence of W. B. Yeats, and a violent defence of Blake's paintings which, at the date when it was written (1913), must have been founded on a genuinely independent judgement. A year later, however, Nevinson is writing an equally vigorous defence of Marinetti, the Futurist poet, afterwards to become the official poet of the Fascist regime. In this essay Nevinson even borrows for a few pages Marinetti's vulgar iconoclasm and glorification of bloodshed, and these passages bring out the strain of perversity that undoubtedly existed in Nevinson's own nature. He was in favour of any cause that was unpopular – his championship of women's suffrage no doubt was partly explained by this – and Marinetti was certainly not popular in 1914. As Professor Murray says: 'He was a fiery partisan with an extraordinary power of understanding the other side', and when one of his lost causes happened to win after all, he tended to lose all interest in it.

Nevinson died towards the end of 1941 at the age of eighty-five. Both Professor Murray and Miss Evelyn Sharpe, the editor of the book, remark that it was unbearable to him to have to look on, aged and helpless, at a bigger war and a war for a clearer purpose than any he had experienced in his youth. He seems to have kept his mental vigour to the last, however; the last essay is dated only a month before his death. Even if one had never heard of him before, this book would be enough to reveal him as an unusual man. He was at once courageous, civilised, and intellectually honest – a combination that grows rarer and rarer as we move further from the nineteenth century. The book contains a couple of good photographs, and is better bound and printed than is usual in these days.

A MUFFLED VOICE

Christianity and Democracy, by Jacques Maritain
(Geoffrey Bles, 5s.)

M. Maritain is never a very easy writer, and his latest book is especially full of those cloudily abstract passages which seem to be so common in present-day French literature and which do not improve in translation. Here are two sentences picked almost at random:

> Democracy is a paradox and a challenge hurled at nature, at that thankless and wounded human nature whose original aspirations and reserves of grandeur it evokes.

> Nothing is easier for human weakness than to merge religion with prejudices of race, family or class, collective hatreds, passions of a clan, and political phantoms which compensate for the rigours of individual discipline in a pious, but insufficiently purified soul.

Both of these sentences, and the hundreds of others like them that are strewn through this book, have a meaning, but one not only has to dig it out from beneath masses of verbiage, one also has to some extent to infer it from the general tenor of the book and from the known direction of M. Maritain's own thought. Considerable passages in the book read like the speeches of a non-belligerent statesman: one knows in advance which side he is on, but one would have some difficulty in proving it. An invisible censor hovers over the pages, and to outwit him it is often necessary to avoid using proper names and change concrete words into abstract ones.

What M. Maritain is saying is that Democracy and Christianity are not incompatible – indeed, they are necessary to one another. A Christian life can hardly be lived in an unjust society, while on the other hand a democracy which is purely secular in inspiration always ends by turning into slavery. Moreover, a Christian society is not necessarily a poverty-stricken one. The desire of the working classes not merely for political equality, but for higher wages and better working conditions, is justifiable and it is the needless starvation of this desire that has made possible the rise of atheistic Communism. Christianity, in short, can be reconciled with material progress.

In our ears this hardly sounds the kind of statement that needs to be uttered with circumspection, but M. Maritain has good reasons for his guarded manner of writing. To begin with, these essays were written in the middle of 1912 when the Axis still appeared capable of winning the war and the Pétain regime was not only still in power but was, to a considerable extent, approved of by Catholics outside France. Secondly, the species of Christian Socialism on which M. Maritain stands has only very recently begun to gain ground and is certainly not representative of the Church as a whole. Primarily, M. Maritain is writing 'at' his fellow-Catholics, and he is well aware of the existing tie-up between Catholicism and reaction. Towards the end of the nineteenth century, he says, 'the working classes sought their salvation in the denial of Christianity; the Conservative Christian circles sought theirs in the denial of the temporal exigencies of justice and love'. The position is no better now, though the defeat of the Axis powers has made it temporarily appear better, and when one remembers the lyrical praises of Fascism that were being uttered by Cardinals and Catholic apologists only a few years ago, it is not surprising if M. Maritain clothes his plea for Christian Socialism in soothing and rather indistinct language.

The thing he does not quite care to admit is the loneliness of his own position. How lonely it is could be seen at the time of the Spanish Civil War, when he was one of the tiny handful of prominent Catholics who kept their heads and refused to make propaganda for Fascism. He is able to argue forcibly that Democracy and social justice are inherent in Christian doctrine and have even been enjoined by the leaders of the Church, but it is difficult to feel that the people for whom he is specially writing will be much impressed. The fact is that the Catholic humanist is a rare animal, like an albino elephant, and must probably remain so. Humanism assumes that man is the measure of all things. Christian doctrine assumes that this world only has a meaning in reference to the next. On paper a reconciliation is possible, but it always breaks down when any concrete problem arises. M. Maritain sees that the drifting-away of the masses from a reactionary Church is inevitable, and would like to retrieve the situation not by the Fascist expedient of keeping the masses ignorant, but by calling the rich to repentance. He is unwilling to admit, or at any rate he does not very clearly say, that religious belief is frequently a psychological device to avoid repentance.

Meanwhile the essential problem remains. Material progress, which is necessary if the average human being is to be anything better than a drudge, has only been achieved at a fearful price. Somehow the religious attitude in life must be restored and yet the only body of doctrine available to the Western world is one which the great mass of people are obviously less and less willing to accept. M. Maritain makes the usual claim that a just society can only be founded on Christian principles. Before making statements of this kind one ought to reflect that only a quarter of the population of the world is nominally Christian and that the proportion is constantly dwindling: also that Hindus or Chinese are not noticeably worse people than ourselves. M. Maritain is a voice crying in the wilderness and rather a muffled voice at that. Nevertheless, considering the people he was writing for and the pressures he was probably subjected to, it must have needed much courage to write such a book at such a time.

---

24 June 1945

MAN FROM THE SEA

The Nigger of the Narcissus, Typhoon and the Shadow Line,
by Joseph Conrad
(Dent: Everyman, 3s.)

Within the Tides, by Joseph Conrad
(Penguin Books, 9d.)

IT has been said that a creative writer can only expect to remain at the top of his form for about fifteen years, and the bibliography which is included in the Everyman reprint of Conrad's short stories seems to bear this out. Conrad's great period was from 1902 to 1915. Within those years he produced not only *The Secret Agent*, *Chance* and *Victory*, but a whole string of brilliant short and long-short stories such as 'Youth', 'End of the Tether', 'Falk' and 'Heart of Darkness'. Also it is only in this period that stories not dealing with the sea predominate in his work.

Of the tales now reprinted (the Penguin book contains four), only one, 'Typhoon', shows Conrad at his best. His name is associated with the sea and with the 'romance' of muddy islands in the eastern archipelagoes, and in a time of paper shortage it was no doubt inevitable that the more obviously picturesque of his stories should be selected for reissue. But even if inevitable it was unfortunate. 'The Planter of Malata', for instance, which occupies nearly half of *Within the Tides*, was not worth reprinting. It simply illustrates the vulgar theatricality which was the reverse side of Conrad's feelings for *noblesse oblige*.

'The Partner', on the other hand, which is included in the same volume, is in essence a very fine story, though it is marred by the queer shyness or clumsiness which made it difficult for Conrad to tell a story straightforwardly in the third person. 'The Nigger of the Narcissus', contains magnificent descriptive passages, but curiously enough the most memorable thing in it are certain irrelevant paragraphs in which Conrad goes out of his way to express his reactionary political and social opinions. In a penetrating essay published some years ago, the sailor writer, George Garratt, pointed out that the whole story can probably be traced back to some encounter which Conrad, as an officer, had had with a rebellious seaman. 'The Shadow Line', is a goodish story, not better or worse than about a dozen others that Conrad wrote. 'Typhoon', of course, was well worth reprinting, but one cannot help feeling sorry that it was not accompanied either by *Chance* or by *The Secret Agent*, and some of the short stories of kindred subjects.

Nearly the whole of Conrad's charm springs from the fact that he was a European and not an Englishman. This is most obvious in his style of writing, which even at his best, and perhaps especially at his best, has the air of being a translation. It is said that for many years he was obliged to translate his thoughts from Polish into French and from French into English, and when he uses phrases like 'his face of a sick goat', or puts the adjective after the noun ('it was a fate unique and their own'), it is possible to follow the process back at least as far as the French. But

Conrad's romanticism, his love of the grand gesture and of the lonely Prometheus struggling against fate, is also somehow un-English. He had the outlook of a European aristocrat, and he believed in the existence of the 'English gentleman' at a time when this type had been extinct for about two generations. As a result he was constantly creating characters in whom a capacity for having adventures, and a capacity for appreciating them, were combined in a way that is impossible in real life. *Lord Jim*, for instance, is an absurdity as a whole, in spite of the brilliant passages describing the scuttling of the ship. 'The End of the Tether' is an example of a story in which Conrad's feeling for personal nobility produces a truly moving effect, but probably an Englishman could not have written it. To admire the English as much as Conrad did, one had to be a foreigner, seeing the English with fresh eyes and slightly misunderstanding them.

The other advantage Conrad derived from his European background was a considerable understanding of conspiratorial politics. He had an often expressed horror of anarchists and nihilists, but he also had a species of sympathy with them because he was a Pole – a reactionary in home politics, perhaps, but a rebel against Russia and Germany. His most colourful passages may have dealt with the sea, but he is at his most grown-up when he touches dry land.

---

8 July 1945

FRENCH FARCE

Nine Tales from les Contes Drolatiques,
by Honoré de Balzac
Translated by J. Plummer, R. Scutt and J. P. Collas
Illustrations by R. A. Brandt
(John Westhouse, 12s. 6d.)

THE *Contes Drolatiques*, now newly translated, are usually considered to be in the tradition of Rabelais, and indeed are sometimes spoken of as though they were a kind of continuation of Rabelais. Balzac himself, in his Prologue, draws the mantle of 'our good master... the prince of all wisdom and all comedy' very closely about him, and here and there attempts an imitation of certain of Rabelais's mannerisms; but the resemblance, if any, is superficial, and the motive for invoking Rabelais in the first place was probably to give a respectable colour to pornography.

The present collection contains nine tales, and the derivation of seven of them seems to be either from Boccaccio or from the narrative poems attributed to Villon. They turn on the immemorial themes of cuckoldry and the swindling of creditors. 'Concerning a Provost who did not recognise things' is an ingenious story in this line. 'The Sermon of the Merry Vicar of Meudon' is direct imitation of Rabelais, fairly successful so far as atmosphere goes, but somewhat pointless as a story, and suggesting, together with various remarks dropped here and there in the book, that Balzac thought of Rabelais as primarily a humorist. 'The Succubus' is a longer story than the rest and different in character. It purports to be an account of the trial, torture and ultimate burning by the Inquisition of a young woman who was believed to be a demon in disguise. The story gives plenty of opportunities for salaciousness and Balzac takes full advantage of them, but his main purpose seems to have been to make a humanitarian protest against bigotry and superstition. The atmosphere and implied moral outlook of this story recall some of Anatole France's stories in the Abbé Coignard series.

It is difficult not to feel that in nearly all of these stories Balzac is simply indulging in dirt and making it respectable by a veneer of archaism. Rabelais was probably regarded as a pornographer in nineteenth-century France, as he certainly was in nineteenth-century England. Archdeacon Grantley, it will be remembered, kept his works in 'a secret drawer beneath his table', and in a well-known poem of Browning's a 'little edition of Rabelais' is part of the general racketiness of a bachelor's chambers. To this day vilely printed paper-covered editions of Urquhart's translation are sold together with *Mademoiselle de Maupin* and the *Complete Works of Aristotle*. But for some reason it has always been the fashion to claim that Rabelais's obscenities are 'healthy' and 'natural' and altogether of a different order from those of, say, Sterne or Petronius. The word 'Rabelaisian' is habitually used to indicate a sort of earthy coarseness which aims only at being funny, and is in no way demoralising: indeed, Rabelais has often been used as a stick to beat such writers as Swinburne, George Moore or D. H. Lawrence. Actually there are passages in his work that are among the most morbid and disgusting ever written, but since it was agreed that he was 'healthy' he could be enjoyed by Puritans, and traces of his influence turn up in unexpected quarters, for instance, Charles Kingsley's *Water Babies*. In declaring himself a disciple of Rabelais, Balzac was in effect proclaiming that his intentions were harmless and was then free to go ahead with what as often as not are imitations of Boccaccio or the *Heptameron*.

The trouble was, as one is bound to feel when reading such stories as 'How the Chateau d'Azay came to be built' or 'The Monk Amador', that between Balzac and Boccaccio there lay the Reformation. In his Prologue Balzac explains that he has ('regretfully', he adds) eliminated the 'old words' which are now regarded as unprintable. The result, almost all the way through, is an unbearable archness: nearly every paragraph refers to something which the reader understands perfectly well, but which can be mentioned only in a sniggering indirect way. When the *Decameron* was compiled, there was not much that could not be said, but in addition these stories were the product of a civilisation which had become almost pagan. There is naughty-naughtiness here and there in Boccaccio's tales, but in general their aim is not to be shocking. Religion is guyed in a manner that the most violent anti-clerical would not adopt in our own day. With centuries of Puritanism behind him, Balzac cannot attain the innocence of Boccaccio. He is conscious all the while of how naughty he is being, and how cleverly he is expressing unprintable meanings by innocent-seeming metaphors. The result is a rather laboured, distasteful facetiousness. At a time when many of Balzac's novels are unobtainable, it seems a pity to have wasted paper on this unsuccessful minor work.

SO RUNS THE WORLD

Man the Measure, by Erich Kahler
(Jonathan Cape, 30s.)

As its name implies, this enormous book (640 pages, with 30 pages of bibliography) is concerned with the problems of humanism, but it is also an attempt to summarise world history from the Bronze Age onwards. The author is himself a somewhat tentative or uneasy humanist. He sees the gradual elimination of religious belief as something necessary to human emancipation, and he accepts the principle of progress and evolution to the point of denying that there is something called 'human nature' which is the same in all ages. Indeed, some of the most interesting passages in his book are those in which he asserts, against Marx and similar thinkers, that motives which we now assume to have almost the status of instincts did not operate until comparatively recently:

> Some modern economists and sociologists have tried to proved
> that there were traces of capitalism as far back as Babylon. But
> what they discovered is not capitalism. Capitalism is not identical
> with wealth and mobile property, it is not identical with money-
> making and money-lending, not even with a mere productive
> investment of property. All this is no capitalism in itself, for all
> this may serve a life principle, alien to economic aims, it may be
> done for a human end, a human purpose, for something a
> human being can enjoy.

The context for this passage is a brief biographical sketch of the first real capitalists, the Fuggers, who financed and almost controlled the Hapsburg Empire, but who, unlike the Italian merchant princes, were unable to use their money for any purpose except making more money. In a rather similar passage Mr Kahler sets out to explain why it was that the physical sciences failed to develop in antiquity. The reason, he says, was not intellectual inferiority or even technical backwardness but simply a different habit of mind:

The Byzantine mathematician and architect Anthemius... was even completely aware of the technical application of steam pressure. He could easily have invented the steam engine, but he used his knowledge only to organise an artificial earthquake as a jest to frighten his friends... The prerequisite for the tremendous technical and industrial progress of our era is the modern concept of nature, and what prevented the ancient peoples from forming this concept was religion... Religion is the one great antagonist of technology and economy.

Throughout most of his book Mr Kahler maintains that the various epochs of human history have been shaped and governed by the ideas that happened to be inside men's heads at the time, and not, as it is now more fashionable to assume, that ideas are merely the reflection of external conditions. It follows that any improvement in human affairs will have to be preceded by a change of outlook and will not be brought about by a mere increase in mechanical efficiency. Even the quite simple problem of making sure that everyone has enough to eat cannot be solved without a 'fundamental shift in the state of mind of people'.

But at the end of his book Mr Kahler seems to fall back upon the notion that human beings can learn nothing except through the suffering imposed on them by external events. A sane society, he says, 'will not be created by the pure idea, it will be tortured out of men through cruel and bitter necessity – how bitter, coming generations alone may know. The ideas of man, the counsel of a new humanism, are certainly the very last things to move the present world to a fundamental change'.

Naturally, much of the later part of the book deals with the rise of totalitarianism. Some of the chapters which discuss this subject suffer from a certain distortion, owing to having been composed, apparently, in 1941 and 1942, when it was none too sure that Germany would be defeated. All the way through, indeed, there is a tendency to claim that all the evils of the modern world originated in Germany, and to discover the causes, even as far back as the days of Arminius.

But in the main this book is intended as history rather than propaganda, and the dilemma of the humanist is finally left unsolved. As long as supernatural beliefs persist, men can be exploited by cunning priests and oligarchs, and the technical progress which is the prerequisite of a just society cannot be achieved. On the other hand, when men stop worshipping God they promptly start worshipping Man, with disastrous results. The humanist has to decide whether what is needed is re-education and a 'change of heart', or whether the indispensable first step is the abolition of poverty. Mr Kahler hesitates between the two positions, but with a tendency to choose the first. The best sections of this book are the purely historical ones: the learning displayed is prodigious.

---

5 August 1945

IN FIELDS OF AIR

The Rescue, by Edward Sackville-West
Illustrated by Henry Moore. Limited Edition
(Secker and Warburg, 21s.)

RADIO programmes are meant to be heard and not read, and Mr Sackville-West's Introduction (or 'Preamble', as he prefers to call it) to *The Rescue* is somewhat more worth reading than the play itself. The play does indeed contain passages which were well worth printing, and the directions as to 'effects' and fading have a technical interest, but anyone who did not listen to the actual broadcast will get more profit from the 'Preamble', which is one of the few serious attempts that have yet been made to discuss the possibilities and the largely unsolved problems of radio drama.

The Rescue, which was broadcast in two parts, each taking forty-five minutes, is a dramatised version of the last few books of the *Odyssey,* sufficiently recast to give it a slightly melodramatic quality. With a few interludes definitely in verse and a few others in colloquial prose, it is mostly written in a highly stylised language which trembles on the edge of verse and has an almost continuous musical accompaniment. Part I shows Penelope hard pressed by the suitors and Part II culminates in the triumph of Odysseus. As nearly as possible the strict dramatic form is followed, and that dreary figure, the Narrator, is got rid of; his place is taken by Phemius the poet and the goddess Athene, who are able to give the necessary explanations while taking part in the action.

One would have to hear this play broadcast to know how well it goes over, but even when one reads the text, there are one or two objections. First, it is questionable whether the *Odyssey* lends itself to radio presentation. With so unfamiliar an art-form as the radio play it is probably wise to choose stories which the listener is likely to know already, but one fact which the microphone brings out is that some stories are much more visual than others. In this case, for instance, the scene in which Odysseus shoots down the suitors with his bow cannot be adequately presented: it has to occur 'off' and be described to Penelope by Eumaeus. Moreover, it is a great pity that a serious piece of work such as this should be pervaded, even faintly, by official propaganda. The parallel between Ithaca occupied by the suitors and Greece occupied by the Germans, though it is not pressed, is definitely indicated in Part II, and there is even, in one place, what appears to be an identification of Odysseus with King George of the Hellenes.

In his 'Preamble' Mr Sackville-West is discussing chiefly the problems of musical accompaniment, but he also has some interesting things to say about radio drama in general. As he points out, radio has made it possible to revive the soliloquy (no longer tolerable on the realistic stage), and to play tricks with space and time which would be difficult even in a film. On the other hand, the difficulty in any broadcast involving more than two or three voices of making the listener understand what is happening where, and who is speaking to whom, has not been fully overcome. It is usually done by means of a Narrator, who ruins the dramatic effect, or by making the characters drop explanatory remarks which are likely to hold up the action and have to be managed very skilfully if they are to be convincing.

As yet these problems have been very little studied. The basic reason is that in England, as in almost all countries, radio is a monopoly. There is only one source of radio programmes, the BBC, which is as though the entire Press from *Comic Cuts* to the *Hibbert Journal* had to be contained within the pages of a single newspaper. Obviously very little time can be set aside for 'highbrow' programmes, which the bulk of the listening public actively dislike, and because the BBC is a semi-official organisation it is subject to interference from all kinds of busybodies who raise an outcry whenever they overhear a programme which strikes them as too intelligent. There is also the financial difficulty. A radio programme costs a great deal to produce – *The Rescue*, with a cast of nearly thirty voices, must have cost hundreds of pounds – and it goes on the air only once, or at most two or three times. It is therefore impossible to have elaborate rehearsals, and indeed it is very unusual for the actors to know their parts by heart. It is also impossible to pay the script-writer a sum that would justify the weeks or months of work that go into the writing of a stage play. These conditions do not favour experimental work.

Meanwhile it is encouraging to see radio plays printed in book form and on good quality paper. If they exist in print they are more likely to be revived, and if it became normal for radio programmes to make more than one appearance it would be easier for those who write them to take them seriously.

---

19 August 1945

TALE OF A 'HEAD'

A Forgotten Genius: Sewell of St Columba's and Radley,
by Lionel James
(Faber and Faber, 21s.)

I F Freud did nothing else for humanity, he at least broke people of the habit of relating their dreams at the breakfast table. The diffusion of psychological knowledge has killed a lot of innocence, and if Dr Sewell, founder of two public schools and headmaster of one, were writing his reminiscences to-day it is doubtful whether he would let slip such a remark as: 'To this hour some of the most delightful, touching, blessed associations I have are connected with the Whipping Room at Radley.' Not that this remark tells the whole story about Sewell, who seems to have done somewhat less flogging than was usual in the mid-nineteenth century, but it does typify the complete absence of self-knowledge which was the strength and weakness of so many of the great Victorians.

William Sewell was the founder of St Columba's College, near Dublin, and later of Radley, of which he was also headmaster from 1853 to 1861. If he is now forgotten, this book, which is mostly a mass of ill-digested documentation, is not likely to make him less so, but the author does show good reason for thinking that Sewell, as much as, or even more than, Arnold was responsible for giving the public schools their present character. He was a High Anglican and a strong Tory, with a 'passionate conviction of the importance of birth', but he was also an educational theorist with considerable foresight and even capable, when planning schools for the aristocracy, of contemplating the creation and maintenance of analogous institutions for the poor. St Columba's was frankly founded with the idea of breeding up an Anglo-Irish gentry which should be reliably loyal and Protestant, and Sewell, who realised that the language difference was one of the roots of the trouble in Ireland, showed his originality by making Gaelic a compulsory subject. His Radley activities had a wider influence.

In the early nineteenth century the public schools were in a very bad way, and it was touch and go whether they survived or not. At even the best-known of them the neglect, disorder, squalor and vice in which the boys lived would be incredible if countless people had not testified to the facts. As a result the number of their pupils was slumping rapidly. Mr James gives some interesting figures bearing on this. Harrow had only 69 boys in 1844, having had 350 half a century earlier. Westminster dropped from 282 to 67 between 1821 and 1841. At Eton it was for a long time impossible even to keep up the complement of 70 King's Scholars, and as late as 1841 only two candidates presented themselves for 35 scholarships. Meanwhile the population was growing, the new moneyed class needed schools for their sons and large day schools which took education seriously were beginning to appear. The older schools might well have vanished altogether if Arnold, Sewell, and a few other gifted men had not saved them by reforming them.

Sewell's eight years at Radley ended in disaster. 'No-one,' says Mr James, 'pretends that finance was his strong point' and the school passed through a period of bankruptcy thanks to some surprising extravagances. But meanwhile he had left his mark upon it and his example had influenced other schools. His reforms seem to have been in the direction of stricter supervision, further development of the prefect system, more emphasis on religious teaching and, above all, encouragement of athletics. He was consciously aiming at the creation of a ruling class and was one of the first people to realise that it was necessary to train administrators for the newly won Empire. His political outlook was in some ways close to that of Disraeli, and his novel *Hawkstone* was dedicated to the romantic aristocrat, Lord John Manners.

Mr James tries hard, but unsuccessfully, to present Sewell as a sympathetic character. Actually he seems, apart from his financial indiscretions, to have been a circumspect person and rather unpopular with his contemporaries. At Winchester he was one of the seven boys who did not join in the famous rebellion; as a young man he was once engaged to be married, but broke off the engagement for reasons he prefers not to mention; at Oxford he had connections with the Oxford Movement, but neatly extricated himself when the storm broke over Tract 90. His Oxford nickname, Sullius (little pig), although a play on his own name, hardly suggests esteem or affection. But Mr James is justified in claiming that he was in his way an important figure and that without his efforts compulsory games, the prefect system and the Whipping Room would probably have played a smaller part in the education of the English upper classes.

---

2 September 1945

CHARLES THE GREAT

Charles Dickens, by Una Pope-Hennessy
(Chatto and Windus, 21s.)

THE perfect book on Dickens, that is a book which would show precisely the relationship between his life and his work, and between his work and his environment, is yet to come, but Dame Una Pope-Hennessy's book assembles so much material and is written in so fair-minded a spirit that it may make further studies of a purely biographical kind unnecessary.

Most of what is written about Dickens is either violently 'for' or violently 'against', according to whether he is being judged as a writer or as a husband. In the long run his reputation has probably been damaged by the fact that Forster's *Life* [*The Life of Charles Dickens*, 1872] suppressed or slurred over various incidents which must have been known to a fairly large circle of people at the time. As a result of this, it was with something of a shock, indeed, with a feeling of having been deceived by Dickens himself, that the public finally learned that this champion of the domestic virtues had at least one mistress, separated from his wife after twenty-two years of marriage, and behaved in a distinctly tyrannical way towards several of his children. Dame Una's book falls into the 'for' class, but she makes no attempt to cover up the facts, and even adds one or two details which have not seen the light before. On the other counts on which Dickens is sometimes attacked, such as his behaviour over money matters, his treatment of his parents and 'in-laws', and his alleged willingness to pander to public opinion, she defends him and generally with success.

The two governing facts in Dickens's make-up were his insecure childhood and his rocket-like rise to fame in very early manhood. He derived, says Dame Una, a 'horror of patronage and distrust of the aristocratic system masquerading as representative government' from his very origins, for his grandfather had begun life as a footman and his father was brought up in the servants' quarters of a country house. But the interlude in his childhood, when his father was in a debtors' prison and he himself worked in a blacking factory in the Strand, must have been a far bitterer and more formative memory. It is clear from the two accounts which Dickens wrote of this episode that his feelings about it were partly snobbish, but were partly also the grief and loneliness of a child who believes himself to be unloved by his parents. Within a dozen years of leaving the blacking factory, however, he was already brilliantly successful, and after the age of about twenty-five he never again knew what it meant to be pinched for money. Only for a very brief period could he have been described as a 'struggling author', and he did not pass through the normal development of first writing bitter books and then becoming 'mellowed' by success. On the whole his books grew more radical as he grew older. *Little Dorrit*, *Hard Times*, or *Great Expectations* do not attack individual abuses more fiercely than *Oliver Twist* or *Nicholas Nickleby*, but their implied outlook on society is more despondent.

Dame Una is less successful as a critic than as a biographer, and her attempts to summarise various of the novels would not be very helpful to anyone who had not read them already. She does, however, give an adequate account of Dickens's attitude to life and to society, and rescues him from the distortions which have been forced upon him by earlier critics, as Dickens was neither a neo-Catholic, nor a Marxist, nor a time-serving humbug, nor a Conservative. He was a Radical who believed neither in aristocratic government nor in class warfare. His political outlook was summed up in his own statement: 'My faith in the people governing is, on the whole, infinitesimal; my faith in the People governed is, on the whole, illimitable' – a statement which, thanks to the ambiguity of the English language, has sometimes been interpreted as meaning that Dickens was an enemy of democracy. Dickens's private character did undoubtedly deteriorate from about the middle fifties onwards, but it would be difficult to show that he ever sold his opinions or lost his tendency to side with the under-dog. The one act of his life which seems to contradict this is his acceptance of a baronetcy: but this was only a few weeks before his death when he may already have been in an abnormal state.

Dame Una's narrative seems to show that the change in Dickens's character dates from his long stay in Paris during the early glittering days of the Second Empire. The society in which he then mingled was far more luxurious and sophisticated than any he had known, and the lymphatic Mrs Dickens, mother of ten children, must have seemed very out of place in it. There was also the demoralising friendship of Wilkie Collins, and Dickens's growing interest in the stage, which took him away from home a great deal and threw him into contact with attractive young women. Like Gissing, Dame Una feels that the intense excitement which Dickens felt, and managed to communicate to his audiences in his public readings, was somehow morbid, and was bound up with the decline in his health. She seems, however, to underrate the morbid streak which had been in Dickens from the beginning. Speaking of his meeting with Edgar Allan Poe in 1842, she says that Poe's macabre stories would hardly have appealed to him 'at this time', although Dickens had already written some intensely horrible scenes in *Oliver Twist*, and also the madman's tale in *Pickwick* which might almost be an imitation of Poe.

PITY AND TERROR

The Brothers Karamazov, Crime and Punishment,
by Fyodor Dostoevsky
Translated by Constance Garnett
(Heinemann, 8s. 6d. each.)

C ONSTANCE Garnett's translations, now to be reissued, were the first full translations of Dostoevsky to be made direct from Russian into English and they appeared in the years immediately preceding the last war. At that date it must have been a wonderful experience to read Dostoevsky. It must have given many readers the feeling that an earlier generation had had from Flaubert and a later one was to get from Joyce – the feeling that here was a country of the mind which one had always known to exist, but which one had never thought of as lying within the scope of fiction. More than almost any novelist, Dostoevsky is able to give his reader the feeling: 'He knows my secret thoughts, he is writing about *me.*' It is hard to think of anything in English fiction to compare, for instance, with the scene near the beginning of *Crime and Punishment,* in which the drunken official Marmeladov describes how his daughter Sonia has been driven on to the streets to support the rest of the starving family.

In the eyes of an English reader, Dostoevsky gained something by his foreignness – Marmeladov's remark that he got drunk in order to repent afterwards was, as people used to say, 'very Russian' – but his basic quality was his enormous capacity for pity. He was sympathetic towards all his characters, even the respectable ones. The breakdown of the hero–villain antithesis, combined with a strict moral code, was something new, and it is not surprising that for a while he seemed a great thinker as well as a great novelist.

At this date, especially when one has just waded through the 800 pages of *The Brothers Karamazov,* one can see faults which were less apparent thirty years ago. The impression one often gets from Dostoevsky is of looking at a series of pictures which are incredibly lifelike except that they are all in monochrome. In a way, all his characters are the same kind of person: there are no exceptional people, or perhaps it would be truer to say there are no ordinary people. Priests, peasants, criminals, policemen, prostitutes, business men, ladies of fashion, soldiers, all seem to mingle easily in the same world: above all everybody tells everybody else about the state of his soul. It is worth comparing the conversations that take place in *Crime and Punishment* between Raskolnikov and the police official, Porfiry Petrovitch, with the kind of conversation that might actually take place in England, between a neurotic university student and an inspector of police. One enormous hurdle which every novelist has to face – the problem of bringing the man of thought and the man of action into the same picture – has been simply by-passed.

Apart from the famous chapter, entitled 'The Grand Inquisitor', *The Brothers Karamazov* is heavy going. Its theme does not seem to justify its vast bulk, about a third of which consists of introductory matter, and passages in it make it easy to believe that Dostoevsky habitually wrote on a corner of the kitchen table and corrected nothing. 'Crime and Punishment' is quite another matter. It is an illustration of the extraordinary psychological insight of this book that one takes Raskolnikov's actions entirely for granted although before the murder is committed, no sufficient motive for it is indicated. It seems quite credible that an intelligent and sensitive young man should suddenly commit a disgusting and almost purposeless crime: and the reason for this must be that Dostoevsky knew exactly what it feels like to be a murderer. A more conscious piece of artistry, forming a wonderful enclave in the book, is the dream of the dying horse by which Raskolnikov's crime is foreshadowed.

Messrs Heinemann intend to reissue the whole series of Constance Garnett's translations, and at eight and sixpence a volume they are good value. One volume to look out for – it is one of the less well known of Dostoevsky's books and not easy to obtain during recent years – is *The House of the Dead*; this describes, under a thin disguise of fiction, Dostoevsky's own experiences as a prisoner in Siberia and contains the never-to-be-forgotten short story, 'The Husband of Akulka'.

THE GREEN FLAG

Drums Under the Windows, by Sean O'Casey
(Macmillan, 15s.)

W B. Yeats said once that a dog does not praise its fleas, but this is somewhat contradicted by the special status enjoyed in this country by Irish Nationalist writers. Considering what the history of Anglo-Irish relations has been, it is not surprising that there should be Irishmen whose life-work is abusing England: what does call for remark is that they should be able to look to the English public for support and in some cases should even, like Mr O'Casey himself, prefer to live in the country which is the object of their hatred.

This is the third volume of Mr O'Casey's autobiography, and it seems to cover roughly the period 1910 to 1916. In so far as one can dig it out from masses of pretentious writing, the subject-matter is valuable and interesting. Mr O'Casey, younger son of a poverty-stricken Protestant family, worked for years as a navvy, and was at the same time deeply involved in the Nationalist movement and the various cultural movements that were mixed up with it. Several of his brothers and sisters died in circumstances of gaunt poverty, which would excuse a good deal of bitterness against the English occupation. He was the associate of Larkin, Connolly, the Countess Markievicz, and other leading political figures, and he had a front-seat view of the Easter Rebellion in 1916. But the cloudy manner in which the book is written makes it difficult to pin down facts or chronology. It is all in the third person ('Sean did this' and 'Sean did that'), which gives an unbearable effect of narcissism, and large portions of it are written in a simplified imitation of the style of *Finnegans Wake*, a sort of basic Joyce which is sometimes effective in a humorous aside, but is hopeless for narrative purposes.

However, Mr O'Casey's outstanding characteristic is the romantic nationalism which he manages to combine with Communism. This book contains literally no reference to England which is not hostile or contemptuous. On the other hand, there is hardly a page which does not contain some such passage as this:

Cathleen ni Houlihan, in her bare feet, is singing, for her pride that had almost gone is come back again. In tattered gown and hair uncombed she sings, shaking the ashes from her hair, and smoothing out the bigger creases in her dress; she is

Singing of men that in battle array
Ready in heart and ready in hand,
March with banner and bugle and fife
To the death for their native land.

Or again:

Cathleen, the daughter of Houlihan, walks firm now, a flush on her haughty cheek. She hears the murmur in the people's hearts. Her lovers are gathering round her, for things are changed, changed utterly: 'A terrible beauty is born.'

If one substitutes 'Britannia' for 'Cathleen ni Houlihan' in these and similar passages (Cathleen ni Houlihan, incidentally, makes her appearance several times in every chapter), they can be seen at a glance for the bombast that they are. But why is it that the worst extremes of jingoism and racialism have to be tolerated when they come from an Irishman? Why is a statement like 'My country right or wrong' reprehensible if applied to England and worthy of respect if applied to Ireland (or for that matter to India)? For there is no doubt that some such convention exists and that 'enlightened' opinion in England can swallow even the most blatant nationalism so long as it is not British nationalism. Poems like 'Rule, Britannia!' or 'Ye Mariners of England' would be taken seriously if one inserted at the right places the name of some foreign country as one can see by the respect accorded to various French and Russian war poets to-day.

So far as Ireland goes, the basic reason is probably England's bad conscience. It is difficult to object to Irish Nationalism without seeming to condone centuries of English tyranny and exploitation. In particular, the incident with which Mr O'Casey's book ends, the summary execution of some twenty or thirty rebels who ought to have been treated as prisoners of war, was a crime and a mistake. Therefore anything that is said about it has to pass unchallenged, and Yeats's poem on the subject, which makes a sort of theme song for Mr O'Casey's book, has to be accepted uncriticised as a great poem. Actually it is not one of Yeats's better poems. But how can an Englishman, conscious that his country was in the wrong on that and many other occasions, say anything of the kind? So literary judgement is perverted by political sympathy, and Mr O'Casey and others like him are able to remain almost immune from criticism. It seems time to revise our attitude, for there is no real reason why Cromwell's massacres should cause us to mistake a bad or indifferent book for a good one.

---

11 November 1945

CYCLE OF CATHAY

A Harp with a Thousand Strings,
compiled by Hsiao Ch'ien
(Pilot Press, 21s.)

Mr Hsiao Ch'ien has no official status and no directly political aim, but the books he has published during the past few years have done their bit towards improving Anglo-Chinese relations. His present book is a mixed anthology of a rather curious kind. It consists partly of translations from Chinese literature and folklore, partly of appreciations of Chinese life and culture by European writers. The Chinese extracts are mostly from biographies or autobiographies, though there are also poems, proverbs, fairy stories, and samples of popular humour; the European writers deal with subjects as diverse as philosophy and entomology, and range in time between Sir John Mandeville and William Empson.

A large part of Mr Hsiao's purpose is to show the variations in the European attitude towards China from the days of Marco Polo onwards. China enters fully into the European consciousness about the end of the seventeenth century, and is the subject of a ferocious attack in *Robinson Crusoe*, some passages from which are quoted here. Defoe had previously written a pro-Chinese pamphlet, but one gets the impression in *Robinson Crusoe* that he is angry and frightened at the thought that there should exist a large, powerful and highly civilised country which is not Christian. However, as Mr Spraigue Allen's essay shows, China gets on the whole a good Press in the eighteenth century; so good, indeed, as to provoke protests from both Wesley and Dr Johnson.

The conception of the Chinese as both wicked and comic comes later and is perhaps not unconnected with the Opium Wars and commercial penetration generally. Mr Hsiao quotes a hostile essay by de Quincey, some mildly disparaging remarks by John Stuart Mill, and also Lamb's 'Dissertation upon Roast Pig', which expresses the kind of amused patronage which was to be one of the normal attitudes for nearly a hundred years. Lytton Strachey's attitude in the Chinese passages in his essay on Gordon is essentially the same as Lamb's. On the other hand, there are Lowes Dickinson's 'Letters from John Chinaman', whose sentimental praise of China is insulting in a more subtle way. It is only in the last few years that the Chinese have begun to be regarded as human beings, and perhaps the obsolescence of the word 'Chinaman' marks the change of outlook.

There is a pleasant essay on Marco Polo by Miss Eileen Power, two essays on Chinese literature by Mr Arthur Waley, and a great deal of varied information about musical instruments, porcelain, gardening, butterflies, alligators, and much else. Among the fragments of travel literature the account of Lord Macartney's journey to Jehol in 1793 is an exceptionally vivid and readable piece of reporting.

The bulk of the translations from the Chinese are arranged under the headings 'The Evolution of Chinese Women' and 'The Evolution of Chinese Men'. They start in the third century AD and they end in the 1940s. Among other things they include the surprising story, told by himself, of Sun Yat-sen's kidnapping at the Chinese Embassy in London in 1896. The most charming piece of all is the story of the married life of the painter Shen Fu in the late eighteenth century, a period when China was peaceful and prosperous and 'men strove to be refined and women accomplished'. Other extracts show the clash between the family and the individual, and the baleful influence of the mother-in-law. A poem of the third century, so skilfully translated that the allusions are easy enough to follow, describes the suicide of a young couple who are in effect sacrificed on the altar of filial piety. How hard the fight against the family system has been one can gather from the crude iconoclastic attitude of some of the later writers.

Although they include an occasional gem like 'He who rides a tiger cannot dismount', the Chinese proverbs are rather disappointing and many of them would be better described as precepts. They do not have the crude earthy quality of European proverbs, the aim of which is usually to puncture fine attitudes. The book includes a selection of Chinese songs with music, numerous plans illustrating the date marks and symbolic signs on Chinese pottery, and a table showing the landmarks in the development of Chinese culture from Neolithic time onward. It is a scrappy book which will not please the scholarly, but there can be few people who would not get profit by dipping into it here or there.

---

18 November 1945

TELLER OF TALES

Novels and Stories, by Robert Louis Stevenson
Selected with an Introduction by V. S. Pritchett
(Pilot Press, 15s.)

WHEN one is confronted with a selection, an abridgment or an anthology, it is always difficult not to start off with a complaint. Why, one is tempted to ask, has such a brilliant masterpiece as A been omitted, while something so obviously second-rate as B has been included? And complaints are liable to be particularly bitter in the case of a writer like Stevenson, about whom there are two opposite and even hostile schools of thought, the one regarding him as a serious novelist and the other as a master of burlesque.

The present selection – which is certainly good value so far as bulk goes – includes 'The Suicide Club', 'Thrawn Janet', *Travels with a Donkey*, *Kidnapped*, *The Beach of Falesá*, *The Master of Ballantrae*, and *Weir of Hermiston*. It will be seen that Mr Pritchett inclines very strongly towards Stevenson's more serious work, although in his introduction he analyses with some severity Stevenson's shortcomings as a novelist and a thinker. He has included only one example of the burlesque (it is hard to know just what to call these writings: perhaps highbrow thrillers would be the right expression), and that one, 'The Suicide Club', is only a part of *The New Arabian Nights. Treasure Island* is rejected on the ground that it is a boys' book, and *Dr Jekyll and Mr Hyde* because it is 'available in a recent edition' – a rather unsatisfactory reason at a time when no book is reliably available. Apart from *The Beach of Falesá* there is nothing from the *Island Nights Entertainments*, though surely any selection from Stevenson should have included 'The Bottle Imp'; also, in a less fantastic and more genuinely horrible vein, 'The Body Snatcher'. On the other hand it seems doubtful whether *Travels with a Donkey* should come under 'novels and stories'.

Mr Pritchett treats Stevenson primarily as a novelist, and considers that he was always at his best when writing of his native Scotland. He claims, rightly, that Stevenson's gift for narrative was quite outstanding, and admits that he had irritating tricks of style, though he appears to find them bearable. He also admits that Stevenson's range of thought was narrow and deeply marked by his puritanical origins. What he does not say, however, is that just this combination of qualities made Stevenson a superb writer of semi-comic melodramas, while making him tiresome and sometimes even morally disagreeable in his serious moments. Stevenson is to be seen at his very worst in his essay on Villon, where thoroughly bad writing and hypocritical indignation are combined. There is a sort of empty strenuousness about him, a temperamental puritanism, not richened by any definite religious belief, which comes out in his laboured manner of writing. He seems to be constantly saying to the reader 'Look what an effort I am making!' and the cumulative effect is very trying to anyone who likes his English plain.

In his burlesque Stevenson tends to write in a somewhat plainer manner, but in any case a touch of the baroque does no harm when he is dealing with figures like Mr Malthus and Prince Florizel. And the horror themes, which answered to some deep need in his nature, set his imagination free and temporarily cured his moralising tendency. Neither 'The Bottle Imp' nor *Dr Jekyll and Mr Hyde* has any discernible moral, and that is part of their charm.

The more orthodox of Stevenson's devotees will be glad to get *Kidnapped* and *The Master of Ballantrae* in one volume: the heretics will be chiefly sorry that the whole of 'The New Arabian Nights' was not printed, but they will also be thankful for the inclusion of *The Beach of Falesá*, which not only has a sort of poetic touch in its 'Tyrolean harps' but contains some shrewd character touches of a kind that Stevenson did not often achieve. The fragment of *Weir of Hermiston* is well worth reading for the portrait of the hanging judge. Mr Pritchett speculates on the possible ending of the book, and concludes that if Stevenson had finished it he would probably have spoiled it. A more important problem, an answer to which would cast much light on the nature of puritanism, is whether Stevenson does or does not admire the disgusting brute whom he is depicting. Mr Pritchett decided that this book must be 'pure Stevenson' and that he must leave out the various books which were written in collaboration: a pity, for any selection of Stevenson's best work ought to include *The Ebb-Tide*, a powerful and sinister story in which his narrative gift and his equivocal moral attitudes are both at their most marked.

---

2 December 1945

A NIPPING AIR

The Condemned Playground, by Cyril Connolly
(Routledge, 10s. 6d.)

THE playground that Mr Connolly is referring to is the lost world of the 1930s (some of what he says would apply better to the twenties, perhaps), when literature had not become sodden with politics, and one could play the fool with a good conscience. The pieces reprinted in this book range in date between 1927 and 1944, and though the manner of writing varies remarkably little, the approach becomes more serious and less purely literary as time goes on. Among the earlier pieces are essays on Joyce, Gide, Swift, Sterne and Chesterfield: among the later, essays on psychoanalysis, Barcelona during the Spanish Civil War and the early death of the late Lord Knebworth, and a brilliant article written in 1943 looking back on the achievements of 1843.

In between are some relics of Mr Connolly's short and turbulent career as a novel-reviewer, including a blistering parody of Aldous

Huxley, entitled 'Told in Gath'. 'Like most critics,' he says, 'I drifted into the profession through a lack of moral stamina... Not that I despise criticism... But I wish I had been a better critic and that I had not written brightly, because I was asked to, about so many bad books.' He did, however, contrive to speak his mind about some of the bad books, even when he was a regular contributor to a weekly paper. Here are some excerpts from an article entitled 'Ninety Years of Novel-Reviewing':

> The reviewing of novels is the White Man's Grave of journalism;
> it corresponds, in letters, to building bridges in some impossible
> tropical climate... For each scant clearing made wearily among
> the springing vegetation, the jungle overnight encroaches twice
> as far... An unpleasant sight in the jungle is the reviewer who
> goes native. Instead of fighting the vegetation he succumbs to it,
> and running perpetually from flower to flower, he welcomes each
> with cries of 'genius'!

This is followed by some rather more serious articles on the contemporary English novel, and later in the book there are appreciations of E. M. Forster and Somerset Maugham. Some of Mr Connolly's judgements on the English novel are extremely acute. Almost certainly he is right in saying that the rigid English class system, which narrows the range of nearly everyone's experience, is responsible for the thinness of subject-matter in the average novel, and indirectly responsible for the present decadence of the English language. But at this stage of his career Mr Connolly rather marred his critical writing by an indiscriminate admiration for everything American. 'The American novelist, Hemingway, Hammett, Faulkner, Fitzgerald, O'Hara, for instance,' he says, 'write instinctively for men of their own age, men who enjoy the same things... English novels always seem to be written for superiors or inferiors, older or younger people, or for the opposite sex.'

This is too sweeping. To begin with, since he excepts a number of English writers from his general condemnation, Mr Connolly is in effect comparing the best American novels with the worst English ones. And in any case the violence in American novels, which he seems to admire, means in most cases that the characters are detached from the circumstances in which the average human being has to live. Nor is the sham-simple style, with the word 'and' pushed in at every opportunity like the pellets in potted grouse, much more bearable than the 'Mandarin' style which Mr Connolly justly despises.

Several of the essays on novels and novel-reviewing were written in a phase of Anglophobia, and it is interesting throughout this book to follow the ups and downs of Mr Connolly's affection for his own country. His relationship with England resembles a marriage in which tears and broken crockery are followed by exhausting reconciliations, but which is bound to end in the divorce court sooner or later. In 1929 he repudiates England altogether, in 1940 he rather admires her, but in 1943 he finds France superior in the things that matter most. Spain is perhaps the country that he loves best of all. Some of what he says is shallow and unfair, and too much coloured by the assumption that civilisation exists in order to produce works of art. But that is the reverse side of the urbane hedonism which makes him so readable a writer. This is an intelligent and amusing book, doubly welcome at a time when high thinking and low writing are the general rule.

---

16 December 1945

BATTLE GROUND

Science and the Creative Arts, by William Bowyer Honey
(Faber, 6s.)

During the last few years a number of writers have attempted, in no case very satisfactorily, to bring about a reconciliation between the scientist and the artist. The controversy is obscured by all kinds of jealousies and misunderstandings and vitiated from the start by the fact that modern men can neither stop worshipping Science nor imagine a genuine scientific civilisation. Mr Honey attacks the problem from several angles but, though he says some useful things incidentally, he appears to contradict himself and ends up with what is almost a surrender to the scientific attitude which he starts out by attacking.

The first and longest essay in the book is devoted to showing that human nature contains a large irrational streak with which Science is not competent to deal. The very existence of Art, especially the most 'useless' arts, poetry and music, proves this. Art serves no discoverable biological purpose. It cannot be satisfactorily related to the struggle for survival and, above all, works of art cannot be produced synthetically. It is easy enough to explain away the artistic impulse in Freudian or Marxian terms, but this brings us no nearer to understanding the difference between a good work of art and a bad one. The difference is perceived, as it were, instinctively, and the only practical test that can be applied is that of survival. In other words, aesthetic feeling is extra-logical, and the failure of the scientist to explain or control it weakens his claim to be a legislator for mankind. Most people who are capable of being moved by poetry, music or the plastic arts would agree with this, though it is a pity that this essay should be written largely 'at' Dr C. H. Waddington, who can hardly be accused of scientific arrogance or philistinism.

The second essay is entitled 'Science and Ethics', and here Mr Honey is on much more shaky ground. Ethical values, he says, are as irrational as aesthetic ones and cannot be explained as the product of the evolutionary process:

> Energy may be rewarded, like intelligence and the power of planning, but the other moral virtues are positive handicaps in the struggle for existence. Nature puts a premium on treachery and cunning, not on trustworthiness or fair dealing, on aggressive and possessive self-assertion, not unselfishness, compassion and love for our fellow-men, on predatory competitiveness, and a ruthless destruction of our rivals, not tolerance and disinterested service. If Science is to say that it cannot accept any standard of value not discoverable in nature and the process of evolutionary advance then these must be the values in question.

It is very doubtful whether this is true. Even in the animal world the gregarious and peaceful creatures are usually the most successful. The sheep will outlive the wolf. Among human beings, almost every quality looked on as 'good' is a quality tending to make it possible for men to live together in communities: or else it is a relic of some earlier attitude which was once supposed to have a utilitarian purpose, such as warding off the vengeance of jealous gods. In this section of the book Mr Honey does not make out a satisfactory case and he is inclined to overplay the duality of matter and spirit.

The final essay is called 'Science and the Arts in a new social order', and the words 'new social order' bring with them their usual implication. We are to have a planned, rationalised world with no wastage, no exploitation, no disorder, no poverty, no gross inequalities – in short, the sort of world that we all want and may even get if the atom bombs do not blow us to pieces first. But at the same time the State is not to be an end in itself, and there is to be the most complete freedom of thought so long as it does not issue in open rebellion.

It is perhaps rather hopeful to expect that intellectual liberty will exist in a highly organised society but, what is more to the point, in this context, is that the artistic impulse must suffer or at least must change if the machine triumphs as completely as Mr Honey wants it to do. He is slightly contemptuous of those who idealise the past, but he does not seem to see that, by destroying the creative element in ordinary labour, the machine has altered the status of the artist. In a fully mechanised age, art must either cease to be an individual activity or it must finally sever its connection with usefulness. Presumably the machine has come to stay, and presumably Art in some form will survive. The question is *how* it will survive, and it is just there, where the real problem begins, that Mr Honey stops. The outlook implied in this final essay is not easy to reconcile with that of the first one. This is an inconclusive book and in places none too readable, but it raises some good talking points.

FAR AWAY, LONG AGO

The Nineteen-Twenties, by Douglas Goldring

(Nicholson and Watson, 12s. 6d.)

THE 1920s are now far enough away for any dispassionate and painstaking book about them to have historical value, even if it consisted merely of personal reminiscences. The twenties were an interesting period. The political crimes and errors which were then committed led to the rise of totalitarianism and to the Second World War, but there was also a brief burst of prosperity during which personal liberty flourished and the arts were taken seriously as they are not likely to be again in our lifetime. Anyone who lived in Paris in the late twenties and knew Ford Madox Ford, Harold Monro, D. H. Lawrence, and the Sitwell family ought to be able to make an interesting book.

Unfortunately, Mr Goldring is not content either to write a documented history of the period or to fill up the gaps in the biographies of the various eminent men whom he has known. Instead of sticking to a time scheme his book consists, in effect, of a series of essays on such subjects as the General Strike, the 'new morality', the League of Nations, or life on the Riviera, and he is liable at any moment to break into a long tirade which is only doubtfully connected with his ostensible subject-matter. The two main targets of his invective are the Conservative Party and the United States, and his unwillingness to miss a chance of taking a crack at either of them leads him into many a digression.

The most valuable part of the book deals with the 1917 Club, which during the later part of the last war became the rallying point for the holders of every kind of unorthodox opinion, and was frequented by men as diverse as Ramsay MacDonald, H. W. Nevinson, H. G. Wells, Aldous Huxley, Francis Birrell, Clement Attlee, and E. D. Morel. Mr Goldring knew Morel over a period of years and supplies some interesting facts about this heroic but rather forgotten man. The first President of the 1917 Club was Ramsay MacDonald, who was also, according to Mr Goldring, its most eminent bore. Mr Goldring claims that he was never at any time taken in by MacDonald – a claim which has been made by so many people from 1931 onwards as to make one wonder how it was that MacDonald ever rose to be leader of the Labour Party and Prime Minister.

Part of the trouble with Mr Goldring's book is that certain of his views have changed since 1920, and he is over-anxious to show that he is guilty of no inconsistency – and more, that views which he now considers to have been wrong were, in fact, the right views at the moment when he held them. He appears to have been in favour of a compromise peace in 1917, and, when the war was over, to have been violently opposed to a vindictive peace settlement, with annexations, indemnities, and the fastening of a 'war guilt' clause upon Germany.

Now, on the other hand, he is in favour of annexations, indemnities, and drastic punishment of war criminals, and is even inclined to feel that the Versailles settlement was not so bad as it seemed at the time. Thousands of English intellectuals have gone through a similar development, but the conventional Left-wing outlook of 1920 and that of to-day are not compatible, and cannot be made to appear so without warping the facts at some point or other. Mr Goldring's solution is to lay all the blame for both past and present ills on the Conservative Party and the 'old school tie' mentality. The Tories strangled the Weimar Republic and nourished Hitler, and they have simultaneously discouraged internationalism and put the interests of their class above those of their country. No doubt this is part of the truth, perhaps even three-quarters of the truth, but at this date it hardly seems worth saying, and it blinks [sic] the fact that Conservative policies, both internal and external, were accepted by the mass of the British people until the results of them became flatly intolerable.

Mr Goldring's chapter on America, entitled 'Those United States', is frankly an outburst of Americophobia, but it contains some worth-while comments on the lack of contact between ordinary British and American citizens and on the practical disappearance of British books from the United States market. The section on 'Art and Letters' rescues the names of a few half-forgotten magazines from oblivion, but the critical passages are shallow, even when Mr Goldring is dealing with those writers who were his contemporaries and whom he might be expected to understand best. This is a scrappy, unsatisfying book, and it does not even have an index.

SENSITIVE PLANT

The Collected Stories of Katherine Mansfield
(*Constable, 15s.*)

KATHERINE Mansfield was only thirty-four when she died, and, what is perhaps more important, she had always expected to die young. This must have affected her attitude towards her work, and was no doubt the reason why she stuck to short stories instead of embarking on a novel which she might never live to finish. Two longish stories in this collection, 'Prelude' and 'At the Bay', have the appearance of being fragments of a projected novel, and there are other pieces, in essence sketches rather than stories, which suffer by having a *dénouement* thrust upon them, whereas they would succeed well enough if they were merely passages in a full-length book.

It is customary to describe Katherine Mansfield's work as 'slight' and to say that it has not worn well. Actually her output was respectable – about sixty completed stories of various lengths, apart from juvenilia – and in their texture the best of her stories do not 'date'. The character-touches seem as exquisite as ever. In 'The Daughters of the Late Colonel', the two crushed, elderly spinsters are suffering under the presence of the nurse who has attended their father's death-bed, and who is 'simply fearful about butter':

Josephine could hardly bear that. But 'I think those things are very extravagant,' was all she said.

'But, whey?' asked Nurse Andrews beaming through her eyeglasses. 'No one, surely, would take more buttah than one wanted – would one?'

'Ring, Con,' cried Josephine. She couldn't trust herself to reply.

And proud young Kate, the enchanted princess, came in to see what the old tabbies wanted now. She snatched away their plates of mock something or other and slapped down a white, terrified blancmange.

There are many other passages equally good. To pick out 'terrified' as the exact epithet for a blancmange, to sum up a lifetime of middle-class womanhood in the phrase 'fearful about butter' was just what Katherine Mansfield could do. What has not worn so well is the subject-matter of her stories or one should perhaps say the underlying mood. She writes nearly always about hopeless, decaying people, or about children and young people who want something from life without knowing what it is that they want: at any rate, not about people who have a definite purpose and are acting on it. It is implied throughout her work that the one great virtue is sensitiveness, and some of her best stories, such as 'Marriage à la Mode', are simply the record of a tiny spiritual failure, a lapse into vulgarity. Inevitably, some of the disasters she describes seem less important now than they did twenty years ago, and the almost complete lack of social criticism – even implied criticism – throughout her work is very striking. All the interest centres on the individual and on tiny gradations of conduct. Mixed up with this is the feeling that if possible one should avoid growing up – a feeling which sometimes leads to a sort of pretty-prettiness, as in 'Something Childish but very Natural'.

The emphasis on sensibility was fairly general among the writers of Katherine Mansfield's time, and no doubt she herself was much influenced by Chekhov. But the consciousness of having only a short time before her probably contributed towards narrowing her range, and caused her at times to over-write – not in the sense of producing purple patches but in the sense of straining after an immediate effect. In a way it is a fault of her work that there are no dull passages in it; everything is on the top note. Towards the end, when she had almost given up hope of regaining her health, she abandoned writing for a while; she wanted to write again, she said, but 'differently – far more steadily'. The 'different' books of which she spoke were never written, but we may guess that they would have been longer, wider in range and less intense.

This collection contains some unfinished stories, and also notes for stories, one or two of which are little works of art in themselves. But it hardly seems fair to Katherine Mansfield to have included the set of stories entitled 'In a German Pension', which she wrote when she was 19 and afterwards suppressed. As Mr Middleton Murry explains in his Introduction, she refused a number of times to republish the book, but finally, on his insistence, agreed to do so if she could add a preface. She never wrote the preface, and one would think that this would have been a sufficient reason for not reissuing the book. It is true, however, that these early stories are much better than she seems to have thought them. This is a well-produced book, and by current standards, very good value for fifteen shillings.

27 January 1946

HOW TO ESCAPE

Horned Pigeon, by George Millar
(Heinemann, 10s. 6d.)

THE late war has already produced a number of 'escape' books, and though they are not all alike – Mr Millar's book, indeed, includes about three times as much violence and sensationalism as the average book – they have common features which seem to make possible certain generalisations on this subject. To begin with, war prisoners seem to be far more intent on escaping, and to have a far better chance of doing so, then ordinary criminals, in spite of the enormous handicap of being in a foreign and hostile country. Secondly, officers seem to escape relatively more often than 'other ranks'. Thirdly, the escape almost never succeeds at the first attempt, and is often finally brought off by some unpremeditated act such as jumping from a train.

Mr Millar was taken prisoner by Rommel's Army in Libya in the autumn of 1942, handed over to the Italians, and later transferred to Germany when Italy went out of the war. He escaped early in 1944, worked his way through France and Spain to England, then was sent back to France to take part in the Resistance Movement (this is described in his earlier book, *Maquis*), and fetched up in the spring of 1945 as a *Daily Express* correspondent in the same part of Germany from which he had made his escape.

The story is mixed up with domestic complications which it would, perhaps, have been better to leave out of a book of this type: but the most fascinating part of it is the description of his earlier, unsuccessful attempts to escape, and of the conditions in the Italian camps when it had not yet become obvious that the Axis must lose the war. There was filth, vermin, starvation and misery of every description, and Mr Millar considers that in the transit camps in North Africa the prisoners were deliberately reduced to the condition of scarecrows so that they could be exhibited in Italy as samples of British 'degeneracy'. He himself, for some time after his capture, was suffering from dysentery and from malnutrition, but when he reached Padua in Italy and began to get his strength back on somewhat better food, he started organising his escape.

The most obvious way of getting out of prison is to dig a tunnel. War prisoners, especially officers, are able to do this because they have a great deal of time on their hands, and if they are imprisoned in a fortress, there is usually a cellar in which to store the removed earth. Consequently the same features appear in all these stories: the fearful struggles underground with home-made tools, the confederates outside who raise distractions at critical moments, the civilian clothes made out of blankets or altered uniforms and dyed with ink or wine, and the dummies placed in the beds on the night of departure. But these attempts are seldom successful.

Another way is to use bluff or bribery. Mr Millar and two comrades made an exceedingly bold attempt to walk out of the front gate dressed in Italian uniforms, and were only frustrated by a piece of bad luck. Having been recaptured they were beaten up in an atrocious manner, and later sent to a punishment camp. Here there was further tunnelling, and later, when Italy surrendered and the Germans seized the camp, Mr Millar and others attempted to hide themselves on the premises, with the idea of escaping when the rest of the prisoners had been removed. On the way into Germany a few people jumped off the train, and most of them were shot by the guards. When Mr Millar finally made his escape it was by jumping from a train: but by that time the Nazi regime was beginning to crumble, and there existed a network of underground organisations from which an escaped prisoner could get aid.

The latter part of the book is concerned with his journey across France and Spain, ending up in the British Consulate at Barcelona. The book is perhaps over-stuffed with detail, but it contains much that is of historical value, and has the advantage of not being coloured by any strong political predilection. Thus Mr Millar notes that some of the

French deportees who sheltered him in Munich, and who were doing all they could to sabotage the German war machine, were nevertheless supporters of Pétain whose Government they considered to be a good one. Of great interest, too, are his descriptions of the Russian prisoners who used to climb the barbed wire of their compound, tearing their hands to pieces in the process, in order to have a meal of bread and jam in the British compound, which they paid for by singing songs. Although in places it is written in a tiresome and egotistical way, so far as its material goes this is one of the best war books that have yet appeared.

10 February 1946

AS I WAS SAYING

The Democrat at the Supper Table, by Colm Brogan
(Hollis and Carter, 8s. 6d.)

NARCISSISM is a normal motive of novelists, including some of the best novelists. To act with firmness and daring in moments of danger, to right injustices, to be a dominating personality, to exercise fascination on the opposite sex and to horsewhip one's private enemies – these things are more easily achieved on paper than in real life, and it is an unusual novel that does not contain somewhere or other a portrait of the author, thinly disguised as hero, saint, or martyr. This is particularly noticeable in conversational novels, to which class Mr Brogan's book belongs. Without actually imitating Chesterton, Mr Brogan has obviously been influenced by him, and his central character has a Father Brown-like capacity for getting the better of an argument, and also for surrounding himself with fools and scoundrels whose function is to lead up to his wisecracks.

The action – or rather the series of discussions of which the book consists – takes place in a private hotel. The 'I' of the story describes himself as a Democrat and also appears to be a Catholic: sharing the supper-table with him are a Jewish Communist, a schoolmaster of advanced views, an Indian Nationalist, a business man, a poet, and the proprietress of the hotel. The three first-named are frankly stooges. The business man, on the other hand, is allowed to show occasional gleams of common sense, while the poet is an enigmatic character, inclined at times to take sides with the narrator, and the proprietress is the typical Chestertonian female, a being devoid of logic but possessing a wisdom which goes beyond that of the mere male. As the arguments turn chiefly upon the questions of free enterprise versus State control and the extension of the school-leaving age, the experienced reader can foresee in advance a good deal of what each of the debaters will say.

Nevertheless, when one compares this book with its predecessors of ten or twenty years ago, one cannot help being struck by the retreat that Conservativism – using this word in a wide sense – has already had to make. Mr Brogan is defending capitalism, and he expends considerable ingenuity in showing that Britain would have a better chance of recapturing her share of the world markets with a 'free' economy than with nationalised industries. He does not, like Chesterton, pretend that it would be possible to step back into the Middle Ages and that great blocks of the people are yearning to do so. He even defends mass production and is ready to accept the principle of social insurance, though he is opposed to making it compulsory. He opposes a unitary educational system and the raising of the school-leaving age, but on the other hand he wants to spend more money on the infant schools, and he does not say, as similar thinkers would have said a little while ago, that parents should have the right to decide whether their children are to be educated or not. In effect the book is a rearguard action – a defence of the past, but inspired by a consciousness that there is not very much left to defend.

However, the conversations follow the usual pattern. The Communist is a bad-blooded creature who drags references to Soviet Russia into almost every sentence. The schoolmaster is a windbag. The Indian is a mass of vague uplift and imaginary grievances, and even the business man, hard-headed in his own line, is taken in by the Dean of Canterbury's sermons. As for the narrator, he is a paragon of wit, learning, intellectuality, broad-mindedness, and common sense, and if he finally fails to convert the others to his point of view it is because their minds have already been rotted by the follies of modern education.

The trouble with all books of this kind is a sort of querulousness that arises from not really having a practical programme to offer. Mr Brogan is probably aware that there will be no return to *laissez-faire* capitalism, just as Chesterton must have been aware, at moments, that there would be no return to peasant proprietorship. Probably too, he is aware that it is not much use telling people that compulsory education, compulsory social insurance, control of investments, and direction of labour add up to slavery, since even if it is true, the great mass of the people would far rather have slavery than the alternative.

The world is going in a certain direction that he does not like, but he is unable to think of any other direction in which it could actually be induced to go. So he takes the essentially defensive line of pointing out the absurdities and monstrosities of 'advanced' thought – which, after all, is not very difficult. But it is not by these methods that anyone who is not in agreement with him already will be brought to think twice about Communism, feminism, atheism, pacifism, or any of the other -isms that Mr Brogan dislikes.

---

24 February 1946

BURMESE DAYS

The Story of Burma, by F. Tennyson Jesse
(Macmillan, 10s. 6d.)

Burma Pamphlets:
7 – *The Burman: an Appreciation,* by C. J. Richards
8 – *The Karens of Burma,* by Harry I. Marshall
(Longmans, 1s. 6d. each)

B URMESE history is legendary until the eleventh century and remains hazy until the mid-eighteenth century, when the Burmese finally overcame the original inhabitants of the country, the Talaings. Miss Tennyson Jesse's book is not intended to be primarily a chronicle of events, and she rightly skates over the earlier period and concentrates on the real turning-point in modern Burmese history – the annexation of Upper Burma in 1885. The mistakes then made, she thinks, were responsible for the failure of the British to build up a sound and popular administration, and hence were partly to blame for the collapse of 1942.

The behaviour of the British in Burma has perhaps not been so blameless as Miss Tennyson Jesse makes it appear, but it is certain that if the Burmese had not lost their independence to the British they would have lost it to some other Power, probably France. Geographically, Burma is an isolated country, and for centuries the Burmese had remained exceptionally ignorant of the outside world. It is curious to reflect that in 1820, or thereabouts, a Burmese army was sent to invade India, with orders to bring back the Governor-General in chains and, if necessary, to march on and capture London. Once Lower Burma had been annexed, Upper Burma was bound to follow sooner or later, but even so the drunken King Thibaw and his wife Supayala made every mistake that it was possible to make. British and Indian traders were insulted in unbearable ways, while Thibaw's periodical massacres of his own subjects – he celebrated his accession to the throne by executing his brothers, to the number of 80 or thereabouts – dismayed even the British anti-imperialists. When the invasion finally happened, Thibaw's regular army dispersed without fighting, though bands of guerrillas kept up the struggle for years afterwards.

The great error, Miss Tennyson Jesse thinks, was to abolish the monarchy. Thibaw had to be deposed, but another prince should have been put upon the throne. As it was, the symbol of authority to which the Burmese had been accustomed for centuries was destroyed and indirectly the power of the priesthood, on which the moral life of the country depended, was greatly weakened. The old order was broken up, and Burma was burdened with a system of law, administration, and education which was alien to the country and which never took root. As a result, violent crime flourished, the priesthood took to politics, the universities turned out an unemployed intelligentsia which became the backbone of the Nationalist movement, and the entire lower ranks of the administration were incurably corrupt. At the same time Burma remained in many ways very backward, and practically all large-scale trade remained in the hands of the British, or of Indians and Chinese. Even the armed forces were recruited mainly from non-Burmese peoples. Naturally, resentment mounted up, and though the Japanese invaders may not have enjoyed very much active support, loyalty to the British regime was hardly a factor in the situation, so far as the Burmese proper were concerned.

Miss Tennyson Jesse's views are shared by other observers sympathetic to Burma, and no doubt they contain part of the truth. She implies, however, that it would have been better to encourage Burma to emerge only very slowly from the Middle Ages and that, above all, we should have tried to preserve the Buddhist religion in its full parity. Underlying this is probably the belief that if we had not tactlessly forced Western institutions on Burma, an anti-British Nationalist movement would never have grown up. This seems very questionable. National consciousness, which in the circumstances could only be anti-British, was bound to develop by one route or another, and it was the promise to modernise the country rapidly that gave Japanese propaganda much of its appeal. Miss Tennyson Jesse seems everywhere to minimise the importance of Asiatic Nationalists and colour-consciousness. She puts the number of the Burmese fifth column during the 1942 campaign at 5,000, which must surely be a serious under-estimate. This book is a useful popular survey provided that the reader bears in mind that it is written from the angle of what might be called benevolent imperialism and, while genuinely affectionate towards the Burmese, is decidedly over-charitable towards the British.

No. 8 in the Burma Pamphlets is an informative though naïvely written study of the Karens, the largest minority of Burma and the chief source of Christian converts. No. 7 is a well-meant tribute to the Burmese character, but it is difficult to believe that any Burmese would enjoy reading it. One gets the impression that the creatures being described are some kind of charming but unreliable animal. And is it not about time to drop the word 'Burman', which has a faintly patronising air, in favour of 'Burmese'?

BLACK COUNTRY

Charity Main, by Mark Benney
(Allen and Unwin, 7s. 6d.)

I T is questionable whether Mr Mark Benney's book should be described as a novel, though it is cast in fiction form. Perhaps a documentary novel, counterpart of the documentary film, would be the right name for it. It is a study of wartime conditions in the coalfields, with the main emphasis on the complicated hereditary struggle between miners and owners.

In 1944 Francis Johnson, an Industrial Relations Officer in the Ministry of Fuel, arrives at a small mining village and takes a room in a miner's cottage. He is fairly well received by the men, is made free at the Club and the Welfare Institute, acclimatises himself to local customs and even tries the experiment – a truly heroic one for anyone not bred to the trade – of occasionally doing a day's work at the coal face.

Mr Benney describes faithfully the cramped underground world where the feeble beams of the Davy-lamps lose themselves in the clouds of coal dust, and where the 'travelling', which is a mere preliminary of work, means walking a mile, two miles – perhaps three or even more – through galleries four or five feet high. If anything he rather under-emphasises the strain of the miner's job: his hero, having reached the coal face, retains enough strength to do a little work there, which is more than most middle-aged Civil Servants would be capable of doing. Various types of mine are described, including some of the older ones where there is no shaft, but merely an enormous stone staircase descending into the mountain-side. But this is merely background, as is the history of a typical mining village given in a separate chapter towards the end of the book. The essential subject is the embittered atmosphere of the coal industry as a whole, and the part played in it by the psychology of the miners themselves.

As this is wartime, the trouble in the coalfields is not over-production and unemployment, but under-production and absenteeism. Three things especially impress themselves upon Johnson. One is that the British coalmines are so hopelessly antiquated that working conditions cannot be made tolerable in any short space of time, and modernisation cannot be tackled at all until the mines are nationalised. The second is that the bad state of the industry is due to the shortsighted greed of the mine-owners, who have been efficient only in marketing their coal and have treated their employees like animals as long as it was safe to do so. And the third is that the mentality the miners have developed in their age-long struggle makes it impossible to introduce any large-scale improvement except by strategy.

Early in his investigations he discovers with a shock that the miners are not always strictly honest in their dealings. They will, for instance, put forward what is really a claim for higher payment and disguise it as a demand for increased safety precautions. Or they will cling to grievances which have ceased to be justified – for example he finds them believing that the royalties which were nationalised in 1938 are still being paid in 1944. Then again they are suspicious of strangers and hostile to innovations, and will tolerate monstrous abuses, such as being made to pay for their own lamps, if these are sanctified by local custom. But, by degrees, the picture falls into perspective. The miner, he realises, has learned from centuries of experience and tradition that the only safe tactic is always to oppose the boss, or, when the Government steps into the bosses' place, to oppose the Government.

This attitude has almost hardened into an instinct. The miner well knows that every advantage he enjoys – the right to organise, co-operative stores, safety regulations, pit-head baths – has been won by his own efforts against bitter opposition. Where a decent building exists in the desolate mining villages, it has usually been paid for by the miners themselves. And the isolation of mining communities, the almost communal life in which everyone knows everyone else's earnings, makes for group activity and hence for a militant outlook.

In the end Francis Johnson is sacked from his job for an indiscretion. Before leaving he submits a report containing certain recommendations which no doubt are Mr Benney's own. The immediate need, he thinks, is for an investigation by a team of trained and independent observers into the causes of mining unrest. He ends by stating that while the coal-owners must in no circumstances be allowed to remain in control of the industry the miners are not capable of running it either. The

Government must take over, and must be fully aware beforehand of the sort of opposition it will have to meet. Hence the special importance of understanding the psychology produced by living in small, close-knit communities and doing hard, dangerous, and ill-paid work. This is a very readable as well as an informative book.

24 March 1946

VOICE OF MADRID

The Clash, by Arturo Barea
(Faber and Faber, 12s. 6d.)

THE third and final volume of Arturo Barea's autobiography covers the period 1935–39, and is therefore largely a story of Civil War. His private struggle and the failure of his first marriage cannot be separated from the general social tension of which the war was a result; and in his second marriage, which took place about the end of 1937, personal and political motives are even more closely intermingled. The book starts off in a Castilian village and ends up in Paris, but its essential subject is the siege of Madrid.

Mr Barea was in Madrid from the very start of the war, and remained there almost continuously until vague but irresistible political pressures drove him out of the country in the summer of 1938. He saw the wild enthusiasm and chaos of the early period, the expropriations, the massacres, the bombing and shelling of the almost helpless city, the gradual restoration of order, the three-sided struggle for power between the common people, the bureaucracy, and the foreign Communists. For about two years he held an important post in the Foreign Press Censorship, and for a while he delivered the 'Voice of Madrid' broadcasts which scored a considerable success in Latin America. Before the war he had been an engineer employed in the Patent Office, a would-be writer who had not actually written anything, a believing Catholic disgusted by the Spanish Church, and a temperamental Anarchist with no close political affiliations. But it is most of all his peasant origin that fits him to describe the war from a specifically Spanish point of view.

At the beginning fearful things happened. Mr Barea describes the storming of the Madrid barracks, the flinging of live people out of upper windows, the revolutionary tribunals, the execution ground where the corpses lay about for days. Earlier, in describing the condition of the peasants and the behaviour of the landlords in the little village where he used to spend his week-ends, he has indicated part of the reason for these barbarities. His work in the Censorship Department, although he realised it to be useful and necessary, was a struggle first against red tape and then against backstairs intrigues. The censorship was never watertight, because most of the embassies were hostile to the Republic, and the journalists, irked by stupid restrictions – Mr Barea's first orders were not to let through 'anything which did not indicate a Government victory' – sabotaged in every way they could. Later, when the Republic's prospects temporarily improved, there was further sabotage of the news at the editorial end, Italian prisoners being tactfully described as 'Nationalists' in order to keep up the fiction of non-intervention. Still later the Russians tightened their grip on the Republic, the bureaucrats who had fled when Madrid was in danger came back, and the position of Mr Barea and his wife was gradually made impossible.

At this period of the war there was a general elbowing-out of those who had borne the brunt in the early months, but there was the added trouble that Mr Barea's wife was a Trotskyist. That is to say, she was not a Trotskyist, but she was an Austrian Socialist who had quarrelled with the Communists, which from the point of view of the political police, came to much the same thing. There were the usual episodes: sudden incursions by the police in the middle of the night, arrest, reinstatement, further arrest – all the peculiar, nightmare atmosphere of a country under divided control, where it is never quite certain who is responsible for what, and even the heads of the Government cannot protect their own subordinates against the secret police.

One thing that this book brings home is how little we have heard about the Spanish Civil War from Spaniards. To the Spaniards the war was not a game, as it was to the 'Anti-Fascist Writers' who held their congress in Madrid and ate banquets against a background of starvation. Mr Barea had to look on helplessly at the intrigues of the foreign Communists, the antics of the English visitors and the sufferings of the Madrid populace, and to do so with a gradually growing certainty that the war was bound to be lost. As he says, the abandonment of Spain by France and Britain meant in practice that Nationalist Spain was dominated by Germany and Republican Spain by the USSR; and as the Russians could not then afford to provoke open war with Germany, the Spanish people had to be slowly bombed, shelled and starved into a surrender which could be foreseen as early as the middle of 1937.

Mr Barea escaped into a France where foreigners got black looks and the man in the street heaved a sigh of relief at the Munich settlement; finally he left France for Britain on the eve of the larger war. This is an exceptional book, and the middle section of it must be of considerable historical value.

WILLOW PATTERN

Letters from John Chinaman and Other Essays,
by G. Lowes Dickinson
(Allen and Unwin, 7s. 6d.)

The Englishman's Country, edited by W. J. Turner
(Collins, 21s.)

L ETTERS *from John Chinaman* is to-day much the best-known of Lowes Dickinson's writings, but it does not compare well with some of his other essays on China, such as those that were reprinted recently in *A Harp with a Thousand Strings*. In the present selection it is interesting to compare the rather hysterical enthusiasm of the title-piece with much more balanced judgement on China which Dickinson uttered a dozen years later, after he had actually visited the country. The 'Letters' were published in 1901, and the driving force behind them was indignation at the barbarities which had just been committed in the crushing of the Boxer Rebellion. The later piece was published in 1918, together with two other essays on India and Japan.

Although he greatly underestimates the power of Asiatic nationalism, some of Dickinson's later observations are extremely shrewd. In the

'Letters' he speaks of Chinese civilisation as though it were something static and wellnigh perfect, its greatest virtue being its refusal of the machine and of the values of commercialism: by 1913 he has grasped that the ancient cultures of the Oriental countries are in fact rapidly disintegrating, and that it is only by adopting industrialism that these countries can save themselves from foreign conquest. Curiously enough, of the three essays, the one that seems to show the most insight is that on India, a country which Dickinson did not like and professed not to understand. He has some particularly good remarks on the sudden collapse of aesthetic standards which always follows the introduction of European manufactured products, and suggests that the perfect natural taste which nearly all Orientals seem to possess, so long as they are left to themselves, may be no more than a petrified traditionalism. His account of the effects, especially in India, of Western education is also very penetrating, particularly since the problem of the unemployed intelligentsia had not become acute at that date.

From this kind of thing it is curious to turn to the 'Letters', with their monotonous insistence on the superiority of Chinese civilisation:

Among such a people there is no room for fierce indecent rivalries. None is master, none servant; but equality, concrete and real, regulates and sustains their intercourse. Healthy toil, sufficient leisure, frank hospitality, a content born of habit and undisturbed by chimerical ambitions, a sense of beauty fostered by the loveliest Nature in the world, and finding expression in gracious and dignified manners where it is not embodied in exquisite works of art – such are the characteristics of the people among whom I was born... When I review my impressions of the average English citizen, impressions based on many years' study, what kind of man do I see? I see one divorced from Nature, but unreclaimed by Art; instructed, but not educated; assimilative, but incapable of thought... His religion is conventional; and, what is more important, his morals are as conventional as his creed. Charity, chastity, self-abnegation, contempt of the world and its prizes – these are the words on which he has been fed from his childhood upwards. And words they have remained, for he has neither anywhere seen them practised by others, nor has it ever occurred to him to practise them himself. Their influence, while it is strong enough to make him a chronic hypocrite, is not so strong as to show him the hypocrite he is.

The whole essay is psychologically interesting and may be compared with the writings of Carlyle, Lafcadio Hearn, and other Englishmen and Americans who have developed an emotional attachment to more or less imaginary foreign countries. However, unlike some of the others, Dickinson did grow out of his allegiance and come to realise that all generalisations purporting to show that this country is 'good' and that country is 'bad' are false. Of the other essays in this book, the best is a discussion of human immortality. Modestly, but persuasively, Dickinson argues that there is a certain amount of reason for thinking that the soul is immortal, and that on the whole life after death is to be desired. Rather surprisingly, he ends by suggesting that the claims of spiritualism deserve serious examination.

The Englishman's Country, a composite book, written by Edmund Blunden, John Betjeman, and others, gives a pleasing, though perhaps rather too idyllic, picture of life in Britain outside the great towns. By far its best features are its coloured illustrations, of which there are many. Particularly good reproductions are of two water-colours by Turner (one of them of Oxford in a curious lurid evening light), another water-colour by Constable, and two lithographs, one of Liverpool in 1846 and the other of Dawlish in 1817.

---

21 April 1946

WHY FRANCE FELL

Plea for Liberty, by Georges Bernanos
(Denis Dobson, 8s. 6d.)

WHEN George Bernanos's 'Letters to the English' were first written, about the beginning of 1941, no translation of them was published, and they were not easy to obtain in the original French. In the present book they are supplemented by a 'Letter to the Americans' and a 'Letter to the Europeans', both written a little while before the United States entered the war.

The original 'Letters' were a direct reaction to the French defeat of 1940, and their message, if not actually irrelevant, seems less stirring now than it must have seemed then. A tendency towards rhetoric – that is, a tendency to say everything at enormous length and at once forcibly and vaguely – seems to be a common failing with present-day French writers, and M. Bernanos is not free from it. Indeed, one might read his eighty vehement pages and come away having learned no more than that the author is on the one hand a Catholic and on the other an opponent of Marshal Pétain. However, that is in itself a complicated position, and it must be said in M. Bernanos's favour that he is not trying simply to do propaganda, but to explain *why* France had collapsed and how it had been possible for fairly well-meaning people to collaborate in her ruin.

In the main the 'Letters' are an onslaught on the French bourgeoisie, using the word more or less in its accepted economic sense. The bourgeoisie, with its commercial mentality, knew that war does not pay, could imagine no policy except appeasement, and, given the opportunity, might have brought off the same kind of sell-out in 1918 as it did in 1940. Even if some kind of miracle or accident – an outbreak of disease in the German Army, for instance – had suddenly reversed the fortune of war, the bourgeoisie would have made the same use of victory as it actually made of defeat: that is, its one object would have been to restore order, safeguard private property, and put the common people in their place:

The Bourgeoisie despises the people but it fears them... The trouble with the French bourgeoisie to-day is that while it is rich and powerful enough to render useful service to the community its origins are too base for it to rise to a conception of disinterested service, one that doesn't pay. It makes a great to-do about all the precious 'values' which it sets out to defend, always naively using the possessive pronoun. It says OUR Law and Order, OUR Property, OUR Justice... Because I write as I do, the intellectuals in the pay of the bourgeoisie try to make out that I am a demagogue. In fact, I am a man of Old France or rather, of France; for a thousand years of history are not to be wiped out by a hundred and fifty years of wretched fumbling... *'There are no more privileges – there are only duties.'* That was the ruling principle of the French popular monarchy, which still claims my loyalty.

In denouncing the French bourgeoisie, M. Bernanos does not claim that they were merely crooks. 'Our elites,' he says, 'had principles, they crawled with principles as a corpse with maggots.' But they had lost their traditions and had become – in spite of the fact that on the whole clericalism and reaction were in alliance – non-Christian. On the other hand the common people had remained both patriotic and Christian without knowing it. 'The people no longer go to Mass... but the image they bear within them, deep in their very souls, without knowing it, is of a society which never actually existed, but for whose unbelievable advent their ancestors waited, century after century: the city of true accord, under the seal of brotherhood.'

There is a good deal in M. Bernanos's romantic royalism with which it would be easy to quarrel. He is inclined to see in 1789 the source of all the ills from which France suffers and, while believing in the common people, is a disbeliever in democracy. No doubt it is true that the French Revolution was essentially the victory of a commercial middle class, but it is also true that the Revolution established certain principles which Pétain and his followers were consciously bent on destroying. Indeed, one fact this book brings out is that the division in French society was far greater than anything existing in Britain; over several generations, important sections of the nation had refused to accept the regime under which they lived. M. Bernanos wants to see the Catholics, the royalists, and the proletariat on one side, and the republicans, the business men and the Fascists on the other – an improbable constellation, which is only credible at all because he himself happens to combine honesty and pugnacity with a love of the past. His political principles, followed to their conclusions, are probably nearer to those of Pétain than to those of Mandel or Blum: but his hatred of lies and tyranny necessarily leads him – as it had led him in 1938 when most of his fellow-Catholics were acclaiming Franco's 'crusade' – in the opposite direction.

In reading this book one must not forget the date at which it was written and the equivocal attitude of millions of Catholics both in Europe and in the Americas. Much that it says needed saying at that time, and the pity is that it was not translated into English five years earlier.

---

5 May 1946

GO TO THE ANT

Of Ants and Men, by Caryl P. Haskins
(Allen and Unwin, 10s. 6d.)

PHYSICALLY ants are about as unlike men as they could well be, but in their behaviour they present a sort of parody of human activities, and their social organisation is so much more efficient than our own that it can be used not merely for purposes of analogy but as an object-lesson by means of which we can criticise our own institutions. Dr Haskins's book does in passing supply a great deal of information about the habits of ants, but his main aim is to decide whether any real parallel exists between ants and human beings. Can we profitably 'go to the ant' as Solomon advised? Does the physical and social evolution of the ant cast any light on the probable direction of our own development?

His book is full of strange and – from the point of view of the ordinary, insect-hating person – rather horrible things. Some of the facts which he casually mentions are stranger than anything in human society – stranger in the sense that the institutions of ants are so much more various and more fully developed. For example, whereas man has domesticated perhaps fifty species of birds and animals, ants have domesticated some three thousand species of insects. Then, again, there is the extraordinary differentiation of function in ants, showing itself not only in the division into sexed and sexless types, but most sensationally of all in the variation in size. Sometimes, in the same nest, the queen or soldier may be several hundred times the bulk of the ordinary worker. These creatures, having the same size-relation to one another as a dog and a mouse, co-operate in apparent amity, each being perfectly specialised for its own job. Thus, the famous 'parasol' ants live by cultivating a species of fungus which they grow in a compost of chewed leaves. The cutting and carrying of the leaves is done by relatively large ants, but the gardens are attended to by tiny 'minims'.

There are grain-storing ants, whose hoards have sometimes been so large as to become the subject of human litigation, carnivorous ants, slave-making ants – these have perhaps the most astonishing habits of all – and there are also exceptionally adaptable ants which appear to have changed their way of life in a quite short space of time and replaced more conservative species over large areas of the earth. But there are strange gaps in the horrible efficiency of the ants, and one of these is their toleration of parasites. Apart from the many kinds of aphid which the ants keep as 'cows', there are other insects which manage to live a robber existence inside their nests, and others which are apparently kept as pets, possibly because they give off a pleasant smell. Sometimes these become so numerous that the whole economy of the nest is upset and the ants die off together with their guests.

Dr Haskins comes to no definite conclusions as to whether we can or cannot anticipate our own developments by observing that of the ants, but he is inclined to consider that, so far as ants go, totalitarianism represents an advance on democracy. The more primitive, less successful ants are comparatively democratic in their social structure, whereas the wonderfully organised communities of the more highly developed species have much in common with both Fascism and Communism. But it remains true, as he admits throughout, that ants are individually so different from ourselves as to make any comparison only doubtfully valid. Ants live in a different world from ourselves and it is questionable whether they are conscious as we understand consciousness. Each ant comes out of its cocoon knowing what it needs to know and then, without any attempt at independent activity, repeats a pattern which in some cases has been repeated for millions of years. Sometimes the stupidity revealed is almost unbelievable. Take the habits of the parasitic ant, *Bothriomyrmex decapitans* –

> Shortly after having gained entry into populous formicaries of
> the host colony, the queens of this species seek out the brood
> mothers of the communities considerably larger than themselves.

Mounting the backs of the rightful owners the *Bothriomyrmex* females spend the next several days in sawing off from the top the heads of these brood queens. As soon as the heads drop the impostors are adopted by their foster-workers.

Similar manoeuvres are attempted in human politics, but they are not tolerated so easily and it is difficult not to feel that we have more control over our own destiny than even the most gifted kinds of ant. Still, when one considers their boldness, their fecundity, their power of living in almost any climate and on almost any kind of food and, above all, their unquestioning loyalty to their own kind, one is left thinking that it is a good job that ants are not larger.

---

10 November 1946

TROUBLED LAND

Politics, Economics and Men of Modern Spain,
1808–1946, by A. Ramos Oliveira
(Gollancz, 30s.)

M R Oliveira indicates his main thesis by putting the word 'modern' and the date '1808' side by side in his title. Spain has undergone changes since the Spanish people rose against Joseph Bonaparte, but certain root problems have persisted unsolved through every kind of regime, and the almost innumerable civil wars are, as Mr Oliveira says, 'only one civil war'. The book lives up to its title and has many useful chapters of background material, and sketches of outstanding personalities alternating with other chapters of straight history. The Second Republic of 1931 only makes its appearance about halfway through, and Franco's insurrection only receives seven chapters out of a total of forty-five.

Early in the book Mr Oliveira notes that Spain suffered forty-three military *pronunciamientos* [uprisings], eleven of them successful, between 1814 and 1923. A little later he tabulates the various regimes which have flourished throughout his whole period, classifying them as 'R' for revolutionary or reformist, or 'C' for counter-revolutionary or conservative. Not only have 'R' and 'C' alternated as regularly as night and day, but except during the 'Restoration' period (1874–1931) no one faction has succeeded in remaining in office for more than ten years. This pendulum movement was almost more disastrous in its results than an unbroken despotism would have been. Every attempt at reform was certain to be undone a few years later, and no progressive government ever had time to get the real levers of power into its own hands. Thus, the central problem of Spain, the agrarian problem, has remained almost untouched for more than a hundred years.

Spain is an agricultural country in which 1 per cent of the population owns, or did own till very recently, 50 per cent of the land. The attempted Liberal reforms in the early nineteenth century actually had the effect of increasing the number of landless labourers. Mr Oliveira gives an interesting survey of the Spanish agricultural system, in which he shows that the main stronghold of the land-owning aristocracy is the wheat- and olive-growing areas. These people (referred to all the way through as 'the oligarchy') have not only clung to their land and their political power through every vicissitude, but have deformed the whole economy of the country in their own favour, discouraging every other kind of agriculture and preventing the development of industry. The bankers have managed to make their peace with the aristocracy, but the industrial entrepreneurs have been almost as much an oppressed class as the workers, and Spain's rich mineral resources have either been neglected or have been controlled by foreign capital. In such circumstances a strong, coherent middle class could not grow up and the great mass of the people, illiterate and half-starved, either remained apathetic or expressed themselves by outbreaks of violence. Convents and churches were already being burned by the populace as early as the 1830s.

The characteristic Spanish movement of the Left was Anarchism, which shaded off into Utopianism at one end and into sheer banditry at the other. The 'oligarchy' knew no way of dealing with discontent except by crushing it, and the Liberals did nothing, either because they could not, or because they were frightened by the prospect of red revolution, or because the stifling intellectual atmosphere made them waste their energies on secondary issues such as anti-clericalism. So the history of Spain continued to be stagnation punctuated by rifle shots, while political, military and economic power always remained in the same hands.

Mr Oliveira's chapters dealing with the recent Civil War are perhaps less satisfactory than the rest of the book. They give only a brief account of the first six months of the war, in many ways its most interesting period, and devote rather too much space to the putsch by Colonel Casado, which overthrew the Negrin government [see also p. 22] and led to the capitulation. Mr Oliveira, who was, and still is, a close associate of Dr Negrin, is generous enough not to emphasise very strongly the foolish and sordid part played in the war by British policy, but the figures he has given earlier, of British capital holdings in Spain, tell their own tale. This is a valuable book, and it assembles information, especially about Spanish industry and agriculture, which it would probably not be easy to find elsewhere.

---

1 February 1948

A LOST WORLD

India Called Them, by Lord Beveridge
(Allen and Unwin, 18s.)

LORD Beveridge's biography of his parents is primarily, as he says, a study of their characters, but most readers will probably value it more as a picture of British India in the forgotten decades between the Mutiny and Kipling's *Plain Tales from the Hills*.

Both the Beveridges, Henry and Annette, came from a commercial middle-class background, Scottish in the one case, Yorkshire in the other. They went out to India with an intense interest in Oriental affairs, but with no imperialist traditions or connections. Henry had passed top into the Indian Civil Service in 1857 – one of the very first batch of 'competition wallahs'. He was the best type of Scottish intellectual: agnostic, mildly but obstinately radical, ambitious but not supple enough to succeed in an official career. Throughout life he never seems to have budged from an opinion because of outside pressure, and his views on

India were exactly the wrong ones to hold at that date. He knew that India could not yet be independent, but he held that the aim of British rule should be 'to prepare for its own extinction' and that the first step towards this – the Indianisation of the services – should be greatly accelerated.

A generation earlier these views would have seemed reasonable to Macaulay: a generation later much of what Henry Beveridge advocated was within sight of happening. But the period covered by his career, 1858–93, was a bad period in Indian–British relations. Among the British, imperialist sentiment was stiffening and an arrogant attitude towards 'natives' was becoming obligatory. The greatest single cause was probably the cutting of the Suez Canal. As soon as the journey from England became quick and easy the number of Englishwomen in India greatly increased, and for the first time the Europeans were able to form themselves into an exclusive 'all white' society. On the other side the Nationalist movement was beginning to gather bitterness. Henry Beveridge supported unpopular reforms, wrote indiscreet magazine articles, and in general stamped himself as a man of dangerous views. As a result he was repeatedly passed over for promotion and spent most of his career in subordinate jobs on fever-stricken islands of the Ganges delta.

Annette, his wife, was first and foremost his intellectual companion, but her development was very different. Coming out to India under Indian sponsorship to run a school for Bengali girls, she started out with much more vehemently pro-Indian views than her husband, but in the end swung round to a position that could almost be called Conservative. Part of the reason was that she was repelled by the Indian attitude towards women. In her old age, in England, she was to be a local secretary of the National Women's League for Opposing Woman Suffrage.

After retirement the two of them had what almost amounted to a second lifetime of thirty-five years, filled up with heavy literary labours. Annette translated Persian fairy tales and learned Turki at sixty; Henry spent twenty years in translating the Persian history of Akbar. Towards the end Annette grew so deaf that they could only communicate in writing. They died in 1929, within a few months of each other. Besides some good photographs, the book contains a fascinating table setting forth the exact composition of an Anglo-Indian household in the eighties. From this one learns just why it was necessary for the Beveridges – a couple with three children, living very modestly by European standards – to have thirty-nine servants.

MEN OF THE ISLES

The Atlantic Islands, by Kenneth Williamson
(Collins, 18s.)

THE Faeroe Islands, to judge by Mr Kenneth Williamson's photographs, are almost completely treeless. They are volcanic islands rising in perpendicular cliffs out of cloudy stormy seas, with their cultivable soil distributed in such narrow pockets that the farmer cannot even use a plough, but has to do everything with a clumsy handleless spade. They have no natural wealth except their fisheries. Nevertheless, whereas most of the island groups fringing Britain are being rapidly depopulated, these others, even poorer and barer, have quadrupled their population in the last hundred years.

Perhaps this is partly because the Faeroese have succeeded in remaining owner-peasants, with no landlord class and no very great differences of wealth. Most of the land is cultivated on the primitive strip system, and the grazing grounds are owned communally. Mr Williamson, who was stationed in the Faeroes for several years during the war, found the Faeroese a tough, simple, rustic people, but by no means uncultivated, for the local schools are fairly good and a proportion of the children are sent to Denmark to finish their education. They are of pure Viking stock and still speak their ancient Norwegian dialect, only rather unwillingly using Danish for official purposes. Except perhaps in the folklore (there is a story of a seal-wife which seems to have an Irish sound) the original Celtic inhabitants have left hardly any traces.

How essentially poor the islands are can be seen from the local diet, which consists quite largely of whale meat and sea birds. With scanty soil and rather chilly summers, it is not worth growing grain, and the chief crops are hay and potatoes, which means that not many sheep or cattle

THE OBSERVER YEARS ▨ 217

can be kept through the winter. Apart from mutton dried in the wind like biltong, the people's animal food has to come out of the sea. The annual massacre of the whales – schools of them are driven into the harbour of Thorshavn, the capital, and there slaughtered with bill-hooks, turning the sea crimson in their death-struggles – is an important event; the hunting of the sea birds is even more so. The Faeroese eat not only gannets, which are eaten in some other places, but guillemots, gulls, cormorants and, above all, puffins. Mr Williamson is an enthusiast for Faeroese cookery, but most of the dishes he describes are slightly horrible to read about. Their key-note seems to be the combination of fishy and greasy meat with sweet sauces.

The Faeroese are exceedingly hospitable. Any stranger arriving at a farm-house, Mr Williamson says, is assumed to be dying of starvation and has to act accordingly. It must be a little difficult to respond when one is offered boiled puffins with strawberry jam.

Nationalism is not yet strong in The Faeroes, and only a very few of the inhabitants objected to the islands being occupied by Britain during the war. Moreover, The Faeroes were our most reliable source of fish throughout the war and, at one time, were responsible for three-quarters of the British supply. All through the dark days of 1940 and 1941, when the Iceland boats refused to sail without air escorts, which Britain could not provide, the tiny Faeroese boats plied to and fro, their sole armament one Bren gun each. They were bombed, machine-gunned, blown up by mines and even torpedoed. But they also made a good deal of money which has been employed in bringing the fishing fleet up to date on the assumption that the trade with Britain will continue. One would like to learn for certain from some authoritative source that this hope is not being disappointed.

DOWN UNDER

My Caves, by Norbert Casteret
Translated by R. L. G. Irving
(Dent, 15s.)

H OW many people in Great Britain would know without consulting a dictionary that spelaeology has something to do with caves? Probably not many, for though pot-holing has its Pennine enthusiasts, cave-exploration has never ranked as a widely popular pastime. Even the vocabulary of the full-time spelaeologist is full of words like '*siphon*' and '*chatière*' which have no exact equivalent in English.

It is otherwise in France, which is exceptionally rich in caves, especially in the Pyrenees and the Dordogne. Some of them extend for stupendous distances under ground, though France does not contain any single cavern as large as the one near Trieste, into which it would be possible to put the Roman church of St Peter's, dome and all. Before one can even start exploring some of the larger caves, it is often necessary to climb or be lowered down a perpendicular pot-hole which may descend as much as 1,000 or 2,000 feet. Once at the bottom one may find an underground stream on which it is possible to travel for miles at a stretch in a rubber boat, but often one has to crawl – much use is made of the technical term 'reptation', meaning a worm-like movement – down galleries barely wider than one's body, with slimy mud or sharp stalagmites underneath one.

Much of the travelling has to be done in complete darkness, for all kinds of lighting apparatus are awkward to carry and liable to be damaged by water. Often a promising exploration is cut short by a 'siphon', that is, a point at which the roof of a cave descends below the surface of the stream that flows through it. There is no way of passing a 'siphon' except by diving underneath it, without knowing in advance whether the ledge of rock extends for a few feet or 50 yards.

Mr Casteret, a lifelong spelaeologist, naturally insists on the scientific and practical value of his chosen pastime. It has led to the discovery of important new reserves of water, it has taught us much of what we know about palaeolithic man, and it has also increased our knowledge of the habits of bats. But it is clear enough from his descriptions of his adventures that the true spelaeologist is not moved by any utilitarian consideration, but by a mysterious urge to get as deep under ground as possible and to penetrate to places where no human being has ever been before. Some of these places, with their monstrous stalactites like cathedral pillars, are astonishingly beautiful, as the photographs in Mr Casteret's book show. In some of the more accessible caves, on the other hand, life is made horrible by evil-smelling clouds of bats, creatures which it is difficult to love, though Mr Casteret defends them warmly.

The equipment used in exploring caves is extremely elaborate and ingenious. Ladders are made of steel wire so delicate that a yard of ladder weighs only about three ounces. Rubber boats which will support a man can be carried, when deflated, in a rucksack. For very deep descents, the spelaeologist is strapped into a parachute harness and lowered on a wire to which a telephone is attached. The kind of clothes that are worn are also important, not only because it is desirable to keep dry, but even more because it is important not to get stuck. More than one spelaeologist has died of starvation because his coat rucked up when he was trying to force his way through a narrow 'cat run'. There are, of course, other dangers, not to mention such discomforts as having to swim across underground rivers whose temperature is only a degree or two above freezing. However, human beings vary in their notion of what constitutes pleasure, and spelaeology is no more dangerous and uncomfortable than mountaineering and is perhaps more useful. The photographs in this book, all of them taken by magnesium flash in circumstances of the utmost difficulty, are excellent.

'MR SLUDGE'

Heyday of a Wizard, by Jean Burton
(Harrap, 10s. 6d.)

DANIEL Dunglas Home, the original of Browning's 'Mr Sludge', has the curious distinction of being the only spiritualist medium – at any rate the only 'physical' medium – who was never caught out. His life was lived in a blaze of publicity, and a considerable literature has accumulated round it. The Czar Alexander II, the Empress Eugénie, the King of Prussia and a respectable section of the British aristocracy devoutly believed in him; so did writers and scientists like Ruskin, Bulwer Lytton, Thackeray, Sir William Crookes, Elizabeth Browning and Harriet Beecher Stowe. On countless occasions Home floated through the air, usually in a horizontal position, materialised spirit hands out of nothing, extracted tunes from musical instruments without touching them, and caused heavy pieces of furniture with which he was not in contact to skip about the room like ballet dancers. And in only one very doubtful instance was any evidence of trickery produced against him.

Moreover, nothing that is known of Home's private life suggests that he was a conscious fraud. He was something of a social climber and made two wealthy marriages, partly as a result of his spiritualistic activities, but he was not venal. He would accept expensive presents such as jewellery, but he refused money payments and he would not 'perform' to order. He dismayed his fellow-mediums by deriding 'dark séances' and exposing some of the tricks by which 'manifestations' are normally produced. And though he had some bitter enemies, such as Robert Browning, his relationships with other people and his general manner of life make it very difficult to believe that he was a vulgar impostor.

And yet – a point that Miss Jean Burton fails to emphasise – there must have been imposture of some kind. Many of the stories that are told of Home are frankly incredible, all the more so because everything has the appearance of being above board. Unlike all other 'physical' mediums, Home accomplished some of his most astonishing feats in daylight or strong artificial light, and very often they were tricks of a kind that could not be reproduced by a conjurer, except on prepared ground. For example, William Howitt, author of *The History of the Supernatural*, deposes to having seen a table rise off the ground and turn over until its top was perpendicular, a flower pot which was standing on it remaining in place 'as if screwed to the surface'. The table then sailed into the next room and took up a position above another table, where it remained suspended in the air. It is clear that things of this kind cannot actually have happened. One could begin to believe in them only if there were other recorded instances, and no similar claims have been successfully made for any medium since Home. But one does not solve the problem by writing off the accounts of Home's séances as 'all lies' or 'all imagination'. For, after all, why should reputable and intelligent people conspire to tell stories which were bound to get them laughed at? One must conclude that Home, whether he was conscious of it or not, had some kind of hypnotic power which enabled him to induce delusions in whole groups of people.

Miss Burton hardly discusses this question. Her book is essentially a biography, and she simply relates the facts of Home's life with very little comment, not even definitely rejecting the suggestion that he was an ordinary fraud. The late Mr Harry Price's introduction does not take the matter much further, though he throws out what is probably a useful hint by classifying Home as a 'poltergeist medium'. Home, whose heyday was in the sixties and seventies, did not work under what would now be considered test conditions, and the people who attended his séances are long since dead, but it might be possible to learn more about the nature of his powers by closely examining the records that remain.

His most celebrated feat – and very justly celebrated if it really happened – was to float out of one window and in at the next, three stories above street level. This was very minutely described by two witnesses, but their accounts have been analysed in Mr Bechhofer Roberts's book on spiritualism, and elsewhere, and shown to be full of inconsistencies. Miss Burton's book makes amusing reading and it is useful in that it assembles a great deal of information and indicates other sources, but what is most needed is a critical examination of the evidence on which Home's reputation rests. For the phenomena of spiritualism, like the pranks of the poltergeist, are not interesting in themselves. What is interesting is the question of how people can be induced to believe in them, and there, perhaps, this paragon among mediums could be made to yield us a little more information.

PRIME MINISTER

Mr Attlee: An Interim Biography, by Roy Jenkins
(Heinemann, 12s. 6d.)

WHEN one is writing of a living person, and especially of a statesman whose leadership one accepts, it is not easy to preserve a critical attitude. However, this unofficial or semi-official biography remains well on the right side of hero-worship, while at the same time it brings out the unspectacular qualities which have enabled Mr Attlee to keep his feet through very difficult times and to out-stay many more brilliant men.

Mr Attlee first won his Limehouse seat in 1922, but his personal connection with the constituency started over forty years ago and has been almost unbroken ever since. He went there in the first place to become a part-time helper at a public-school mission. In those days he was still a strong Conservative: at Oxford, he tells us, he had 'admired strong ruthless rulers' and 'professed ultra-Tory opinions'. Within a year, however, as a result of what he saw in the East End, he was a member of the ILP [Independent Labour Party] and the Fabian Society, and he soon became active as a pamphleteer and street-corner speaker.

It was partly because of this long connection with a single constituency that he was one of the few Labour MPs who kept their seats in the calamity of 1931 and the thinning of the ranks gave him a chance of showing his talents which he might not otherwise have had. But, as Mr Jenkins rightly emphasises, his accession to the leadership of the Parliamentary Labour Party was not simply an accident brought about by Lansbury's resignation.* It had to be confirmed by the Party and it was the result of Mr Attlee's proved abilities. Even when he was Leader of the Opposition he was not generally looked on as the likeliest man to become Prime Minister if Labour won the next election. During the war years, however, his reputation grew

THE OBSERVER YEARS ◼ 223

steadily, in spite of his somewhat embarrassing position as second-in-command to a Conservative Premier, which naturally caused murmurings from time to time within his own party.

Mr Jenkins usually, though not invariably, defends Mr Attlee's political judgements. Certainly he was very right in resisting the pre-war clamour for a Popular Front, which would simply have weakened the Labour Party without bringing any electoral advantage. On the other hand, he must share some of the blame for the contradictory policy of simultaneously demanding a firm stand against Germany and opposing rearmament, which created a bad impression all over Europe. It is unfortunate that Mr Jenkins has chosen to take his narrative no further than the 1945 General Election. This is not so definite a turning-point as it appears, since the difficulties which the Labour Government now has to contend with were partly created in the two or three years before it took office. Probably it was an error on the part of the Labour Party not to get out of the coalition when it became clear that the war was definitely won. Had it done so, it would have avoided inheriting the Yalta and Potsdam agreements and would have had time to make clear its position on certain issues which were afterwards obscured or falsified in the election campaign.

The book contains a fairly full account of Mr Attlee's early days as a boy at Haileybury and an undergraduate at Oxford. One learns with a certain feeling of appropriateness that as a cricketer he was a poor batsman and bowler, but a good fielder. The photographs are undistinguished, but curiously enough they confirm the *Daily Mail's* statement – made at the time of his becoming Leader of the Opposition – that Mr Attlee's head is the same shape as Lenin's.

* George Lansbury's pacifism led him to resign as leader of the Labour Party in 1935, over Labour's hostile response to the Italian invasion of Ethiopia.

FOR EVER ETON

Eton Medley, by B. J. W. Hill
(Winchester Publications, 30s.)

IT is hard to disentangle admiration from dismay when one learns that Eton in 1948 is almost exactly what it was in 1918. If any change at all can be inferred from the photographs in Mr Hill's book it is that the boys now go about bareheaded, owing to the lamentable shortage of top hats. Otherwise their clothes are just the same, and so is everything else. The procession of boats, lighted by fireworks, still glides down the river on the Fourth of June, the Wall Game is still played amid seas of mud, the flogging block is still there, a bit chipped by the bomb which hit Upper School, but doubtless still serviceable.

Mr Hill says that a New Zealand Air Force officer, in England during the war, wrote asking him for an account of Eton and its educational system. The subject was too large to be dealt with in a letter, and Mr Hill embarked instead on a careful description of Etonian daily life with many photographs and a few reproductions of old engravings.

His book is pleasantly written as well as informative, but it is unavoidably – and, indeed, almost unconsciously – an apology for a form of education that is hardly likely to last much longer.

At the end Mr Hill remarks mildly that Eton will no doubt change as the years go on, but that he hopes that the changes will be self-imposed and not too rapid. And he points out, as a mark of vitality, that since the war more people than ever have been willing to pay the very large fees that are demanded. But unfortunately more is involved than the attitude of parents. Whatever may happen to the great public schools when our educational system is reorganised, it is almost impossible that Eton should survive in anything like its present form, because the training it offers was originally intended for a landowning aristocracy and had become an anachronism long before 1939. The top hats and tail coats, the pack of beagles, the many-coloured blazers, the desks still notched with the names of Prime Ministers had charm and function so long as they represented the kind of elegance that everyone looked up to. In a shabby and democratic country they are merely rather a nuisance, like Napoleon's baggage wagons, full of chefs and hairdressers, blocking up the roads in the disaster of Sedan [1870].

On the other hand, Eton will presumably remain a school, which it is physically well suited to be. It has magnificent buildings and playing-fields and, unless it is finally swallowed by Slough, beautiful surroundings. It also has one great virtue which is fairly well brought out in Mr Hill's book, and that is a tolerant and civilised atmosphere which gives each boy a fair chance of developing his own individuality. The reason is perhaps that, being a very rich school, it can afford a large staff, which means that the masters are not overworked; and also that Eton partly escaped the reform of the public schools set on foot by Dr Arnold and retained certain characteristics belonging to the eighteenth century and even to the Middle Ages. At any rate, whatever its future history, some of its traditions deserve to be remembered. The price of this book is surely hard to justify.

---

22 August 1948

THE WRITER'S DILEMMA

The Writer and Politics, by George Woodcock
(The Porcupine Press, 10s. 6d.)

' ANY honest artist', writes Mr George Woodcock, 'is an agitator, an anarchist, an incendiary', and this bold statement can be taken as the key-note of his book. It is a book of collected essays, rather heterogeneous in character and dealing more with individuals than with generalities, but always coming back to that painful and – as it seems to-day – almost insoluble problem, the relationship between literature and society.

In the opening essay the problem is stated directly. In our own age a serious writer cannot ignore politics as he could in the nineteenth century. Political events affect him too nearly, and he is too much aware of the fact that his seemingly individual thoughts are the product of his social environment. He therefore attempts, as so many writers of the past twenty years have done, to take a direct part in politics, only to find that he has entered a world in which intellectual honesty is regarded as a crime. If he toes the line he destroys himself as a writer, while if he refuses to do so he is denounced as a renegade. This drives him to take refuge in dilettantism, or, perhaps even worse, to alternate between one attitude and the other. Only by embracing Libertarian Anarchism, Mr Woodcock maintains, can the writer make himself politically effective without losing his integrity: and he at any rate demonstrates successfully that Anarchism is not the same thing as woolly-minded Utopianism. He does not, however, fully meet the objection that Anarchism is simply another -ism and that all movements involving large groups of people tend to be alike in their intellectual atmosphere.

This essay is followed by another on political myth-making, and then by three studies of revolutionary thinkers whose writings are less known in Britain than they might be: Proudhon, one of the founders of the French Socialist movement; Herzen, the friend and financial supporter of Bakunin; and Kropotkin, the biologist and sociologist whose inventive and pragmatical outlook makes him one of the most persuasive of Anarchist writers. After this there are essays on a series of contemporary writers – Silone, Koestler, Graham Greene, and others – most of whom are alike in combining a 'Left' outlook with hostility to orthodox Communism. Silone comes nearest to winning Mr Woodcock's complete approval, but he treats Graham Greene with marked friendliness – Greene, it seems, though a Catholic, is *anima naturaliter anarchistica*, Koestler is condemned because of the change of front which he makes, or seems to make, in *Thieves in the Night*, a book which condones the totalitarian methods that he had previously attacked in *Darkness at Noon*.

Among the other essays there is one on the sociology of hymns – an excellent subject, but too shortly treated since Mr Woodcock is interested almost exclusively in the revivalist hymns and does not discuss the medieval Latin hymns and their translations, nor, on the other hand, the occasional modern specimens (such as those of Henry Newman) which possess literary value.

THE DEFENCE OF FREEDOM

Gandhi and Stalin, by Louis Fischer

(Gollancz, 10s. 6d.)

'GIVEN a shelf of freedom on which to stand', writes Mr Louis Fischer, 'and using the crowbar of individual power, Gandhi undertakes to move the earth.' It sounds splendid, of course. But, since it is apparently offered as the basis for a political programme, one feels inclined to ask: What would Gandhi do if he *wasn't* given a shelf to stand on?

The fact that this question is never clearly answered vitiates the whole book. In outline Mr Fischer's argument is simple enough. Russia is a danger to world peace and must be resisted: we, the Western nations, can resist successfully only if we make our own democracy work: the way to do this is to follow the teachings of Gandhi. As to the first two propositions, they can hardly be disputed, and Mr Fischer does useful work in setting them forth. He puts the case against the Stalin regime in a vigorous journalistic style, backed up by his long personal experience of Russian conditions, and he rightly emphasises, what is still not sufficiently grasped in this country, that the struggle between Russia and the West may be decided by the attitude of the coloured peoples. At present we are losing the battle for Asia and Africa, and to win it will mean a change of attitude which is not yet within sight of happening. But the invocation of Gandhi in support of a merely 'progressive', anti-totalitarian programme is a *non sequitur*.

The fact is that Gandhi's political methods were almost irrelevant to the present situation, because they depended on publicity. As Mr Fischer admits, Gandhi never had to deal with a totalitarian Power. He was dealing with an old-fashioned and rather shaky despotism, which treated him in a fairly chivalrous way and allowed him to appeal to world opinion at every step.

It is difficult to see how his strategy of fasting and civil disobedience could be applied in a country where political opponents simply disappear and the public never hears anything that the Government does not want it to hear. Moreover, it appears that when Mr Fischer tells us that we should follow Gandhi's teaching, he does not actually mean that we should follow Gandhi's teaching. He wants to prevent the expansion of Russian imperialism, non-violently if we can, but violently if we must: whereas Gandhi's central tenet was that you must not use violence even if the alternative is defeat. Asked to give an opinion on the German Jews, Gandhi apparently answered that they should have committed mass suicide and thus 'aroused the world' – an answer which seems to embarrass even Mr Fischer. Most of Mr Fischer's political conclusions are such as any person of good will can agree with heartily, but the attempt to derive them from Gandhi seems to be founded on personal admiration rather than genuine agreement.

28 November 1948

CULTURE AND THE CLASSES

Notes Towards the Definition of Culture, by T. S. Eliot

(Faber and Faber, 10s. 6d.)

IN his new book, *Notes Towards the Definition of Culture*, Mr T. S. Eliot argues that a truly civilised society needs a class system as part of its basis. He is, of course, only speaking negatively. He does not claim that there is any method by which a high civilisation can be created. He maintains merely that such a civilisation is not likely to flourish in the absence of certain conditions, of which class distinctions are one.

This opens up a gloomy prospect, for on the one hand it is almost certain that class distinctions of the old kind are moribund, and on the other hand Mr Eliot has at the least a strong *prima facie* case.

The essence of his argument is that the highest levels of culture have been attained only by small groups of people – either social groups or regional groups – who have been able to perfect their traditions over long periods of time. The most important of all cultural influences is the family, and family loyalty is strongest when the majority of people take it for granted to go through life at the social level at which they were born. Moreover, not having any precedents to go upon, we do not know what a classless society would be like. We know only that, since functions would still have to be diversified, classes would have to be replaced by 'élites', a term Mr Eliot borrows with evident distaste from the late Karl Mannheim. The élites will plan, organise and administer: whether they can become the guardians and transmitters of culture, as certain social classes have been in the past, Mr Eliot doubts, perhaps justifiably.

Birth and choice

As always, Mr Eliot insists that tradition does not mean worship of the past; on the contrary, a tradition is alive only while it is growing. A class can preserve a culture because it is itself an organic and changing thing. But here, curiously enough, Mr Eliot misses what might have been the strongest argument in his case. This is that a classless society directed by élites may ossify very rapidly, simply because its rulers are able to choose their successors, and will always tend to choose people resembling themselves.

Hereditary institutions – as Mr Eliot might have argued – have the virtue of being unstable. They must be so, because power is constantly devolving on people who are either incapable of holding it, or use it for purposes not intended by their forefathers. It is impossible to imagine any hereditary body lasting so long, and with so little change, as an adoptive organisation like the Catholic Church. And it is at least thinkable that another adoptive and authoritarian organisation, the Russian Communist Party, will have a similar history. If it hardens into a class, as some observers believe it is already doing, then it will change and develop as classes always do. But if it continues to co-opt its members from all strata of society, and then train them into the desired mentality, it might keep its shape almost unaltered from generation to generation. In aristocratic societies the eccentric aristocrat is a familiar figure, but the eccentric commissar is almost a contradiction in terms.

Something wrong

Although Mr Eliot does not make use of this argument, he does argue that even the antagonism between classes can have fruitful results for society as a whole. This again is probably true. Yet one continues to have, throughout his book, the feeling that there is something wrong, and that he himself is aware of it. The fact is that class privilege, like slavery, has somehow ceased to be defensible. It conflicts with certain moral assumptions which Mr Eliot appears to share, although intellectually he may be in disagreement with them.

All through the book his attitude is noticeably defensive. When class distinctions were vigorously believed in, it was not thought necessary to reconcile them either with social justice or with efficiency. The superiority of the ruling classes was held to be self-evident, and in any case the existing order was what God had ordained. The mute inglorious Milton was a sad case, but not remediable on this side of the grave.

This, however, is by no means what Mr Eliot is saying. He would like, he says, to see in existence both classes and élites. It should be normal for the average human being to go through life at his predestined social level, but on the other hand the right man must be able to find his way into the right job. In saying this he seems almost to give away his whole case. For if class distinctions are desirable in themselves, then wastage of talent, or inefficiency in high places, are comparatively unimportant. The social misfit, instead of being directed upwards or downwards, should learn to be contented in his own station.

Pessimism

Mr Eliot does not say this: indeed, very few people in our time would say it. It would seem morally offensive. Probably, therefore, Mr Eliot does not believe in class distinctions as our grandfathers believed in them. His approval of them is only negative. That is to say, he cannot see how any civilisation worth having can survive in a society where the differences arising from social background or geographical origin have been ironed out.

It is difficult to make any positive answer to this. To all appearances the old social distinctions are everywhere disappearing because their economic basis is being destroyed. Possibly new classes are appearing, or possibly we are within sight of a genuinely classless society, which Mr Eliot assumes would be a cultureless society. He may be right, but at some points his pessimism seems to be exaggerated. 'We can assert with some confidence,' he says, 'that our own period is one of decline; that the standards of culture are lower than they were 50 years ago; and that the evidence of this decline is visible in every department of human activity.'

This seems true when one thinks of Hollywood films or the atomic bomb, but less true if one thinks of the clothes and architecture of 1898, or what life was like at that date for an unemployed labourer in the East End of London. In any case, as Mr Eliot himself admits at the start, we cannot reverse the present trend by conscious action. Cultures are not manufactured, they grow of their own accord. Is it too much to hope that the classless society will secrete a culture of its own? And before writing off our own age as irrevocably damned, is it not worth remembering that Matthew Arnold and Swift and Shakespeare – to carry the story back only three centuries – were all equally certain that they lived in a period of decline?

2 January 1949

OUR NATIVE HUMOUR

The English Comic Album,
compiled by Leonard Russell and Nicolas Bentley
(Michael Joseph, 15s.)

IT is generally admitted that the standard of English comic draughts-manship deteriorated after 1850, but the collection of drawings now published shows, at any rate, that the standard has risen sharply during the past fifteen years. Even if there is no Rowlandson or Cruikshank alive to-day, a period in which Low, Giles, Nicolas Bentley, Ronald Searle, and Osbert Lancaster are all at work simultaneously is not doing so badly.

The collection starts about a century ago, when the self-contained 'joke picture' was just coming into being. Unfortunately this was also the period at which English humour was being 'purified' for the benefit of a new, largely feminine, public. It is painful to compare, for instance, Tenniel and Charles Keene, or even Edward Lear, with 'Phiz' and Cruikshank. Indeed, the funniest pictures that Messrs Russell and Bentley have been able to find in the late middle of the century are some satires on drunkenness by an anonymous postcard artist.

The eighties and nineties were dominated by George du Maurier, and others of the same school, who simply drew naturalistic sketches to go with jokes which, when they were funny, could have got along equally well with no picture. There was also Phil May, Sir Max Beerbohm (who, however, did his best work about twenty years later), and two gifted Frenchmen, Caran d'Ache and Godefroy, apparently included here because of their influence on English draughtsmanship.

The whole period between roughly 1900 and 1930 is a very bad one. Its redeeming features were Sir Max Beerbohm's caricatures and George Belcher, a social historian rather than a comic draughtsman. Otherwise, nearly all the so-called comic drawings of that time are either weakly naturalistic or display the kind of silly facetiousness that can be seen in, for instance, the Shell advertisements.

This type of drawing still predominates, but since the 1930s the 'American joke' has naturalised itself. It is no longer assumed that every magazine-reader is a member of the upper middle classes, whose one great terror in life is of being made to think and, above all, it has come to be accepted that a comic drawing ought to be funny in itself and ought to convey a meaning without further explanation. Mr Bentley's lumbering Amazon of the hockey field hardly needs the 'Pass, Gwyneth!' printed beneath her, and Mr Lancaster's diptych on the march of progress has no caption and needs none. It is true, however, that the long Victorian caption had its charm. In the hands of a writer like Thackeray it was sometimes a small work of art in itself, and it could be made so again, as Mr D. B. Wyndham Lewis showed some years ago in a book produced in collaboration with Mr Topolski.

It is difficult to review an anthology without raising a few complaints. Low is not represented by his best work, and neither is Sir Max Beerbohm. Thackeray does not get a fair showing, and Leech would have been better represented by some of his illustrations to Surtees than by his contributions to *Punch*. And since both advertisements and comic strips are included, might there not have been at any rate one seaside postcard? But this is a well-balanced collection, and the most jaded reader can hardly glance through it without laughing several times.

EXCLUSIVE CLUB

The Great Tradition, by F. R. Leavis
(Chatto and Windus, 12s. 6d.)

THE subtitle of Dr Leavis's book is 'George Eliot, Henry James, Joseph Conrad', and the bulk of it consists of studies of those three writers. There is also a shorter essay on Dickens's *Hard Times* and an introductory essay in which Dr Leavis attempts, not altogether convincingly, to fit his chosen authors into a coherent pattern.

There are, it seems, only four 'great' English novelists: the three names above, and Jane Austen, who is not here discussed at length. Among modern writers, only D. H. Lawrence can be said to have carried on the tradition. Others who are mentioned with approval are Peacock, Emily Brontë, and T. F. Powys, while Fielding, Hardy and Joyce are admitted to have talent, though of a bad kind. The remaining English novelists are not only inferior but – this at least is the impression one carries away – reprehensible.

The best essay in the book is that on Conrad. This does the thing that criticism can most usefully do – that is, it draws attention to something that is in danger of being neglected. Writing at a time when every novelist was expected to have some kind of regional affiliation, Conrad had the label 'the sea' stuck so firmly upon him that the excellence of his political novels has hardly been noticed even to this day. He is remembered as the author of *Lord Jim*, and not of *The Secret Agent* and *Under Western Eyes*, books which are not only far more grown-up than any that could have been written by an English writer at that date, but also have a structural beauty that Conrad did not often achieve. His best books, largely ignored in his lifetime, still need advertising, and Dr Leavis's essay will assist in the process. The Dickens essay, too, may gain new readers for *Hard Times*, a first-rate novel which is often rejected even by the faithful on the ground that it is 'not like Dickens'.

But just where the 'tradition' comes in it is not easy to say. Clearly the four writers whom Dr Leavis has picked out as 'great' do not exhibit any sort of continuity. Two of these 'English novelists' are not English, and one of them, Conrad, derives entirely from French and Russian sources. One has the impression that what Dr Leavis most wants to do is to induce in the reader a feeling of due reverence towards the 'great' and of due irreverence towards everybody else. One should read, he seems to imply, with one eye always on the scale of values, like a wine-drinker reminding himself of the price per bottle at every sip.

And he has a magisterial manner of writing which is, if anything, somewhat emphasised by sudden lapses into colloquialism ('isn't' for 'is not', etc.). 'Remember, boys,' one seems to hear a voice saying intermittently, 'I was once a boy myself.' But though the boys know that this must be true, they are not altogether reassured. They can still hear the chilly rustle of the gown, and they are aware that there is a cane under the desk which will be produced on not very much provocation. To be caught reading George Moore, for example, would be good for six of the best. So also with Sterne, Trollope, and perhaps Charlotte Brontë. Thackeray is permitted reading so far as *Vanity Fair* is concerned, but not otherwise. Fielding may be read – on half-holidays, say – provided that you remember that he is definitely not 'great'. On the other hand, in reading Bunyan or Defoe or Dickens (apart from *Hard Times*), the important thing to remember is that they are not novelists.

One would be a little more ready to accept Dr Leavis's guidance if, for example, he were not an admirer of T. F. Powys. However, his three main essays perform some useful expository work, especially at moments when he is able to forget his quarrels with other critics, Lord David Cecil in particular. But surely a book on the English novel ought at least to mention Smollett, Surtees, Samuel Butler, Mark Rutherford, and George Gissing?

INDEX

Abyssinia, 2, 3, 4
Acland, Sir Francis Dyke, 12
Acland, Lady, 12
Acland, Sir Richard, 12–14, 67
Africa, 75, 160, 228
agriculture, 62, 103, 129, 139
Aitken, Captain Max, 66
Alexander II, Czar, 221
Alexander, Horace, *India Since Cripps*, 122, 124
Algeria, 35
Allen, C.K., *Democracy and the Individual*, 102–3
American Civil War, 116
American novels, 187–8
American Volunteer Group (AVG), 144
Anarchism, 138–40, 214, 227
Anglo-Catholic movement, 94
Anthemius, 170
anti-Semitism, 93, 94, 104–6
ants, 211–13
Appleton, G., *Buddhism in Burma*, 143–5
Arabs, 6–9
aristocracy, literary taste, 125–6
armed forces, relation to society, 99–101
Arnold, Matthew, 161, 232
art, 188–9, 190
Asia, 75, 107, 228
Asquith, H.H., 12
Atlas Mountains, 6–7
Attlee, Clement, 64, 191, 223–4
Auden, W.H., 152
Austen, Jane, 234
Austria, 55–9, 61

Balogh, Thomas, 118
Balzac, Honoré de, *Nine Tales from les Contes Drolatiques*, 166–8

Barcelona, 153, 186, 196
Barea, Arturo, *The Clash*, 204–6
Barham, Richard, 151
Barrès, Philippe, *Charles de Gaulle*, 84–5
Barzun, Jacques, *Romanticism and the Modern Ego*, 130–32
Basques, 22
Baudelaire, Charles, 155–7
Bavaria, 57
Bazaine, François, 36
BBC, 172–3
Beaverbrook, Lord, 68
Beerbohm, Sir Max, 233
Belcher, George, 233
Belgium, 39, 61
Belloc, Hilaire, 92, 110, 118
Benney, Mark, *Charity Main*, 202–4
Bentley, Nicolas, *The English Comic Album*, 232–3
Berlin, 55
Bernal, J.D., 118
Bernanos, George, *Plea for Liberty*, 208–11
Besant, Annie, 77, 78
Betjeman, John, 208
Bevan, Aneurin, 69–71
Beveridge, Annette, 215, 216
Beveridge, Henry, 215–17
Beveridge, Lord, 21; *India Called Them*, 215–17
Bevin, Ernest, 66
Bible, 99
Birrell, Francis, 191
birth-rate, France, 30
Blaisot, General, 37
Blake, William, 97, 136, 161
Blouault, M., 28
Blum, Léon, 53
Blunden, Edmund, 208
Boccaccio, Giovanni, 167, 168
Boileau, Nicolas, 132
bombing, Second World War, 40–41

Borkenau, Franz, 118
Bracken, Brendan, 63–4, 65
Bridges, Robert, 148, 150
Britain: Allied occupation of Germany, 57, 58–61, 62; anti-British sentiment in France, 52; as a democracy, 102–3; Diggers, 138–9; Home Guard, 10–12, 26–8; imperialism, 35, 36; and India, 3–4, 146–8, 215–17; Irish Civil War, 100; 1942 Budget, 5–6; 1945 general election, 63–8, 224; post-war public mood, 4–6, 19–21
British Army, 20, 27, 85
British Union, 93
Brogan, Colm, *The Democrat at the Supper Table*, 197–9
Brogan, D.W., *The American Problem*, 141–3
Brontë, Charlotte, 235
Brontë, Emily, 234
Browning, Elizabeth, 221
Browning, Robert, 110, 167, 221
Brumwell, J.R.M., *This Changing World*, 117–19
Brussels, 41
Budapest, 41
Buddhism, 144, 201
Bunyan, John, 235
Burke, Edmund, 77
Burma, 86, 122–4, 143–5, 199–201
Burton, Jean, *Heyday of a Wizard*, 221–3
Butler, H.W., 64
Butler, Samuel, 235
Byron, Lord, 117, 131

Calicut, 77–8
Calverley, Charles, 151
capitalism: Fascism and, 91, 92; laissez-faire, 104, 113, 114, 198, 199; motivation for, 169; status of writers under, 126